TARMAC TO TOWERS

Praise for *Tarmac to Towers*

'Infrastructure is the backbone of economic growth, and this book brilliantly captures the essence of how comprehensive development in real estate, transportation, construction, smart cities and utilities can drive not just economic progress but also social transformation. The book dives deep into the multifaceted world of infrastructure, illustrating how each element, from metros to Tier-2 and Tier-3 cities to rural areas, contributes to the larger picture of national development. This book is not just a chronicle of infrastructure development but a powerful argument for considering infrastructure as a basic right and a call to action for governments to be accountable to their citizens. It eloquently discusses how equal access to infrastructure can democratise opportunities, whether it's through reliable electricity, accessible roads, fast internet or quality education and healthcare. The detailed accounts of policy recommendations, quality improvements and industry-specific journals provide invaluable insights into the sector's evolution over the past twenty-seven years.'

—Amitabh Kant, India's G20 Sherpa & Former CEO of NITI Aayog

'Having experienced the ebbs and flows of India's infrastructure sector from the trenches, it is nice to see a different perspective, and Pratap Padode's *Tarmac to Towers* attempts to peel the onion, as it were, for a better understanding of how things work in India. There is no denying that India's growth story can only be fuelled by infrastructure development, and with her growing population, one can safely assume that India will continue to dominate globally with her strength in demography and demand. However, the transformative impact of this growth will lie in making it more inclusive, where infrastructure will have a key role to play. With Composite AI poised to rewrite ground rules, and the likelihood of 50% of current activities going redundant to robots, reskilling and upskilling will be critical and a vehicle to propel inclusive development. The key to combat the threat of global warming lies in widespread use of Renewables; no effort can be spared to push this aspect to the top of the world's agenda. Again, India has both the resources and the heft to lead the charge. All these aspects have been deftly woven into an engaging tapestry by Pratap and as he concludes, now is the time for Viksit Bharat. The stage is set, all that is required is political will, investor confidence and 1.4 billion Indians collaboratively pursuing a path of infrastructure, progress and sustained development in positive manner. Pratap, in his inimitable style, has brought out the nuances of what needs to be done in a very nice manner. The book is worth going through.'

—S.N. Subrahmanyan, Chairman & Managing Director, Larsen & Toubro

TARMAC TO TOWERS

THE INDIA INFRASTRUCTURE STORY

PRATAP PADODE

Published by Westland Business, an imprint of Westland Books, a division of Nasadiya Technologies Private Limited, in 2024

No. 269/2B, First Floor, 'Irai Arul', Vimalraj Street, Nethaji Nagar, Alapakkam Main Road, Maduravoyal, Chennai 600095

ISBN: 9789360458485

10 9 8 7 6 5 4 3 2 1

Typeset by Mukul
Printed at Parksons Graphics Pvt. Ltd

Dedicated with gratitude and love …

To Gurumayi, whose blessings have always illumined my path and guided me towards my purpose.

To my parents, Vijaysingh Padode and Laxmi Padode, whose unshakeable spirit has been the wind beneath my wings, encouraging me to explore fearlessly.

To my wife and partner, Falgun—my rock, my confidante and my best friend—who has stood by me through every trial and triumph.

To the entrepreneurs, innovators and business leaders who have bravely borne the risks and endured the adversities caused by brutal bureaucracy and apathetic legal systems;

And who, despite facing countless challenges and obstacles, remain steadfast in their commitment to building a stronger, brighter nation.

The unwavering spirit, unrelenting perseverance and unshakeable faith in India's potential are the true engines of our nation's growth. May these struggles be recognised, efforts be rewarded and contributions be celebrated.

'We worry about making our parents proud when we should be focused on making our children proud. The responsibility of each generation is not to please our predecessors—it's to improve conditions for our successors.'

—Adam Grant

Contents

Introduction

'You and I come by road or rail. But economists travel on infrastructure!' These were the memorable words of former British prime minister and 'Iron Lady' Margaret Thatcher.[1]

Indeed, infrastructure is the backbone of economic growth. Encompassing a gamut of aspects—from real estate to transportation, construction, smart cities, utilities—it is an umbrella whose whole is much greater than the sum of its parts, jumpstarting growth and employment and transforming quality of life. And today, it is a mantra in India, with metros, Tier-2 and Tier-3 cities and rural areas voting and vying for infrastructure and development.

Infrastructure is the enabler of the fulfilment of potential. Today, it is also a call for a right of 'equal opportunity'. Some citizens may have access to electricity 24/7, road access to reach markets easily, access to fast internet, good education institutions and healthcare centres. Such people would have an unfair advantage over others who do not have these facilities. Access to coaching in cricket today can give you a shot at getting into the Indian Premier League. Access to a video camera may allow a teenager to become a sensation on YouTube or Instagram. Having a train stop at a small village station may open a flood of opportunities for farmers who need to take a long, winding and often treacherous road to reach city markets. More and more governments are now becoming accountable to their citizens for providing infrastructure as a basic right.

My tryst with infrastructure and construction began after my chartered accountancy. In fact, after trying my luck with acting in films, my father and I co-founded a publishing startup with an investment magazine, *Dalal Street Journal*, its name styled after *The Wall Street Journal*. The magazine was a huge success from the mid-1980s to the mid-1990s, when the Indian economy began faltering and financial scams brought the country to the brink.

I then articulated in an editorial that India could pull itself out of its precarious financial state by launching projects that could help its large population earn daily wages. Serendipitously, it was at that time that former prime minister Atal Bihari Vajpayee launched the Golden Quadrilateral project, connecting the four corners of India by road. By then, in 1996, I had launched a magazine called *Construction Update*, which was then renamed *Construction World* for trade professionals, and then I plunged, heart and soul, into the sector. Over the years, I set up an infrastructure thinktank called FIRST Construction Council (in 2003) and went on to publish sector-specific journals like *Infrastructure Today*, *Equipment India*, *Power Today*, *Project Reporter* and *Indian Cement Review*.

In my twenty-seven years of engagement with infrastructure, I have seen the entire evolution of the sector and contributed to raising the standards of building, construction and infrastructure. I have lobbied for change, raised my voice against irresponsible quality of construction, recommended policies, conducted conferences featuring international and national thinkers, innovators and policymakers and sown the seeds of thought for the building of a strong nation.

How did it start, how did it go, how is it going and how can it continue? For context, past, present and future, I decided to embark on this project. My book examines the period between 1995 to 2024 and the shifts and starts in policies and attitude towards infrastructure development—from the halcyon days of growth to the logjam and policy paralysis reached in 2012 and the reinjection of fuel after Prime Minister Narendra Modi entered the picture.

He completed a decade at the helm in 2024 and has got a mandate for a third consecutive term. Thus, specifically, from 2012 to 2023, I use my monthly editorials, which tracked the country's major decisions and issues in construction and infrastructure, to provide a ringside view of the journey to the reader. These editorials may be the best captured account of major events in the sector. Further, I encapsulate what trajectory India is likely to follow given the current dispensation.

India is currently a shining beacon amid trailing global economic growth. We have certainly come a long way. But let us deconstruct the journey.

During UPA 1 (2004–09), the Indian economy recorded the highest growth ever recorded in GDP terms at 9.5%, 9.6% and 9.3% for the years 2005–06, 2006 –07 and 2007–08. Even during UPA 2 (2009–14), the economy recorded high growth during 2010–11 and 2011–12, with a GDP growth of 8.6% and 9.3%. Yet it collapsed to 5% by 2012–13. What did we do that growth fizzled out and our economy went into a downward spiral?

The Narendra Modi government picked up the baton from UPA 2 after securing a majority as the National Democratic Alliance (NDA) in the general elections in 2014. After initially struggling to make headway, the demonetisation and GST interventions took the wind completely out of its sails. But, incredibly, while the deadly pandemic could have been the last straw, the economy saw a robust revival. How did this happen? What was done right? What is still not being done right?

Despite India becoming the toast of the world, our private capital continues to remain shy and is just about stepping out of the shadows. What makes it risk-averse? Our demographic dividend demands that we grab the moment and chase high growth. What's holding us back? What do we as a nation need to do to fulfil our undeniable promise and potential?

These and several more questions have remained confounded in political dogfights, where it is difficult to separate fact from fiction. This book attempts to inform, explain, and give expert insight into how realistic our aspiration is to becoming a global power by transforming India.

Metrics of Success

- Our GDP is growing the fastest. In 1992, the GDP of France was $1.4 trillion; the UK's was $1.2 trillion and India was $0.28 trillion. In 2023, the GDP of France was $2.92 trillion, the UK's was $3.15 trillion and India's was $3.75 trillion.
- Six of the seven largest economies in the world are projected to be emerging economies in 2050 led by China (1st), India (2nd) and Indonesia (4th)
- The US could be down to third place in the global GDP rankings.[2]
- India leads the world in digital payment transactions with 127 billion digital transactions in 2022–23.
- India has built the world's largest optic fibre network, with a length of 647,759 km laid and 205,549 panchayats covered.
- We are the leading provider of satellite launch services, with 431 satellites launched for thirty-four countries.
- Banking the unbanked, India is home to the world's largest financial inclusion initiative—the country has opened 497 million new bank accounts.
- India is the second-largest consumer of data in the world, with over 14 million GB used just in first quarter of 2022. Significantly, our cost of data is one of the lowest in the world.
- We have the second-largest road network in the world: the US has 6,832,000 km, India has 6,700,000 km and China has 5,200,000 km. The country built 80,000 km of new highways in the past nine years alone.
- The Indian Railways is the second-largest rail passenger traffic carrier in the world—it carried over 7 billion passengers in

FY2022–23. It is also the fourth-largest rail freight carrier, carrying 1,512 million tonne of freight in 2022–23.

- In terms of steel production, India is now the second-largest producer by country (in millions of metric tonne). In 1980, the US stood at 101.4 m; China was at 37.1 m and India was only at 9.5 m. In 2000, China took the lead at 128.5 m, the US stood at 101.8 m and India was at 26.9 m. In 2020, while China surged ahead at 1,064 m, India, too, made its mark at 100.3 m, while the US stood at 72.7 m.
- India is the third-largest domestic aviation market in the world, with over 294 million passengers in 2022–23.
- We have the world's third-largest startup ecosystem, with over 99,300 recognised startups as on 31 July 2023.
- India is the third-largest producer and consumer of electricity in the world. Further, the country's power capacity grew by 40% from 305 GW in 2016 to 423 GW in 2023.
- India ranks fourth in the world in installed renewable energy capacity. Capacity has jumped to 178 GW—the country has more than doubled its capacity in eight years.
- India is home to the world's highest bridge—359 m above the river Chenab in Dharot, Jammu & Kashmir, with a 1.315-km-long steel arch structure supported by piers. It is also home to the world's longest tunnel above 10,000 ft—the 9.02-km Atal Tunnel connects Manali to Lahau in the Spiti Valley in Himachal Pradesh.
- Global private equity giant Blackstone Group has announced its plan to invest $2 billion annually in India. This decision underscores the company's long-term commitment to the Indian market, where it has already established substantial assets worth $50 billion. This investment strategy is driven by the high returns Blackstone has historically achieved in the Indian private-equity sector, alongside its significant

footprint in the real-estate market, which has positioned it as one of the largest landlords in the country.

- The diaspora has attained eminence and CEOs of top companies are of Indian origin, including the CEO of Alphabet Google, Microsoft, YouTube, Adobe, World Bank Group, IBM, Albertsons, NetApp, Palo Alto Networks, Arista Networks, Novartis and even Starbucks! And finally, India is the first country to land on the South Pole of the Moon and the fourth country to step on the moon!

Sector	2014 Figures	2023 Figures
Freight Loading (Railways)	1,097.57 million tonnes	1,512 million tonnes
CAPEX (Railways)	₹65,455 crore	₹260,200 crore
Track Construction	1,983 km	4500 km
Electrification (Railways)	730 route km	6,577 route km
Port Cargo Handling Capacity	1399.99 million tonnes pa	Over 1,610 million tonnes pa
Cargo Handled by Major Ports	800.52 million tonnes	795 million tonnes
Vessels Handled	Not specifically mentioned	21,846 vessels
Highway Construction	Approx. 12 km/day	Average of 34 km/day
Total Road Length	~54 lakh km	63.73 lakh km
National Highways Length	91,287 km	146,145 km
Number of Airports	74	148
Rural Roads Constructed (PMGSY)	3.81 lakh km	7.55 lakh km

Sector	2014 Figures	2023 Figures
Rural Electrification	~84% coverage	Near 100% coverage
Piped Water Supply	Limited coverage	Significant expansion under Jal Jeevan Mission
Piped Gas Supply	Limited coverage	Expanded to more urban and rural areas
Solar Generation Capacity	2.63 GW	66.78 GW
Wind Power Generation Capacity	28 GW	72 GW
Stock Market Capitalisation	~$1.6 trillion	~$3.9 trillion
Number of Start-ups	~350	Over 90,000
GDP	~$2 trillion	~$3.7 trillion
Total Length of Highways and Expressways	Not specifically broken out	Part of total 66.71 lakh km roads
Cement Production Capacity	356 million tonnes	570 million tonnes
Steel Production Capacity	109.85 million tonnes	160.3 million tonnes
Houses Constructed under PMAY (Urban)	The scheme was launched in 2015	Over 1.22 crore houses sanctioned
Houses Constructed under PMAY (Rural)	The scheme was launched in 2016	Over 2.95 crore houses sanctioned

CHAPTER ONE

The Road to 2014

According to the Economic Survey 2010–11, presented by the then Finance Minister Pranab Mukherjee, 'The manufacturing and services sector has registered impressive gains. Savings and investment are looking up while exports are rising.' The survey summed up the expectation of the government when it concluded, 'The real GDP growth is expected to reach the 9% mark in 2011-12 and the next two decades may well see the economy growing faster than it has done any time in the past.'[1]

But that was not to be.

Even before we delve into why that forecast failed, let us look at the seeds sown during UPA 1 that caused a storm in its orchard.

The Infra Mantra

In 1999, the dotcom boom became an obsession, especially after Satyam acquired Rajesh Jain's India World Communications for a reported sum of $115 million. All companies wanted a share in the dotcom valuation and several companies, including S.Kumars (the textile company), India.com, Indya.com and several others, joined the bandwagon.

Similarly, a decade later, it was the turn of the infrastructure companies. The exuberance of infrastructure spending led to many companies jumping into the fray.

To illustrate the rising trend of companies leaning into infrastructure, the following list shows how many of them changed their names to showcase themselves as infrastructure companies.

BSE Code	Old Name	New Name	Date
531261	Tanu Leafin & Investment Ltd	Concurrent (India) Infrastructure	10 June 1999
530773	IVR Constructions Ltd	IVRCL Infrastructures & Projects	1 October 2000
531959	Kumaon Pharmacaps & Chemicals	Newtime Infrastructure	15 March 2002
512048	Hindustan Stockland Ltd	Splash Media & Infra	7 October 2002
532123	BSEL Information Systems Ltd	BSEL Infrastructure Realty	16 October 2003
500390	BSES Ltd	Reliance Infrastructure	27 February 2004
530343	Genus Overseas Electronics Ltd	Genus Power Infrastructures	13 September 2007
530323	Era Constructions (India) Ltd	Era Infra Engineering	11 February 2008
513648	Marg Holdings and Financial Services	Marg Projects And Infrastructure	19 December 2008
531194	Mewar Industries Ltd	Brahmaputra Infraprojects	17 July 2009
531261	Kushagra Software Ltd	Concurrent (India) Infrastructure	16 November 2009

BSE Code	Old Name	New Name	Date
500402	Subhash Projects	SPML Infra	14 May 2010
530215	Victory Aqua Farm Ltd	Kings Infra Ventures	17 May 2010
508860	Diamant Investment & Finance	Diamant Infrastructure	8 June 2010
531959	Intra Infotech Ltd	Newtime Infrastructure	15 November 2010
506016	Jalgaon Re-Rolling Industries	JRI Industries & Infrastructure	22 March 2011
531537	Boss Securities Ltd	Jyothi Infraventures	4 July 2011
501945	Hingir-Rampur Coal Co	Dhenu Buildcon Infra	17 September 2012
512121	Hari Om Traders & Agencies	Delma Infrastructure	19 July 2013
519477	Umred Agro Complex Ltd	Cian Agro Industries & Infra	27 April 2016

Even the media company Zee made a beeline for infrastructure as its subsidiary, which was incorporated in July 1987 as Essel's Amusement Parks (India) Ltd, switched its name to Essel Infraprojects Ltd in February 2007. In fact, it went on to acquire a 11.2% equity stake in Hyderabad-based IVRCL for ₹200 crore with an aim to consolidate its presence in the sector, only to find that the promoter was not ready to play ball, i.e., they were not looking at a strategic investor and therefore were not really happy with the investment that Zee made in IVRCL.

Dilip Buildcon Ltd (DBL), which was founded in 1987 in Bhopal by Dilip Suryavanshi as a proprietorship concern called Dilip Builders, was then incorporated as Dilip Buildcon Pvt. Ltd on 12 June 2006. Dilip Builders was awarded its first major project as EPC contractor for Ansal Housing, which was constructing the largest private residential project in Bhopal. Dilip Builders entered the roads sector by working on five to six road projects in Madhya Pradesh valued between ₹2 crore and ₹3 crore each. The company's revenue at the time was ₹1 crore and it also went on to pick up subcontracting work from Essel Infraprojects. Dilip Builders was acquired by Dilip Buildcon and listed itself in 2016 after it had a full suite of infrastructure capability. Dilip Buildcon managed to continue to grow in scale.

A few realty companies had also started using the suffix 'infrastructure'. The increased number of projects, buzzing order inflows, consistently improving margins and, most important, ample liquidity all set the stage for several of them to join the gravy train.

That said, the bull phase that started in 2003 ended in 2008, at least for the infrastructure companies. In this phase, a lot of small contractors formed joint ventures (JVs) and entered the Indian infrastructure segment. By first executing smaller contracts, several small companies worked their way up to eventually taking up larger projects. The increased competition led to aggressive bids that shrunk margins for everyone involved. While the smaller players initially enjoyed the volumes and lower margins, as they saw some rewards in the form of better valuations in the stock market with bulging order books, the financial collapse of Lehman Brothers, followed by project delays due to tardiness in environment permissions and land acquisition, eventually affected all players. Even though initially the topline showed growth, the profit margin continued to shrink to a point that companies reported huge losses. Companies like Hindustan Construction

Company (HCC), Gammon India, IVRCL, Punj Lloyd, Simplex Infrastructure, Lanco, Era Infra, Marg, Madhucon Projects, Progressive Constructions and so on eventually landed in the throes of bankruptcy.

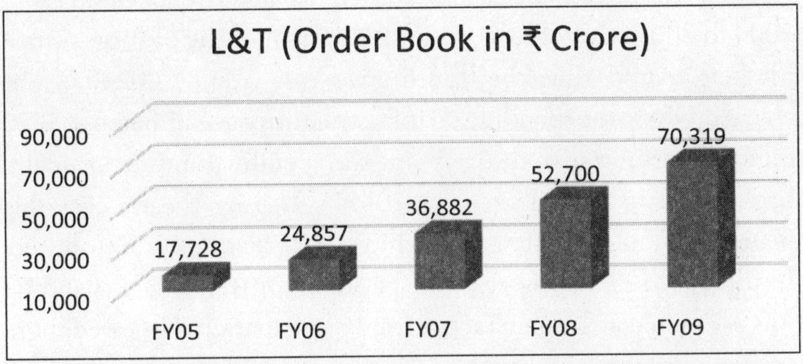

L&T's order book grew with higher allocation for infrastructure projects. It was one company that maintained professionalism and grew at a good pace as its capacity to undertake large orders was its unique strength. Further, it did not compromise on its margins and therefore did not undertake unnecessary risk.

To put things in perspective, from 2004 till 2008 a large chunk of capital through the IPO route or private equity (PE) deals was raised by Indian infrastructure companies. So, fundraising was not an issue.

	IPO / FPO		PE	
Fiscal year	**No. of Issues**	**₹ crore**	**No. of deals**	**$ million**
2004–05	4	6,221	7	92
2005–06	9	4,649	10	613
2006–07	12	6,646	40	2782
2007–08	21	20,647	77	7,824
2008–09	2	845	48	3,805

The Success of PPP Along with Strong Economic Growth

After remaining sluggish for a few years, as the global economic scenario improved, India too started its growth journey. From 2004 to 2008, a lot of foreign funds flowed into the country's stock markets. Amid this, the Tenth Five-Year Plan (2002–07) was charted,where the spending on infrastructure was estimated at $220 billion (within a span of five years, the spending on infrastructure had tripled to ₹6 trillion in 2010–11). During the time of this plan, the public–private partnership (PPP) model was introduced. In the Tenth Plan, private participation in infrastructure spending was estimated at 20%. In fact, private participation witnessed more traction and went higher than the targeted 20%.

The PPP model was another stepping stone in the development of the India infrastructure story. Significantly, the government created a viability gap funding scheme for PPP projects to help promote the sustainability of infrastructure projects. This scheme provided financial support (grants) to infrastructure projects, normally in the form of a capital grant at the stage of project construction (up to 20% of the total project).

The government also set up India Infrastructure Finance Company Ltd (IIFCL) in 2006, which provided long-term debt for financing infrastructure projects. IIFCL provided financial assistance in the following sectors: transportation, energy, water, sanitation, communication, social and commercial infrastructure.

To help finance the cost incurred towards the development of PPP projects (which can be significant, including the costs of transaction advisors), in 2007, the government launched the India Infrastructure Project Development Fund (IIPDF), which supported up to 75% of project development expenses.

In hindsight, the factors that boosted economic growth the world over were the same that caused it to correct finally in 2007–

08. In the run-up to 2007–08, the whole world was booming—even small African countries!

During this boom, the business model, which seemed to be advantageous for contractors, was to amass a good order book, as the reflection of a massive growth in the order book would impel equity analysts to project a high growth for the company and thereby fuel the rise in its share price. Heightened share prices would allow the promoters to borrow and qualify the company for a larger scale of orders. Further, companies were also allowed to collaborate with other, better-qualified companies with impressive balance sheets, and they would present a joint bid for the project. Five of the top ten bidders were foreign players, who were then enjoying lower cost of borrowing and, therefore, had an edge over domestic companies.

In the quest for a higher valuation, companies felt so certain of success that, in many cases, they offered a negative grant to the government—this means they were prepared to give the authorities a fee for giving them the order, with the assurance that they would undertake the cost of the project and collect the return from the use of the infrastructure. In 2009, the beleaguered Reliance Infrastructure had bagged the ₹1,725-crore Pune–Satara project, quoting the highest premium at ₹90.90 crore.

In August 2011, for six build-operate-transfer (BOT) contracts awarded, the National Highways Authority of India (NHAI) had budgeted a subsidy grant of ₹270 crore. But instead, the bidders promised it an income of ₹6,350 crore over the life of the projects. Experts were debating whether this was the result of aggressive competition or an underestimation of potential revenues on the part of government bodies. The results of NHAI's annual pre-qualification exercise showed that competition had intensified. There were ninety-eight unique bidders for fifty-five projects ranging from ₹82 crore to ₹11,350 crore. What the government thought was unviable seemed to have been assessed as very profitable by private-sector bidders, who opted for negative grants. In a round of bidding in 2011, some companies bid so aggressively that the internal rates of return (IRRs) went negative or lower than the cost of capital (the funds raised for the project). For example, the equity IRR for the Khagaria–Purnea annuity project won by Punj Lloyd was 7.8% while the IRR was negative for the Barasat–Krishnagar project.[2]

It does not make economic sense for a company to take a project with a negative IRR, unless it is compensated in some other way, like development rights along the highway. However, even in most of the recent BOT cases, such rights have not been awarded.

According to industry observers, as toll is collected in cash, not every rupee collected is reported. Faulty machines, power failures at the toll gates and theft are various ways of showing lower revenues. Some companies auction a toll booth to outside agencies and are thus assured a minimum return, but the true value of the traffic is far above than that recorded. It cannot be ruled out that the toll collection company is also a front company for the developer. Reportedly, NHAI received ₹1,352 crore as negative grant (upfront payments by bidders) till January 2013 under various highways projects.[3]

As of early 2024, India's overall toll collection had increased by nearly 2.6 times in the past five years from ₹25,154.76 crore in 2018–19. The total toll revenue stood at ₹27,637.64 crore in 2019–20, ₹27,923.80 crore in 2020–21, ₹33,907.72 crore in 2021–22 and ₹48,028.22 crore in 2022–23. The government estimates that total toll collection in India will likely surpass ₹70,000 crore in 2024–25 and rise to ₹130,000 crore by 2029–30.[4]

Fits and Starts

Infrastructure in India during the early 2000s, after its share of delays, always had a woeful start. A classic example is the Noida Toll Expressway (DND Flyway), which was commissioned on 7 February 2001. During the press conference of Noida Toll Bridge Company Ltd I attended at Taj Mahal Hotel in Mumbai, Pradeep Puri, its then president and CEO, made a presentation on the project. The 7.5-km, eight-lane expressway connected Noida to South Delhi across the Yamuna River. Later, in June 2007, it added another 1.7-km, four-lane link to Mayur Vihar. The project cost, at ₹393.17 crore, was as per estimates. It deployed electronic toll collection with a twenty-eight-lane plaza. The project, which began four months before the scheduled commencement date, raised funds through a debenture issue and bonds aggregating ₹70 crore against a paid-up capital of ₹100 crore.

Average traffic rose from 17,140 vehicles in February 2001 and 21,197 in October 2001 to 29,720 in March 2002 and so on, as seen in the table below:

Period	**Traffic** (total vehicles)
February 2001	17,140
October 2001	21,197
March 2002	29,720
March 2003	41,474
March 2004	48,202
March 2005	55,473
March 2006	62,504
March 2007	75,461
March 2008	91,546
March 2009	98,482 (DMRC commences operations in Noida)
March 2010	104,035
March 2011	104,749
March 2012	110,000 (PIL filed in 2012)
March 2013	111,012
March 2014	113,341
March 2015	113,151
Average traffic 2015–16	116,949
Average traffic 2016–17	70,794

The Noida Residents' Welfare Association challenged the levy of toll by the Noida Toll Bridge Co Ltd (NTBCL) as a 'user fee' for accessing the expressway. Cars were charged ₹25 and two-wheelers ₹12. A two-judge bench of the Allahabad High Court comprising justices Arun Tandon and Sunita Agrawal, in a 121-page ruling, said the levy of the toll was 'unfair and unjust' and that the users and commuters were being illegally taxed. The court also declared the clause allowing Noida Toll Bridge to collect toll as inoperative and bad in law. It said that the method of calculating the total project cost of the expressway was arbitrary and against public policy.

The judgment held the collection of tolls on the flyover illegal, effective from the date of the judgment. The order was based on three reasons:

- The manner in which the concession agreement was entered into was contrary to the requirements of equality and fair play under Article 14 of the Constitution of India.
- NOIDA (the authority, not the area) had no power to give the NTBCL the power to levy and collect tolls.
- The manner in which NTBCL was allowed to recover costs and get a guaranteed rate of return of 20% from the project was contrary to public policy.

The court noted in its ruling that ₹810.18 crore had been recovered from toll income since the commencement of the expressway till 31 March 2014. Approximately ₹300 crore more was realised through user fee or toll between 1 April 2014 and 30 September 2016, the court noted. The court ruled that the concept of user fee/toll was to meet the 'cost of construction' plus some reasonable returns on the investment. And, therefore, as soon as the entire cost of construction plus reasonable returns had been realised by way of toll, the bridge and the road were to be exempted from imposition of user fee. The court asserted that there was no justification for continuing the recovery of toll thereafter.

However, based on the formula in the agreement, the cost of the project as per the company's auditor report as on 31 March 2012 was ₹2,339.69 crore, which increased to ₹2,955.1 crore as on 31 March 2013 and ₹3,448.95 crore as on 31 March 2014. Till 31 March 2016, the total cost of the project based on 20% assured returns reached a figure of over ₹5,000 crore. This amount would go on increasing further in view of the formula adopted in Article 14 of the Concession Agreement to determine the total project cost. The court ruled that the total cost of the project could never be recovered and the bridge would never be free from the levy of toll. Further, there was no chance of handing over the bridge to the NOIDA Authority even after thirty years, nor could NOIDA terminate the agreement, as in that eventuality, it would be under obligation to pay the concessionaire an amount equal to the total project cost and returns thereon, apart from other expenses set out in the agreement, outstanding till the termination date. As the accrued total project cost due to the concessionaire had reached an astronomical figure of about ₹5,000 crore as on 31 March 2016, it was almost impossible for NOIDA to repudiate the agreement. Further, in case of termination even on the concessionaire event of default, liability was fixed on NOIDA to compensate the concessionaire for the debt and debt service outstanding in accordance with the agreement. The court viewed that there could not be an agreement by a public body with the aim of generating profits out of the project in favour of a private company at the expense of the common public. The Allahabad High Court order was further validated by the Supreme Court.[5]

Another example was that of IRB Infrastructure, which bagged the contract for construction and recovery of toll of the Mumbai–Pune Expressway. The 94.5-km expressway cost ₹16.3

billion ($200 million) to construct. The first sections opened in 2000, and the entire route was completed, opened to traffic and made fully operational from April 2002. Maharashtra State Road Development Corporation (MSRDC) entered into a concession agreement with IRB Infrastructure in August 2004 to operate and maintain the Mumbai–Pune Expressway as well as to develop, operate and maintain National Highway (NH) 4, which connects Mumbai and Pune. IRB bagged the contract against an upfront payment of ₹918 crore.[6]

The contract, which gave IRB Infrastructure the right to collect toll at a lump sum of ₹918 crore, was for a fifteen-year period. Vivek Velankar, a Right to Information (RTI) activist and president of NGO Sajag Nagarik Manch, cited figures uploaded on the MSRDC website to claim that the expressway's toll proceeds from August 2004 to December 2016 exceeded the target of ₹2,869 crore. The contract ended in August 2019.

IRB bid for the same road stretch again, and it bagged the contract against an upfront payment of ₹6,500 crore and then a staggered payment of ₹850 crore in the second year, ₹850 crore in the third year and ₹62 crore in the fourth year, aggregating to ₹8,262 crore for the concession period of ten years and two months. From ₹918 crore in 2004 to ₹8,262 crore, the collection estimated by the private developer jumped nearly ten times over fifteen years.

These two examples show that while Indian infrastructure was an opportunity, it grappled with evolving sensibilities and was riddled with legal issues and associated risks.

Going Global

In 2011, in our quest to take the infrastructure opportunities in India to the global stage, our magazine *Infrastructure Today*, which held conferences as well as annual awards with KPMG, decided to hold the 'Infrastructure Today Opportunity Conclave' in Manhattan, New York. I met Prabhu Dayal, Consul General, who kindly consented to our proposal to host the conference in the grand Consulate General Building as long as we took care of the hospitality expenses. The fact that the event was being held there added seriousness and authenticity to our event. The building itself has great character; Prime Minister Jawaharlal Nehru was instrumental in its purchase in 1950.

Source: 'About Consulate Building', *Consulate General of India*, https://www.indiainnewyork.gov.in/pages?id=Vy80RENjZGxxTTNDOHN5VkRJSGlJUT09&subid=Vy80RENjZGxxTTNDOHN5VkRJSGlJUT09.

The conference, held on 16–17 September 2011, attracted a lot of attention. We had an encouraging turnout with bankers, institutional investors, engineering firms and technology companies in attendance. The stars of the event included publisher Steve Forbes, who presented a keynote address on the opportunities in India, and Senator Larry Pressler, who participated in the conference. We presented awards to some of the fastest-growing construction companies in India to showcase their growth over a six-year period.

The author with Senator Larry Pressler

We were then approached by Rana Sarkar, President, Canada-India Business Council (C-IBC), who asked us to consider taking the event to Toronto. Back home in India, we managed to convince A.K. Upadhyay, Secretary, Ministry of Road Transport & Highways (MoRTH), to attend the conference and present the PPP opportunity for developers and financiers.

Held in association with the C-IBC at the Westin Harbour Castle, Toronto, on 11 May 2012, the 'Infrastructure Today

India Opportunity Conference' highlighted the contemporary infrastructure environment in India, showcasing opportunities for investors, entrepreneurs and project management firms. Other attendees included senior representatives from Essar Steel, IDFC Private Equity, Morgan Stanley, Delhi Metro Rail Corporation, SBI Capital Markets and IL&FS. They were accompanied by leading Canadian companies and investors, including Canada Pension Plan, Cleantech Group, Hydro One Networks, Reichmann Hauer Capital Partners, KPMG and Export Development Canada. We had an extremely enriching conference, where it was evident that Canadian pension funds and institutional investors were not ready to sink their funds in projects with risks, such as project delays, government interferences and environmental issues. Rather, they suggested that India offer bundled assets in special purpose vehicles (SPVs) once the assets were ready to earn rentals and tolls. They clearly articulated that they were ready to invest in long-term yield-earning assets that were not subject to pre-project completion risks.[7]

The author and family with the publisher Steve Forbes

While we took both these events to the global Meccas of finance, we did not seek any financial support from the Government of India for marketing and showcasing India's opportunities. We were lucky to have encouragement from people like Prabhu Dayal and A.K. Upadhyay as they facilitated our intention of spreading the message about India's grand plans in infrastructure.

Our mission, as I set about forming my magazine and the company, was the idea of 'Nation Building'. The economy and construction market trundled along and the magazine, launched as a bi-monthly by the Managing Director of Gammon India at Mumbai's Ambassador Hotel in September 1996, also limped along. I firmly believed that India needed to launch a large project that would employ lakhs of labourers so that they would earn daily wages and bring about some momentum in the economy.

NHAI, the nodal agency that managed the country's 34,298 km of national highways then, floated global tenders for seven projects worth ₹4,011.45 crore, covering 1,157 km of roads. Successful bidders—individual companies or consortia—would take on the projects on a BOT basis, which would allow them to charge a toll from all commercial and private vehicles using the road till they recovered their investment and assured themselves of an average 18% rate of return. The private sector had begun to explore participation in the highways plan.

So, when Prime Minister Atal Bihari Vajpayee announced the Golden Quadrilateral project, I felt my view had been vindicated. The project got off to a slow start, but I was certain that the government had realised that the way out of this economic downward spiral was through building infrastructure. Our magazines began purring with some activity around the launch of the Golden Quadrilateral plan.

Golden Opportunity

PM Vajpayee announced the Golden Quadrilateral (GQ) project on 24 October 1998, which truly began India's infrastructure story. The ₹50,000-crore plus National Highways Development Programme (NHDP) project aimed to connect Kashmir to Kanyakumari and Silchar to Porbandar. The prime minister laid the foundation stone for the project on 6 January 1999.

The NHDP was launched as a major initiative towards qualitative and quantitative enhancement of national highways, involving the development and four/six laning of about 13,150 km of road at a budgeted cost of over ₹54,000 crore (at 1998–99 prices). It was completed on 7 January 2012 at nearly half the budgeted cost of ₹32,492 crore. At 5,846 km, the GQ was the largest highway project in India then and the fifth longest in the world. For perspective, the Delhi–Mumbai Expressway is 1,352 km long, the Ganga Expressway is 1,047 km long and the Nagpur–Mumbai Expressway (officially, the Maha Samruddhi Mahamarg) is 701 km long. All three are under construction.

In the words of PM Vajpayee, 'The project envisages a Golden Quadrilateral linking the Delhi-Kolkata-Chennai-Mumbai-Delhi circuit, a North-South Corridor connecting Kashmir to Kanyakumari and a similar East-West Corridor connecting Silchar to Saurashtra. It is indeed the largest and the most ambitious infrastructure project undertaken in independent India – a highway to prosperity. The project will not only further integrate our great land through a network of world-class highways, it will also place India on the fast lane to socioeconomic development.'[8]

The programme set by the prime minister included:

- The GQ—Phase 1: The Delhi-Kolkata-Chennai-Mumbai-Delhi circuit, involving 5,846 km of road and costing about

₹25,050 crore. The date of completion was initially set for December 2004.

- North–South and East–West Corridors—Phase 2: From Srinagar to Kanyakumari and Silchar to Saurashtra (Porbandar), involving a distance of 7,300 km and costing about ₹30,000 crore. The date of completion of this project was set as December 2009.
- Port connectivity: The major ports (Haldia, Paradip, Visakhapatnam, Chennai, Tuticorin, Cochin, Mangalore, Mormugoa, Jawahar Lal Nehru Port Trust, Kandla) were also to be connected by about 400 km of roads. Other projects involved about 600 km of road development.
- Rail bridges: As there was to be no railway level crossings in the NHDP, about 250 railway over/under bridges needed to be constructed.

A striking feature of NHDP was that Indian firms had won the majority of contracts. Out of 133 ongoing contracts during 2002, as many as eighty-six contracts worth ₹10,490 crore had gone to Indian firms and thirty-five contracts worth ₹6,115 crore to joint ventures, while twelve contracts worth ₹1,974 crore had gone to foreign firms.

According to a World Bank study, the completion of the GQ alone was expected to result in an annual saving of about ₹8,000 crore (at 1999 prices) on account of fuel savings, reduced wear and tear of vehicles and faster transportation.

To encourage road construction, the central government had offered many incentives, such as total custom duty exemption on road building equipment not being produced in the country (twenty-one such items had been identified); income tax exemption for ten years from NHDP earnings; grant up to 40% for BOT schemes; and exemption from capital gains for NHAI bonds. The government also took several steps to arrange finances for the roads sector. A unique idea was introduced in the form of a nominal cess on both petrol and diesel. The funds so collected were to be put aside in a non-lapsable Central Road Fund (CRF) for the development of a modern road network. This idea itself resulted in an allocation of ₹1,192 crore, ₹5,590 crore, ₹5,962 crore and ₹5,880 crore from the revamped CRF during 1999–2000, 2000–01, 2001–02 and 2002–03, respectively.

The change was tangible and tremendous. For example, while in the previous fifty years, only 556 km of national highways were four-laned, over 14,000 km were being four-laned between 1999 and 2007. This was the first time such large funds had been mobilised for the development of state and rural roads across the country. The total length of national highways in the country was 58,112 km then (in 2023, this had reached 146,145 km). Of this, the length of national highways under the NHDP, port connectivity and other programmes being implemented by NHAI was 14,000 km. MoRTH also took up improvement of riding quality and widening of national highways other than those covered under the NHDP, which constituted a length of 44,112 km. Under the Improvement of Riding Quality Programme (IRQP), riding quality of 23,000 km length was improved during 1999–2002 and the balance length was targeted for improvement by 2003–04.

A November 2012 research paper by US-based thinktank National Bureau of Economic Research pointed out the positive impact of the GQ project on the organised manufacturing sector. '... the GQ upgrades have increased new entry the most in high- and medium-density districts that lie 0-10 km from the GQ network,' it said. 'For instance, moderate-density districts, like Surat in Gujarat or Srikakulam in Andhra Pradesh, that lie on the GQ highway registered more than 100% increase in new output and new establishment counts after GQ upgrades.'[9]

The GQ project also came with its set of challenges, some of which helped to rectify the system. In August 2003, Jharkhand-based project director Satyendra Dubey, in a letter to the prime minister, outlined a list of bad faith (mala fide) actions in a segment of a highway in Bihar. According to Dubey's claims, some big contractors had inside information from NHAI officials, the contractors for this stretch were not executing the project themselves (as stipulated in the contract) but had been subcontracting the work to small builders who lacked technical expertise, and that no follow-up was performed after awarding advances. Dubey's name was leaked by the Prime Minister's Office (PMO) to NHAI and he was transferred against his wishes to Gaya, Bihar, where he was murdered on 27 November 2003.

NHAI eventually admitted that Dubey's allegations were substantiated and implemented 'radical reforms' in selection and contract procedures. After considerable scrutiny by the Central Bureau of Investigation (CBI), Mantu Kumar and three accomplices were arrested and charged with murder. Mantu escaped from court on 19 September 2005 but was recaptured a month later. In 2010, Mantu and two others were convicted of murder and other offenses and sentenced to life in prison.

Many had criticised the NDA government, stating that such a project would be a burden on taxpayers and was bound to fail. Naturally, it had its own share of challenges and difficulties. In the first few years, global economic pressures like Y2K and the slump after the 9/11 terrorist attacks in the US overshadowed the burgeoning India infrastructure story. The GQ project also faced issues like delays in land acquisition and many state-related bureaucracy issues. And the change of government from NDA to UPA in 2004 made its impact felt. However, despite all hiccups, it turned out to be one of the most successful mega-projects, putting India on the global map.

That said, one moot factor was the requirement of funds.

The idea of establishing the CRF set the system of charging cess for construction of roads in the country. Even now, cess is being collected on petrol and high-speed diesel in the nature of additional duty of excise and customs in accordance with the provision of the CRF Act 2000. The act does not provide any terminal date for collection of cess. The rate for collection is as under:

Period	Cess per litre
2 June 1998–28 February 1999	₹1 per litre on petrol only
1 March 1999–31 March 2003	₹1 per litre on both petrol and diesel
1 April 2003–31 March 2005	₹1.50 per litre on both petrol and diesel
w.e.f 1 April 2005 to date	₹2.00 per litre on both petrol and diesel

The Ministry of Finance allocates funds for state governments/ Union Territories (UTs) for development and maintenance of state roads under the Central Road & Infrastructure Fund (CRIF) Scheme as per the provisions of the CRIF Act 2000 amended by the Finance Act 2019.

The cess collected so far per year since the idea was mooted is as under:

Year	Amount collected (in ₹ crore)
2002–03	5,245.00
2003–04	7,453.00
2004–05	9,287.00
2005–06	11,313.71
2006–07	12,206.54
2007–08	13,264.61
2008–09	15,198.23

Year	Amount collected (in ₹ crore)
2009–10	16,590.68
2010–11	16,978.93
2011–12 (April to September) Provisional	8,806.18
2016–17	72,400
2017–18	83,116
2018–19	113,000
2019–20	127,000

Source: 'Realisation of Road-Cess for Construction of Roads' *Press Information Bureau*, 8 December 2011, https://pib.gov.in/newsite/PrintRelease.aspx?relid=78305.

GDP at Factor Cost

Year	GDP at Factor Cost (%)
2000-01	4.3
2001-02	5.5
2002-03	4.0
2003-04	8.1
2004-05	7.0
2005-06	9.5
2006-07	9.6
2007-08	9.3
2008-09	6.7
2009-10	8.4
2010-11	8.4
2011-12	6.9

Source: Economic Survey 2011-2012. Available at https://www.indiabudget.gov.in/budget2012-2013/es2011-12/estat1.pdf.

Ambitious Government Targets

With the government's successful Tenth Five-Year plan (at least in terms of attracting private capital), it was not surprising that the next plan was even more ambitious. To put the figures in perspective, the target for the Eleventh Plan was $500 billion for infrastructure with private participation estimated at 30%. And the high ambitions did not stop here; the Twelfth Plan was estimated at $1 trillion with private participation at 50%.

There was a combination of many factors that led to such ambition, such as the impetus provided by the GQ project, more than sufficient liquidity at lower interest rates and good growth visibility for India Inc. Looking at growth parameters and Indian domestic consumption, more capacities were built in infrastructure-allied sectors, such as cement and steel. These sectors witnessed a great traction and more capacities were built estimating sustenance of demand.

Everyone on the street expected the target to be achieved. And why not, with the Indian economy growing at near to a double-digit figure, ample liquidity, consistently improving foreign fund flows and rising domestic demand? The positivity was visible on the bourses, too, as indices touched all-time highs by the end of 2007.

But then, something happened that took everyone by surprise: the global financial meltdown of 2008, considered the worst economic disaster since the Great Depression of 1929. While the crisis happened in the US, the impact was felt across the globe. And, as expected, it resulted in liquidity flowing back from emerging markets to developed economies. Even India, which had witnessed consistent FII inflow for more than a decade, witnessed a significant outflow. In 2008, FIIs turned net sellers to the tune of ₹53,000 crore.

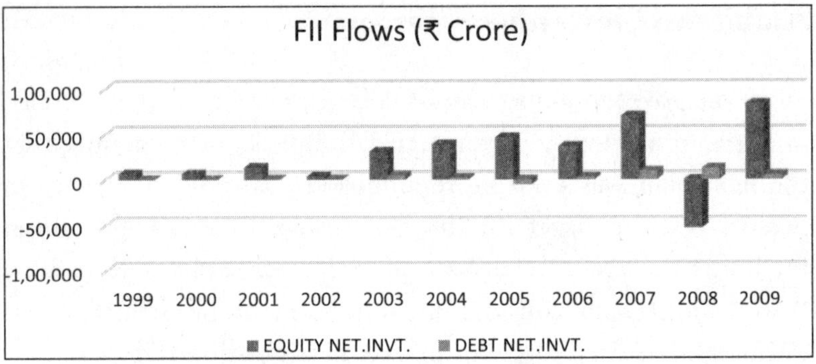

While every sector witnessed a negative impact, capital-intensive, rate-sensitive and debt-laden companies were hit the hardest. The realty, infrastructure and capital goods sectors were severely impacted.

There was a specific reason for this. Looking at the growth rates witnessed from FY2004 to FY2007, it was not only the large companies that had expanded. Even smaller infrastructure companies had gone ahead and expanded, sometimes beyond their means. As stated earlier, with many joint ventures and complex organisational structures, the balance sheets looked large but were heavily debt-laden. This was a period where, expecting better growth prospects, infrastructure companies had raised funds in every possible way. Debt constituents were significantly higher; yet, analysts were justifying the debt in view of the prevailing over-optimistic estimates. Every financial institution had lent funds to infrastructure companies. And a decade later, taxpayers are still paying the price of this hubris. India's public-sector banks have written off ₹10.42 lakh crore in loans in the nine years between FY2015 and FY2023, according to RBI data shared by the Ministry of Finance in the Lok Sabha in December 2023.[10]

Year	Amount written off (in ₹ crore)
FY2015	49,018
FY2016	57,585

Year	Amount written off (in ₹ crore)
FY2017	81,683
FY2018	128,229
FY2019	183,202
FY2020	175,877
FY2021	131,894
FY2022	115,536
FY2023	118,950
TOTAL	1,041,974

Source: 'Rs 10.4 lakh crore NPAs, 9 years: Which banks wrote off, recovered how much?', *Newslaundry*,1 March 2024, https://www.newslaundry.com/2024/03/01/rs-104-lakh-crore-npas-9-years-which-banks-wrote-off-recovered-how-much.

Of this, the banks have recovered ₹1.61 lakh crore. The data detailed twenty-seven bank groups, among which the top five banks that wrote off the highest loan amounts were the State Bank of India (SBI), Punjab National Bank, Bank of Baroda, Union Bank of India and Bank of India. These banks cumulatively lost over ₹6 lakh crore during the nine years and recovered a total of ₹1.9 lakh crore during the period. SBI wrote off the highest amount of loans, worth ₹286,144 crore, during the nine months. It was followed by Punjab National Bank, with a loan write-off of ₹105,478 crore, while Bank of Baroda recorded the third highest write-off at ₹92,174 crore. This was followed by Union Bank of India at ₹78,294 crore and Bank of India at ₹62,537 crore.[11]

While the RBI should have been red-flagging the ills in the economy, it was instead expected to play the role of cheerleader. Former RBI Governor Duvvuri Subbarao was finance secretary (2007–08) before taking over as RBI governor for five years on 5 September 2008. In his recent memoir, *Just A Mercenary? Notes from My Life and Career*, he claims that the Ministry of Finance under Pranab Mukherjee and P. Chidambaram used to pressure the central bank to soften interest rates and present a rosier picture of growth to shore up sentiments.[12]

As the global meltdown happened, it obviously resulted in economic slowdown. Even emerging economies were not spared. Once featuring as among the fastest growing economies in the world, even India witnessed significant decline in GDP growth.

Government Stimulus Efforts

The question is, given that the financial crisis was visible, what action was taken by the government? While other large economies faced major issues, India, with its domestic consumption story and decoupling, was expected to come out of the woods with the least impact.

While the government took some actions, it was not enough. To contain the effects of the global slowdown, it announced three successive fiscal stimulus packages from December 2008 to February 2009, amounting to a total of ₹80,100 crore. These packages were in addition to the already announced post-budget expenditure towards the farmer loan waiver scheme, rural employment guarantee and other social security programmes, enhanced pay structure arising from the Sixth Pay Commission, and so on. As a result, the net borrowing requirement for 2008–09 increased nearly 2.5 times from the original projection in 2008–09, from 2.08% of the GDP to 5.89%.

The second stimulus package had five elements, including a strong focus on interest rate reduction, additional liquidity enhancement to productive sectors, the export sector being offered financial aid and a boost to the infrastructure sector. In this package, the government focused on infrastructure needs wherein the India Infrastructure Finance Company Ltd (IIFCL) raised ₹10,000 crore to refinance infrastructure projects worth ₹25,000 crore. It also envisaged funding of additional projects worth ₹75,000 crore at competitive rates. Funding for these projects to IIFCL was also enabled in tranches of an additional ₹30,000 crore by way of tax-free bonds. In the third fiscal stimulus package, further tax cuts of ₹29,100 crore or about 0.5% of GDP were announced.

India Infrastructure Response

In response to rapidly deteriorating growth, the central government had allowed IIFCL to raise ₹40,000 crore (then 0.7% of the GDP) to help with financing projects (largely for roads and ports) that were being implemented as PPPs. The projects eligible for financing were well-advanced in their design and many were near financial closure—and they had been, or were at, the risk of being delayed on account of the global credit crunch.

The additional resources were made available through the IIFCL refinanced loans originally provided by commercial banks. This had ensured that at least long-term projects were able to proceed and help support aggregate demand and protect jobs during the economic downturn.

However, a few issues stood out in the PPPs. First, there was sectoral imbalance. For instance, while the Eleventh Plan outlay was maximum for the power sector (electricity generation/distribution), central assistance was largely tilted towards the roads sector, i.e. national highway projects. Over 90% of the projects approved by the Public Private Partnership Appraisal Committee (PPPAC) were in the highways sector. As a result, bridges, ports, power and other projects were short of funds.

Second, while the Planning Commission and the Ministry of Finance had cleared the ground as far as policy issues were concerned, the implementing ministries in the infrastructure sector had not kept pace with the process. This created bottlenecks and hampered the speed of implementation. Even Montek Singh Ahluwalia, who was then deputy chairman of the Planning Commission, candidly admitted that logjams at the implementation level led to an underachievement of the $500 billion target laid for infrastructure.[13]

Third, the creation of social infrastructure through PPPs was clearly lagging. Inadequate attention was paid to the creation of rural roads, rural electrification, housing, sanitation and education, which could have speeded up through PPPs.

During the years of high growth, it was assumed that it would continue indefinitely and that there would be no cyclical downturn. Even though the impact of the global financial crisis resulted in an abrupt capital pullout from the capital markets, India managed its stimulus effectively in insulating the slowdown. Despite escaping the crisis with a moderate GDP growth, the government's initiative to revive infrastructure faced multipronged hurdles owing to structural imbalances and funding shortages. One must understand that the link between infrastructure and economic development is a continuous process. Progress in development has to be preceded, accompanied and followed by progress in infrastructure, if we are to fulfil our declared objectives of generating a self-accelerating process of economic development. In my opinion, the UPA government failed to keep the process continuous.

The Games Begin

While it did appear that India was set for greatness in infrastructure development at one stage, the execution blew our reputation to smithereens.

India was awarded the prestigious honour of hosting the Commonwealth Games to be held from 3–14 October 2010 in Delhi. I interviewed Chief Minister Sheila Dikshit and questioned her on several projects that were running way behind schedule. All she did was instruct her secretariat to give us a table of the revised schedule of the completion dates.

Beneath the surface, there was moral corrosion. Just twelve days before the actual date of the opening ceremony, the foot overbridge connecting a car park with the main stadium collapsed as construction crews carried out some last-minute concreting work (the army was called in to rebuild it). At least twenty-three people were reported to be injured. The residential towers, which were intended to host the 6,500 athletes during the games, remained a work in progress. Concerns about incomplete plumbing and electrical work and piles of uncleared rubble were being expressed by associations. The UK officials condemned the still incomplete athletes' accommodation as 'unfit for human habitation'. Only eighteen of the thirty-four towers at the Commonwealth Games village were fully complete.

Finally, India celebrated its best-ever performance in any Commonwealth Games, but this was overshadowed by the exposure of corruption and marred our opportunity to deliver excellence. Suresh Kalmadi, an MP from Pune who served as the chairman of the Organising Committee of the Games, was the mastermind of the one of the biggest scams—₹70,000 crore. He was accused of giving out inflated contracts, including one worth ₹141 crore to Swiss Timing for equipment. The deal was inflated by ₹95 crore. Some of his other colleagues, Lalit Bhanot and V.K. Verma, had also been arrested. Sheila Dikshit refuted allegations of corruption against her government, claiming, 'Everything was done keeping in mind the national interest and prestige.'[14] However, only half of the amount allotted by the budget actually went towards facilities for Indian athletes. They allegedly had to relocate from the official housing units assigned to them to shabby and shady flats. A budget of ₹1,620 crore had been anticipated; the games finally went over budget by ₹11,500 crore.[15]

Scandals Galore

The government set ambitious targets for private investment in infrastructure but neglected to ensure that these projects progressed smoothly, demonstrating a lapse in judgement. This oversight was overshadowed by the impact of significant scandals, such as the 2G and Coalgate scams. These blunders were so severe that they dwarfed the challenges posed by the global recession, positioning the government as its own greatest adversary because of its actions.

The 2G scam pertains to the alleged loss to the exchequer to the tune of ₹30,984 crore and a presumptive loss of ₹1.76 lakh core in the allocation of 122 2G licences in 2008 to telecom companies on a first-come-first-served basis. A. Raja, then telecom minister, was accused of selling 2G spectrum licenses at a very low cost, which resulted in the loss of ₹1,760 billion ($25 billion) in government revenue. He was accused of not following rules and regulations as well as not recognising any advice from the Ministries of Finance and Law and Justice of India while allotting 2G spectrum licenses to telecom operators. The accusations included allegations from CBI after investigating the case that Raja intentionally advanced the cut-off date (from 1 October 2007 to 25 September 2007) to favour some specific firms (Unitech Wireless and Swan Telecom), which were allegedly ineligible for applying for telecom licenses, in return for bribes. Not only was the date cut-off pulled up, on 25 September 2007, the Department of Telecommunications announced on its website that applicants filing between 3:30 p.m. and 4:30 p.m. that day would be granted licenses. Although the policy for awarding licences was first come, first served, which was introduced during Atal Bihari Vajpayee government, Raja changed the rules so it applied to compliance with conditions instead of the application itself.

The Enforcement Directorate claimed that the kickbacks earned from the scam were routed to the DMK-run television channel Kalaignar TV, in which Kanimozhi and Dayalu Ammal, the wife of party patriarch Karunanidhi, held 80% of the shares. CBI argued that Raja incurred huge losses for the state exchequer by undercharging telecom firms. The Comptroller and Auditor General (CAG) of India estimated the total loss to be ₹1.76 lakh crore. Declaring the allocation of 2G spectrum by the UPA government 'illegal' and an example of arbitrary exercise of power, the Supreme Court on 2 February 2012 cancelled all 122 telecom licences allotted on or after 10 January 2008 to eleven companies during Raja's tenure. The Supreme Court said, 'Within two months, TRAI shall make fresh recommendations for grant of licence and allocation of spectrum in 2G band in 22 service areas by auction, as was done for allocation of spectrum in 3G band. The central government shall consider the recommendations of TRAI and take an appropriate decision within the next one month and fresh licences be granted by auction.'[16] In December 2017, a special court acquitted all the accused, including Raja, citing lack of evidence.

Barely had the dust settled over the 2G scandal that the Coalgate scandal rocked the political scene. Barely five months after the spectrum scam, three CAG reports were tabled in Parliament on 17 August 2012. The report on power stated that the Anil Ambani-led Reliance Power got an undue benefit of ₹29,033 crore when the government allowed the use of surplus coal from blocks allotted to Sasan power plant for its other projects. The second audit report on Delhi airport slammed the levy of development fee on passengers and stated that the Ministry of Civil Aviation violated the bid conditions for the benefit of GMR-led Delhi International Airport to over ₹3,415 crore.[17]

The third CAG report was the real damning one! The audit report on coal block allotment showed inefficient and possibly illegal allocation of coal blocks between 2004 and 2009. It estimated a loss to the exchequer to the tune of ₹10.7 lakh crore, but it later toned this amount down to ₹1.86 lakh crore in the final report. The central point of the CAG report that showed improper allocation was though the government had the authority to allocate coal blocks, it was to be done via competitive bidding. But the government chose to take another route and avoided competitive bidding. The CAG observed that the revenue secured from the allottees for allocation was much lower than would have been the case with competitive bidding.

After the CAG submitted its final report to Parliament, Prime Minister Manmohan Singh read out a statement in August 2012 that rebutted the report in the alleged/presumptive loss as well as the reading of the law. He also said that the observations of the CAG were disputed. For its part, the CAG felt the loss could have been avoided, or at least lower, as the procedure for auction of the precious natural resource could easily have been put in place by 2006. The failure to do so meant that twenty-five firms, including Essar Power, Hindalco, Tata Steel, Tata Power and Jindal Steel and Power, received a windfall through coal blocks on nomination basis instead of competitive bidding. The initial CAG report didn't talk about corruption, rather inefficient allocation. After the BJP filed a complaint with the Central Vigilance Commission (CVC), the CVC directed the CBI to probe the matter for corruption. At least a dozen companies were named in the FIR that resulted in a criminal investigation. Accusations ranged from malicious means for securing allocation, overstating net worth and non-disclosure of prior allocation to hoarding.

A report of the Parliamentary Standing Committee said that the allocation of blocks between 1993 and 2008 had been unauthorised. It recommended deallocation of all blocks where construction had not started and forfeiture of bank guarantees in others. Over the course of the investigation, the Supreme Court constituted a special court to try all cases related to the coal scam. In August 2014, three months after the NDA government was sworn in, the Supreme Court quashed 204 coal mine allocations. It found these allocations, made between 1993 and 2011, 'arbitrary and illegal'.[18]

While the Commonwealth Games scam was a blemish on our capability to create infrastructure for an international event, the Coalgate and 2G scams were an outcome of crony capitalism. Resources had been awarded for quid pro quo to friends and associates for decades, highlighting the lack of a transparent mechanism for awarding resources owned by the government where market forces ought to have determined the compensation that would accrue to the government.

As scams surfaced consecutively and the people responsible for approving files, including government bureaucrats, were named and then summoned to the courts, the bureaucracy clammed shut. The complex approval mechanism of projects stalled and then virtually ground to a halt. With government approvals not coming through, private companies began withdrawing from financial commitments and debt proposals. By 2012, bankers began to sense the growing non-performing loans on their books and became much more conservative in lending. The average annual growth of banking credit for 2001–10 was 23.6%. It dropped to below 10% by FY2014–15. Despite having a large pipeline of projects, companies that went ahead got caught in a debt trap as delays in projects caused by delays in approvals led them to borrow more and compromise their sustainability.

Eventually, the coal blocks were deallocated and the price was paid by the allied industries of infrastructure like steel, cement and power. While the company promoters would have benefitted over the previous years for having been awarded coal allocations at a steep discount to market prices, the change in circumstances laid the penalty on the listed entities of the promoters, which bore the brunt of the decision. Deallocation led to higher imports of coal at higher costs and low calorific values. This not only added to the cost but also meant increased cost of raw material. As for telecom, the segment had many foreign partners who had no idea how the licenses were secured by their Indian partners. With cancellation of such telecom licenses, it dented the sentiment of foreign players.

Norway's Telenor, which ran its Uninor brand in a joint venture with realty firm Unitech, invested $1.24 billion for a 67% stake in Unitech Wireless, which held a pan-India Unified Access Services (UAS) license to offer mobile telephony services in each of India's twenty-two circles. It also received spectrum to roll out these services in twenty-one of the twenty-two circles. Later, the fallout with Unitech and the Supreme Court decision led to disastrous consequences for this Norwegian company and it finally wrote off a total impairment loss of ₹5,825 crore during the nine months of 2016 while, previously, in 2012, it had written off ₹3,500 crore worth of India's assets—meaning a loss close to ₹9,325 crore. When Telenor finally exited, it wanted to cut its losses and settled for nothing, despite having 44 million customers and nearly ₹5,000 crore in annual revenues, leave alone the value of its spectrum.

The UAE's Etisalat wrote off more than ₹4,135 crore. Others who lost money included Moscow-based Sistema, which controlled Shyam Sistema Teleservices (SSTL) and Bahrain Telecom.

The Fallout

As bureaucracy turned cold, approvals became infrequent or extremely delayed. Promoters who raised debt ended up waiting for approvals, which proved expensive and piled up huge interest costs of delay. It was during this time that P. Chidambaram, the

Harvard-educated two-time finance minister, was called in to steer India's economy out of a web of economic mess, from a sharp slowdown in growth to a free-falling rupee, from industrial deceleration to rising prices.

Banks, previously generous in their lending to infrastructure sectors, had begun to grow sceptical about financing new projects. This shift led to infrastructure and some real-estate companies securing funds at exorbitant rates, sometimes exceeding 24%. Despite government efforts to assist with financing, bureaucratic challenges and alleged scandals compounded difficulties. Additionally, rising fiscal deficits and increased government borrowing were pushing interest costs higher. The result was a halt in private infrastructure investment owing to government delays, capital shortages and the issues mentioned, with negligible public expenditure in the sector.

Meanwhile, the UPA government's heavy spending on social schemes like MGNREGA, along with subsidies for oil, farming and loan waivers, led to escalated government borrowing. This contributed to the twin deficit problems, worsening the economic climate and keeping interest rates high, thus stifling public participation in infrastructure. The establishment of a Cabinet Committee on Investment did little to change the situation. Ultimately, it was primarily 'policy paralysis' that crippled the entire infrastructure sector.

One minister who singularly stood like the biggest challenge to progress was Minister of State for Environment and Forests Jairam Ramesh. Even when all clearances were received, the majority of projects got stuck in environmental clearances. Add to that, with woes like government organisations delaying payments, the cash generation cycle stalled. Project proposals became a 'snakes-and-ladders' boardgame as illustrated below:

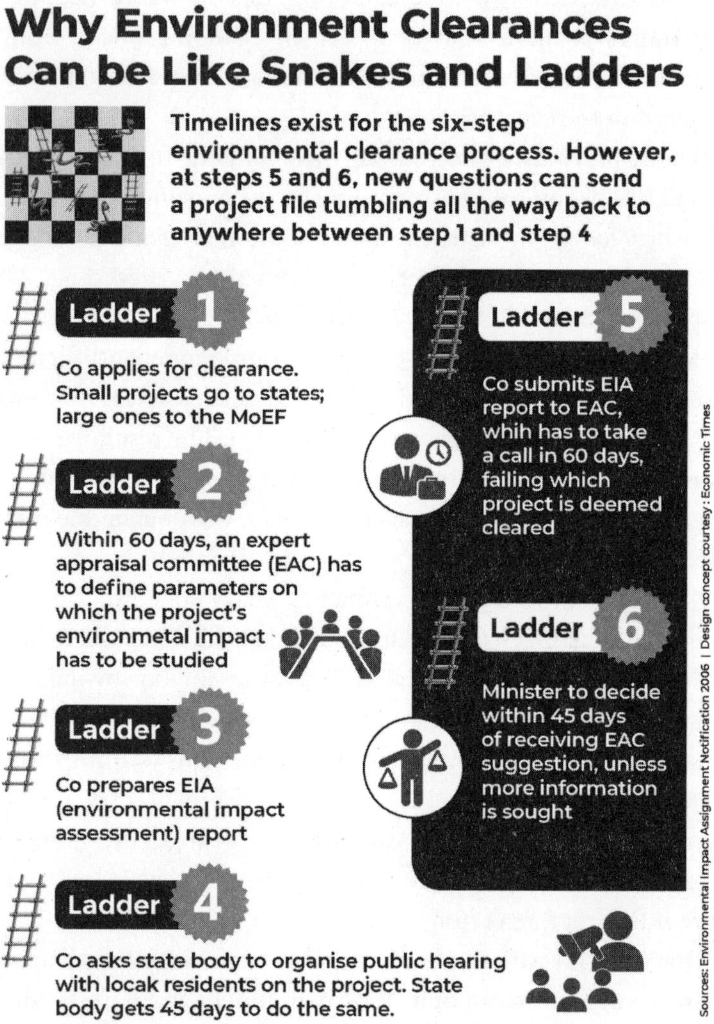

On 14 January 2013, normally a day when new projects get announced, GVK Power and Infrastructure, the developer of Mumbai International Airport, threw in the towel for a road project it was to build in Madhya Pradesh, citing environment and land acquisition delays.[19]

Just a week earlier, GMR Infrastructure, the developer of Hyderabad Airport, terminated its contract to widen a 555-km highway stretch between Kishangarh in Rajasthan and Ahmedabad in Gujarat because the Union government failed to provide land and environment clearances for the project.[20]

GMR and GVK pulled the plug on two high-profile road projects, collectively worth around ₹10,700 crore. The two projects—GMR's ₹7,700-crore Kishangarh–Udaipur–Ahmedabad project, for which it had bid to pay NHAI an annual premium of ₹636 crore (which would increase every year), and GVK's ₹3,000-crore Shivpuri–Dewas project in Madhya Pradesh—among the biggest in the sector. There was a fear that this would lead to a cascading effect.[21]

In GMR's case, the issue was environmental clearance being held up due to forest clearances. The Environment Ministry had begun linking the two (following a Supreme Court judgment), saying that the environmental clearance could not be taken without a forest clearance, thus adding to the delay. Under the 1927 Act, decisions regarding diversion of forest land for non-forest purposes are taken by the state government. The 1980 Act requires additional prior approval from the Centre. So even if the state's Environment Ministry gave its consent to the developer, the Centre could hold the approval back citing forest clearance. This created mayhem for developers.[22]

GVK pulled out of its project citing another Supreme Court judgment, which made environment clearance mandatory in case a concessionaire needed to extract boulders or other minor minerals (which GVK needed to do to clear the path for the highway). GVK gave the repeated inability of NHAI to gain the required clearance as a reason to pull out, citing a force majeure due to the judgment. Now if a concessionaire needed to surface the road and needed such permissions for removing every obstacle, how could anything be constructed to any timeline? The decisionmakers were completely apathetic to the plight of the developers and were somehow under the false impression that the developers were making a whole lot of money from these deals, so this was par for the course.

The question then arose before the courts whether the developers could walk away from their contracts and whether GMR, say, would have to forfeit about 6% of the project cost to NHAI? (At the time, developers needed to pay 1% of the project cost upfront as paid guarantee and then 5% as performance guarantee when the agreement was signed.) The issue was taken to arbitration, where both parties contested the matter. However, the outcome was such that GMR had to adhere to the stipulated contractual obligations, including the forfeiture fee.

Despite this, NHAI Chairman R.P. Singh remained unperturbed. In his view, these large groups were terminating their contracts because of problems raising equity to fund the project considering the market scenario. Expressing that they had been weathering the delays in environment clearances even in the past, he also attributed the pullout to the rise in materials costs. In his view, the viability of various projects was hit hard, mainly because of escalating input costs, lenders' tightening of existing norms and sliding of toll traffic of commercial vehicles owing to the shrinkage of exports that fiscal year. Evidently, the authorities were not in sync with the reality. The obvious response was 'not in my backyard', or to point the finger of blame somewhere else.

Coming back to Ramesh, he took over from outgoing minister A. Raja in May 2009 and quickly became industry's worst enemy. He rejected or put on hold several large industrial projects, citing faulty environment assessments. His tenure as environment minister was marked by extreme public controversies. In August 2010, he created a controversy by cancelling the forest clearance given to the bauxite mine project of Vedanta Aluminium in Orissa's Niyamgiri hills. When his ministry's review arm, the Environment Appraisal Committee, recommended the project despite his objections, he overrode them and cancelled the clearance. He also took a hard stand on mining in Maharashtra's Sindhudurg region and put on hold forty-nine leases given by the state government during Ashok Chavan's reign as chief minister.[23] He called for the demolition of the controversial Adarsh Cooperative Housing Society's thirty-one-storey apartment tower in Mumbai's upmarket Colaba region after it was found to have violated coastal norms.

The controversial nuclear power project at Jaitapur, in Ratnagiri, was another instance of his blow-hot, blow-cold approach. In the wake of protests from activist groups and locals, he had initially called for a pause on the proposed nuclear power plant till a transparent nuclear policy had been formulated. A few days later, the project was hastily accorded the green light following a meeting convened by the prime minister, which ironically coincided with the twenty-fifth anniversary of the Chernobyl nuclear disaster.

Ramesh gave the go-ahead to Korean giant POSCO's steel project in Orissa, citing its 'considerable technological, economic and strategic significance', but he raised objections to the Navi Mumbai airport project. He later cleared it, calling it a 'compromise deal' with the Maharashtra government! The minister gave the go-ahead for resumption of work on the Maheshwar Hydro Power Project in Madhya Pradesh after the PMO's intervention. As for Polavaram irrigation project in Andhra Pradesh, he took action very late, and only after activists exposed violations by the state government. Ramesh averred that work on the Loharinag Pala hydroelectric project in Uttarakhand could not be stopped, as several hundred crores had already been spent and the region needed electricity. But the Group of Ministers (GoM) set up by the prime minister decided to scrap it. Meanwhile, the Environment Ministry devised a 'Go' and 'No Go' system for coal mining. Again, the PM set up a GoM after protests from the Planning Commission and the Coal Ministry. And the Vedanta bauxite mining project in Orissa was scrapped, after Rahul Gandhi lent his support to tribals in Niyamagiri who were opposing the project.[24]

As projects got delayed (a few projects could not even make it to financial closure), interest payments got delayed and further source of financing was unavailable. Debt was getting scarce and with a sell-off visible in the equity markets, raising funds was almost impossible for infrastructure players. Forget the new listings, even listed players who once enjoyed premium valuations could not manage to raise funds. While this was the scenario with small and medium players, eventually large companies with a heavily leveraged balance sheet felt the burden too. Then, inevitably, the defaults began.

Project delays owing to non-availability of land and other government and environment clearances were the dominant reasons why projects were stuck. This caused government organisations to not release payments to contracting companies, leading to arbitration and appeals in long-drawn-out court battles. With money overdue and delayed at the government end, private companies were forced to borrow more at high rates of interest, causing excessive fiscal strain. Some private companies that had taken the risk of BOT models suffered as they had bid aggressively in the hope of a larger initial public offering (IPO) based upon their order-book position. These companies suffered colossal losses as debt repayments and overdue interest led them down a spiral. The non-performing assets (NPAs) of the public and private sector were on the rise in the infrastructure sector.

Wrong Acquisitions and Strategies

While we have discussed the failure of the government in implementing the reforms process at length, the wrong strategies adopted by private companies also must be addressed.

For example, Punj Lloyd, which was supposed to become the new poster boy of the Indian infrastructure space, homed in on gathering expertise in different segments of engineering. It entered a JV with a Saudi prince to form Dayim-Punj Lloyd Engineering

Ltd, another JV with KAEFER GmbH, Germany, a world leader in the insulation business. Further, it entered a JV with Swissport International, a world leader in the ground handling industry.

In FY2007, Punj Lloyd saw its revenue more than treble, with a contribution of 68.6% from overseas markets. A Libyan project also opened the floodgates for the company as it got several contracts in the UAE, Qatar, Saudi Arabia, Oman, Bahrain and Yemen. But in a bid to increase the pace, it wanted a vehicle to open its doors to Europe. As part of this strategy, it acquired a majority stake in Semb Corp Engineers & Constructors and its UK-based engineering services company Simon Carves through Punj Lloyd Pte Ltd (its wholly owned subsidiary in Singapore). The company envisioned that these acquisitions, besides giving it prequalification status for large, complex and higher value bids, would also enable it to pursue opportunities in Europe, China and Southeast Asia. Sembawang was a design-build engineering and construction service firm with core capabilities in process and plant engineering, heavy civil engineerings and building. This did result in a good increase in Punj Lloyd's order book, but at extremely low margins. The company was now offering a complete portfolio of EPC solutions with airports, jetties, MRT/LRT, tunnelling and sewerage, among others. Its projects were spread across many regions in the Middle East, Caspian, Asia Pacific, Africa and South Asia.

While all this looked good on paper, implementation and margins were stretched. What made matters worse was the impact of legacy contracts that were squeezing the bottom lines. In the quest for growth, Punj Lloyd had failed to assess the consequences of the performance bonds it had paid for a £135 million (later increased to £155.8 million) contract from Riyadh-based SABIC. The termination of this contract, due to a failure to conduct due diligence adequately, resulting in the delay of the project, followed by SABIC encashing the performance bonds, led to the company taking a ₹473.06 crore one-time hit later. As a result of this, and the fact that its total debt had soared over six times in just the three years between FY2006 and FY2009, its profit collapsed from an all-time high of ₹358.4 crore in FY2008 to a loss of ₹224.7 crore in FY2009. While in FY2008 it had a total debt of just ₹1,607.2 crore, by the end of FY2014, its total debt had increased by ₹4,640.3 crore to ₹6,247.5 crore. As a result, while in FY2008 it had paid just ₹180.6 crore as interest, in FY2014 it ended up paying ₹882 crore—over 2.7x its EBITDA—as interest!

Similarly, some other players made different but ill-advised moves and suffered. Big players like Reliance Infrastructure, Jaiprakash Associates and IVRCL Infrastructure all pursued growth by making huge bets on contracts with inherent high risks. As margins in this business were not traditionally very healthy, even a slight delay in projects was enough to create a huge rumble in their prospects. The suffering companies had no choice but to sell non-core assets.

This challenging period also saw infrastructure entities offloading non-core assets at significant discounts, deepening losses on assets initially acquired at high valuations. Meanwhile, the Indian infrastructure sector, especially in the early 2000s, experienced aggressive bank lending despite banks' limited domain knowledge, leading to a cycle of stuck cash generation and rising NPAs.

Issues extended beyond domestic financial strategies. Infrastructure firms grappled with external commercial borrowings and foreign currency convertible bonds (FCCBs). The 2008 equity market crash exacerbated the situation, as lenders resisted converting their bonds into equity at diminished rates, increasing the financial outflow for infrastructure companies and impacting the broader corporate landscape in India.

Moreover, Indian companies rarely adopted FIDIC contracts, which are internationally recognised guidelines offering a balanced risk-sharing framework, crucial for mitigating disputes and ensuring project completion. This oversight became particularly problematic given India's infrastructural deficits and procedural delays, a stark contrast to smaller nations like Bangladesh, which implemented these standards more effectively.

As a result, a significant amount of capital became tied up in stalled projects and arbitration. In 2018 alone, about ₹70,000 crore was mired in arbitration, although a 2016 resolution allowed government agencies to pay 75% of the arbitration amount for projects delayed by land acquisition or regulatory issues.

The Downward Spiral

After peaking at 8.9% in 2010–11, the economy began to sputter. India's economic growth rate slipped to 5.3% in the fourth quarter of 2011–12 (against 9.2% in the same quarter in the previous year), the lowest in nearly nine years owing to the poor performance of the manufacturing and farm sectors. GDP moderated to 6.7% in 2011–12.

Somehow, the government had its head firmly planted in the sand. Despite the warnings of economists, it kept insisting India's troubles were simply an outcome of the crisis in the Euro Zone. However, the country's twin deficits for 2011 and 2012—the fiscal deficit at 5.9% and the current account deficit at 3.8% of the GDP—the high interest rates and persistent inflation indicated that many of the problems had arisen out of its own inaction. Global ratings agency Standard & Poor's (S&P) revised its rating outlook for India and stated that if India did not push through reforms, it could be downgraded in the next two years. There was an expectation that S&P could downgrade India from its BBB+ rating to BBB–, which would mean that India would be rated alongside the likes of nations such as Azerbaijan, Benin, Cameroon, Gabon, Grenada, Iceland, Jordan, Senegal and Turkey.

The industry wanted reforms. Finance Minister Pranab Mukherjee was hinting at austerity measures and Prime Minister Manmohan Singh approved the establishment of an investment tracking system to prevent major investment projects from getting mired in bureaucratic procedures and thus delayed.

Clearly, the government was out of its depth. In desperation, it began clutching at some straws; many of these moves backfired. During the third quarter of 2011, a Supreme Court judgment created a stir that echoed round the world.

The Vodafone Case

In May 2007, UK-based mobile operator Vodafone purchased Hong Kong-based Hutchison's telecom business, which included operations in India, for about $11.2 billion. Through the deal, Vodafone acquired a 67% stake in Hutchison-Essar Ltd (HEL) through companies based in Netherlands and Cayman Islands.

Indian income tax authorities sought ₹11,000 crore from Vodafone, which challenged the move. The IT Department maintained that as capital gains were made in India through the deal, Vodafone was liable to pay the tax and issued a show-cause notice asking why it should not be treated as a representative assessee of the Vodafone International Holding. Vodafone challenged the notice before the Bombay High Court, saying it was a share transfer carried outside India. The appeal was rejected by the court in December 2008, which was again challenged by Vodafone before the apex court. The Supreme Court also dismissed Vodafone's appeal in January 2009 and directed the IT Department to decide whether it had the jurisdiction to tax the transaction. However, it observed that Vodafone would be at liberty to challenge the IT department's decision if it went against Vodafone and the question of law would also be open.

The IT Department passed an order in May 2010 that it had competent jurisdiction to treat Vodafone as an 'assessee in default' for failure to deduct tax at source. This decision was challenged by Vodafone before the Bombay High Court. In a judgment on

8 September 2010, it dismissed Vodafone's petition and held that 'the essence of the transaction was a change in the controlling interest in Hutchison Essar Ltd, which constituted a source of income in India'. It said, 'the proceedings initiated by the Income Tax Authorities cannot be held to lack jurisdiction'. This judgment was again challenged by Vodafone before the Supreme Court on 14 September 2010. In an interim order on 27 September 2010, the apex court refused to stay the verdict and asked the IT Department to compute the tax liability of Vodafone.[25]

On 15 November 2010, the Supreme Court asked Vodafone to deposit ₹2,500 crore and a bank guarantee of ₹8,500 crore before the hearing of the case began. It also said that if the case went in favour of Vodafone, the government would have to return the amount to Vodafone along with interest. Vodafone lost the case in the Bombay High Court in 2010 but then again appealed to the Supreme Court. The apex court finally began hearing detailed arguments on 3 August 2011 and reserved its judgment on 19 October 2011.

The Supreme Court's final landmark decision on 20 January 2012 directed the tax department to refund ₹2,500 crore with interest of 4% within two months and asked its registry to return the bank guarantee within four weeks. Delivering the judgment, Chief Justice S.H. Kapadia said, 'The government has no jurisdiction over Vodafone's purchase of mobile assets in India as the transaction took place in Cayman Islands between HTIL and Vodafone.' He further clarified that for the stability of economic operations, investors should know where they stand. He said Hutch Essar, whose Indian operations were acquired by Vodafone, was not a fly-by-night operator and was in India since 1994 and had contributed ₹20,242 crore by way of direct and indirect taxes. There were eight such other cases where the IT authorities were locked in similar battles—all these would now get impacted with this judgment. The IT authorities were desperately seeking to recover tax dues to boost their collections for an economy gasping for breath.[26]

In his book *The Coalition Years (1996-2012)*, released on 13 October 2017, Pranab Mukherjee revisited his contentious decision that followed the Supreme Court decision in Vodafone's favour:

> This decision of mine, born out of my conviction that India's Direct Tax Policy should not discriminate between domestic and foreign entities, was a subject of much debate and remains so to date. The controversy began when I announced in my 2012–13 budget speech that I proposed to amend the Income Tax Act, 1961, with retrospective effect to undo the Supreme Court judgement in the Vodafone tax case.
>
> While the Supreme Court, in an interim order on 15 November 2011, had directed Vodafone International to pay ₹2,500 crore and provide a bank guarantee of ₹8,500 crore, its decision of 20 January 2012 directed the tax department to refund ₹2,500 crore with interest of 4% within two months and asked its registry to return the bank guarantee within four weeks. With the Supreme Court setting aside the judgement of the High Court, it created an unusual situation where the tax department would have to return several thousands of crores to several companies …
>
> Manmohan Singh was convinced that the proposed amendment in the IT Act would impact FDI inflows into the country. I explained to him that India was not a 'no-tax' or 'low-tax' country ...
>
> Later, Sonia Gandhi, Kapil Sibal and P Chidambaram also expressed the apprehension that the retrospective amendments would create a negative sentiment for FDI. I explained to them that FDI comes when there is profitability and not on account of zero tax. Clarificatory amendments

were proposed to make the intent of the legislature clear. This would bring tax certainty and would clarify that India had the right to tax similar transactions. Two more Cabinet colleagues separately advised me to take a middle path, and to reconsider the decision. But I remained resolute.

Here is a chronological summary of events related to the retrospective amendment of the Income Tax Act in India:

1. *15 November 2011*: The Supreme Court, in an interim order, directed Vodafone International to pay ₹2,500 crore and provide a bank guarantee of ₹8,500 crore.
2. *20 January 2012*: The Supreme Court ruled in favour of Vodafone, directing the tax department to refund ₹2,500 crore with 4% interest within two months and return the bank guarantee within four weeks.
3. *The 2012–13 Budget speech*: Finance Minister Pranab Mukherjee announced a proposal to amend the Income Tax Act 1961, with retrospective effect to counter the Supreme Court's judgement in the Vodafone tax case. This amendment aimed to assert the government's right to levy tax on M&A deals involving overseas companies with business assets in India, dating back to 1962.
4. *Reactions to the proposal*:
    - The FM argued that the amendment was necessary to protect India's fiscal interests and prevent revenue erosion.
    - PM Singh and other political leaders, including Sonia Gandhi, Kapil Sibal and P. Chidambaram, expressed concerns that the amendment could negatively impact FDI inflows.
    - The FM explained that India's tax policy treated all taxpayers equally, and the amendment aimed to ensure that foreign investors paid taxes similar to domestic investors.

5. *Internal government debates*:
   - Several Cabinet colleagues advised the FM to reconsider or take a middle path, citing potential negative sentiments for FDI.
   - Despite these concerns, the FM remained resolute, arguing that profitability, not zero tax, drives FDI.
6. *Days before introducing the Finance Bill 2012*: Multiple colleagues, including one with a high-ranking Vodafone official, approached the finance minister seeking reconsideration of the retrospective amendment.

These events highlight the controversy and debates surrounding the retrospective tax amendment and its implications for India's tax policy and foreign investment climate.[27]

The impact of the retrospective tax decision was severe. It cannot be computed in financial numbers. But it ricocheted for several years until it was amended in 2021. In March 2015, based on this legislation, Cairn Energy was asked to pay a tax of ₹29,000 crore.

In days following this retrograde step, international investors were rattled. Harold 'Terry' McGraw III, USIBC chairman and CEO of McGraw-Hill Companies, is reported to have suggested in a letter to US President Barack Obama's deputy national security advisor Mike Froman that with Indian cabinet ministers busy dousing political fires, powerful bureaucrats were running the show in Delhi.

'What is apparent is that political power is devolving to strong state leaders and the vacuum at the Centre is allowing forces in government to move on issues that are harmful to India's investment climate,' McGraw wrote. He also mentioned that there is a 'rut of policy paralysis' in New Delhi. Ron Somers, President of USIBC and an ardent India supporter, was warned just as the Union Budget for FY2013–14 was to be announced that investors had 'myriad alternatives' and 'must compete for capital'. In an article titled 'Indian Economy: Reform or Perish', he advised that India needed to be mindful of declining investor sentiment and ought to create a welcoming environment that attracts investment. He went on to say, 'It is not enough this time to assume that the investment community will suck it up and persevere because of their hunger for India's market.' The article followed within a week of US Secretary of State Hillary Clinton's short-notice trip to India, and clearly reflected the growing anti-India mood in the corporate leadership, which was time and again expressing its frustration over the slow pace of reforms in India. Quite exasperated with the authorities as they deflected criticism aimed at their lethargy to global headwinds, Somers added, 'Not surprisingly, the government of India's public relations machine continues to predict blue-sky growth rates in the mid-7% range, claiming that the current policy paralysis in the country is temporary, even against the backdrop of an anaemic global economic recovery and a continuing European crisis.'[28]

Amid the comments coming from international investors and the US government, Chief Economic Advisor Kaushik Basu made some observations at a lecture at the Carnegie Endowment in Washington on 18 April 2012. While his intention was to highlight the imminent European crisis of 2014, his further remarks, as follows, got him in a pickle:

> I mentioned also, as I have done several times in India, that, thanks to coalitional democracy, there is some slowdown in economic reforms and decision-making. I specifically mentioned that the problem with the GST reform was that the opposition realized this is a good reform. Therefore, it was reluctant to let it happen under the current regime. A single-party majority government would not face this problem. If there is a single-party majority in the next election, that will facilitate such reforms. I argued that some reforms, such as FDI in multi-brand retail, were likely to

happen sooner because in principle they did not need the support of the opposition; and this will give a boost to the mood of the economy.[29]

Even while these events unfolded, another storm was brewing.

The Green 'Block'

Jayanthi Natarajan was noticed by Sonia Gandhi and appointed spokesperson for the Congress party. She replaced Jairam Ramesh as environment minister on 12 July 2011 in the UPA-led government. She served as the Minister of State for Environment and Forests (Independent Charge) from 12 July 2011 to 20 December 2013.

During her term, the single big-ticket project to get conditional clearance was HCC's flagship hill city project at Lavasa near Pune. However, other projects, including those of POSCO and Vedanta, remained stalled, irking domestic industry and shaking the confidence of foreign investors. Despite securing clearances from the minister, POSCO faced land acquisition hurdles in Odisha, while Vedanta continued to be engaged in a legal battle with the ministry over its mine in Niyamgiri in Odisha.

The word on the street said that only the style of functioning of the minister was different—industry still found it difficult to start projects on time owing to delay in clearances. Unlike Ramesh, Natarajan maintained a very low profile and had limited interaction with the media. So, the media attention the ministry enjoyed during Jairam Ramesh reduced. Other than that, nothing really changed—the projects continued to pile up without a decision.[30]

On 20 December 2013, Natarajan resigned from the Council of Ministers. On 5 November 2014, she wrote a letter to Congress President Sonia Gandhi, which became public on 30 January

2015. In the letter, she recalled the sequence of events that led to her resignation as PM Singh allegedly conveyed to her that Sonia Gandhi wanted her for party work and therefore wanted her to resign from her ministerial position. She went on to say that she had never been told of any issues regarding her work prior to 20 December 2013 and that she felt that some analysts speculated that she might be projected as the focal point for the perceived failure of the economy at the time.

On 13 January 2014, a report in *Indian Express* had claimed that nearly 350 files had been held back by Natarajan and her office. As many as 180 of these files were recalled and retrieved from Natarajan's residence on 22, 23 and 24 December 2013 unsigned. About 119 files were signed but were held back by the former minister for some reason and another fifty signed files were retained by her staff. Twenty-eight of these files were sent to Natarajan in 2012, while two to three date back to 2011. On 2 January 2014, an office memorandum titled 'Status of files submitted to the Office of the then MOS (IC) E&F Jayanthi Natarajan' was issued to all divisional heads in the Ministry of Environment and Forests, sharing the list of the files sent back. This memorandum—as accessed by the newspaper—asked all divisions, sections and units to go through these lists and 'indicate whether apart from the listed files, any other file is still pending with the Office of the then MoS (IC)'.[31]

Why was Jayanthi Natarajan in the eye of a storm?

Apparently, the 350 files with her were worth ₹10 trillion in projects that were held up under various pretexts, as per estimates made by various infrastructure ministries. According to an internal government analysis carried out in early December 2013, out of major projects worth ₹14 trillion that had sought the Centre's help for unclogging red-tape hurdles, the Environment Ministry was responsible for delays in case of investments of over ₹5 trillion. These were projects that had approached the government for help with clearances under the aegis of the Cabinet Committee on Investment (CCI), a panel of ministers set up to resolve procedural delays plaguing industry.

Further, projects worth another ₹4 trillion, for which clear deadlines had been set to resolve policy issues, continued to be held up, as per senior government officials in different ministries. In addition, projects worth a further ₹1 trillion, identified by the Gujarat government as hit by red tape, were stuck at the green ministry. One of the biggest areas of concern, discussed at the highest levels of the government and the Congress high command after complaints by CEOs as well as top Cabinet ministers, had been the Forest Ministry's apparent reluctance to overhaul its norms and processes for granting clearances.

The projects stuck for clearances included three major rail linkage projects involving investments of ₹100 billion (₹10,000 crore), which could boost India's coal output by 300 million tonne a year. Had this been done then, India would not have spent such a huge forex spend to import coal in 2022. (In FY2022, India imported 208.93 million tonne of coal worth ₹2.28 trillion).[32]

Private Participation

The GQ project and the NHDP programme set the ball rolling for private contractors to grow along with the pace of infrastructure growth.

The boom in investments between 2004 and 2012 was led by the private sector. As much as 60% of the new investment proposals during this period of exuberance were by the private sector. The government's share increased after this boom period. However, its role was never sufficiently countercyclical. It did not offset the fall in private investments.

Research body Centre for Monitoring Indian Economy (CMIE) had stated that projects worth ₹4 lakh crore were completed in FY2012, the highest in the previous few years. The corresponding numbers were ₹3.4 lakh crore and ₹3.8 lakh crore, respectively, for the previous two years. CMIE reported with elation that the existing pipeline of projects was strong enough to sustain for the next several years and FY2012 had seen a dramatic pickup in the completion of some outstanding projects. According to CMIE, at the end of March 2012, outstanding investment in projects amounted to ₹140 lakh crore, which was six times the country's annual gross fixed capital (GFC) formation. It reported that the pipeline of outstanding projects was so large that even if no new project were announced for the next four to five years, the Indian economy could continue to grow at a brisk pace.

Data compiled by CMIE suggested that total completion during FY2012 was estimated at around ₹4 lakh crore. This would be the highest project completion seen by the industry in a single year. From ₹66,187 crore in 2003–04, project completion had increased to ₹3.8 lakh crore in 2009–10. It then moderated a bit to ₹3.4 lakh crore in 2010–11. CMIE's analysts expected the number to double to ₹8.3 lakh crore in 2012–13, if the completion rate went up by 100%.

	New projects		**Projects completed**		**Projects shelved**	
	No.	**₹ crore**	**No.**	**₹ crore**	**No.**	**₹ crore**
FY2009–10	4,044	1,672,678	1,710	384,520	539	276,230
FY2010–11	5,052	1,655,251	1,732	338,845	377	165,222
FY2011–12	3,194	1,021,584	1,575	315,329*	522	315,329*
*CMIE estimates the final figure to be a little over ₹4 lakh crore						

Source: Malini Bhupta, Rajesh Bhayani and Katya Naidu, 'Project completion highest in years, pipeline robust', *Business Standard*, 19 April 2012, https://www.business-standard.com/article/economy-policy/project-completion-highest-in-years-pipeline-robust-112041902022_1.html.

But trouble was on the horizon. While the project completion graph was on the ascendant, new project announcements were diving to all-time lows. CMIE reported that new investment announcements fell to a thirty-three-quarter low of ₹58,494 crore in the September 2012 quarter. Net investment announcements by the private sector (at ₹35,368 crore) and the government (at ₹23,126 crore) were the lowest since the September 2004 quarter. Barring Kerala, Punjab and Himachal Pradesh, investment announcements during the April–September period in 2012 remained substantially lower than the average in the previous four quarters. All industries, except for steel, electricity distribution and road transport, saw a sharp fall in new investment announcements. In fact, new investment announcements had been falling for the previous three years. From ₹3 lakh crore in 2003–04, new announcements peaked at ₹22.6 lakh crore in 2008–09. Promoters went shy thereafter and announcements fell gradually to ₹16.6 lakh crore in 2009–10, ₹15.08 lakh crore in 2010–11, ₹10.3 lakh crore in 2011–12 and further to ₹3 lakh crore in the first half of 2012–13, according to CMIE. The fall in the September 2012 quarter was exceptionally steep.[33]

Private capital started to become sceptical and hold back its enthusiasm. The problem began with projects not receiving due permissions, which resulted in costs ballooning and projects ultimately becoming unviable. Meanwhile, private developers who had over-ambitiously taken on more than they could chew felt a liquidity squeeze as several of their projects got stuck midway owing to land acquisition or other environment-related issues. The delays caused project economics to go haywire, and developers finally found several of them unsustainable.

The Need to Fast-track

With GDP growth slowing down to a nine-year low of 6.5% in 2011–12, the PMO had approved the setting up of an investment-tracking system to monitor and fast-track the implementation of projects with an individual outlay of ₹1,000 crore.

While the National Manufacturing Competitiveness Council would track all public-sector projects with an investment of ₹1,000 crore and above, the Department of Financial Services would monitor such projects in the private sector. A year later, when the project progress seemed to make no headway, PM Singh set up a project monitoring group (PMG) to track large investment projects, aiming to fast-track approvals for stalled projects and boost investor confidence. FM P. Chidambaram then put up a list of about 215 such projects, where banks had funded over ₹7 lakh crore. The time and cost overruns being faced by these projects was also documented, as well as the action required to remove the implementation bottlenecks.[34]

The Ministry of Finance documented projects worth ₹1.46 lakh crore as pending because of the absence of regulatory clearances in the sectors of power, steel, highways and cement. These projects did not include mega projects like the $12 billion POSCO steel project and $90 billion Delhi–Mumbai Industrial Corridor, which were also delayed on various counts like clearances and land acquisition.[35]

The idea of a high-powered body to give speedy clearance to infrastructure projects was initially mooted by Chidambaram. He had suggested the body be called the National Investment Board (NIB). Chidambaram's proposal had, however, evoked sharp criticism from the Environment Ministry, which had argued that the NIB would dilute its powers to address green concerns. The decision on establishing the NIB was then deferred by the Cabinet, as the prime minister wanted more interministerial discussions and a consensus on the proposal.

Meanwhile, Environment Minister Jayanthi Natarajan was opposing any move to bypass the required green clearances for mega projects and, accordingly, she wrote to the PM. In her view, the proposal seemed to have been mooted only for the benefit of large firms and investors while having no provision for redressing the concerns of the people affected by projects. Meanwhile, Chidambaram was red-flagging that there were over 100 projects, each involving an investment of ₹1,000 crore or more, that had been delayed because of various reasons.[36]

Break-up of 86 delayed projects in all sectors as on March 2012	
Delay by	**No. of projects**
1–12 months	34
13–24 months	17
25–60 months	24
60 months and above	11
Railways: Break-up of 11 delayed projects	
Delay by	**No. of projects**
1–12 months	2
13–24 months	1
25–60 months	3
60 months and above	5
Power: Break-up of 32 delayed projects	
Delay by	**No. of projects**
1–12 months	9
13–24 months	8
25–60 months	11
60 months and above	4

Source: Dilasha Seth, 'Nearly half of central projects worth over Rs 1,000-cr delayed', *Business Standard*, 15 July 2012, https://www.business-standard.com/article/economy-policy/nearly-half-of-central-projects-worth-over-rs-1-000-cr-delayed-112071502010_1.html.

In fact, when *Construction World* magazine conducted a survey in 2013 on why several of the ₹1,000 crore-plus projects were delayed, we found a host of reasons and observations.

'There is a huge list of projects and hundreds of thousands of crores of sanctions are pending,' stated RK Gupta, then managing director of the Dedicated Freight Corridor Corporation of India, had stated.[37] Of the 195 infrastructure projects costing ₹1,000 crore and more at the time, eighty-four were delayed. Several projects had been stalled owing to litigation around small parcels of land. Chief bottlenecks included land acquisition, environment and forest clearances and financial closures. Coordination issues between various agencies were major bugbears too.

Even after financial closure of projects, banks would not release the funds unless 80% of the land was provided by the client. Even if projects were stalled, resources deployed at site needed to be maintained. The running costs resulted in huge cashflow deficits. Revenue generation slowed down, leading to a working capital and cashflow crunch, as running costs needed to be incurred. Finally, increase in input costs over the period led to huge cost escalations. In the absence of a dispute resolution mechanism and arbitration, the situation turned from bad to worse. Arbitration awards were challenged and contractors had to bear the delay until the matter of appeal was settled. There were also concerns relating to the non-availability of assured funding. All this led to curbing of the enthusiasm of private capital.

The PMG was set up in July 2013 as a secretariat for the CCI. By early 2013, it was estimated that projects with investments of ₹22 lakh crore were logjammed. Project promoters began defaulting on debts and banks started piling up bad loans. A study by Axis Capital shows that bad loans and stressed assets of banks rose from 3.4% of total infrastructure loans in FY2011 to 17.4% in FY2013. Worse, the scenario scared prospective investors away. Between FY2009 and FY2013, the study notes, new project investments showed a negative CAGR of 32%.[38]

Industry had been flagging the issue for nearly three years. Individual industrialists, too, had taken up the matter with senior ministers and officials. The Planning Commission, according to

Deputy Chairman Montek Singh Ahluwalia, was the first to ring the warning bell.[39] The commission had been tracking, since 2010, the quarterly progress of annual targets set by six infrastructure ministries. Reports on these were going to PM Singh.

However, it was only in 2012, after economic growth began to falter and leading industrialists from the power sector met PM Singh, that the problem was addressed seriously. Pulok Chatterjee, principal secretary to the PM, started holding regular meetings to push infrastructure projects. The Twelfth Five-Year Plan recommended the establishment of a National Investment Approval Board (NIAB) headed by the PM to speed up large infrastructure projects. It suggested the Transaction of Business Rules be amended to allow NIAB, comprising key ministers, to give statutory clearances to projects of over a certain size.

At a National Development Council meeting in September 2012, P. Chidambaram pitched for a National Investment Board—the NIAB with a different name. In December, this became the CCI, with the mandate to clear projects worth more than ₹1,000 crore. But the problem required more focused attention than ministers meeting once or twice a week. It also turned out that decisions taken by the CCI were not being implemented. Chidambaram then suggested the PMG as a secretariat, which could do the groundwork for CCI meetings and resolve purely administrative issues, as well as monitor the implementation of CCI's decisions. IAS officer Anil Swarup was driving the Rashtriya Swasthya Bima Yojana—the health insurance scheme for the poor that wowed international lending agencies—and was due to return to his Uttar Pradesh cadre. But he was given a year's extension and put in charge of the PMG in July.

A senior official at the power ministry, dealing with billions of dollars of stalled power generation investments, estimated that nearly 40% of unresolved issues holding up major projects originated in the Environment Ministry and even though there were other ministries, such as coal, railways and road transport, which needed to resolve project-related hurdles, the Environment Ministry surpassed all of them put together.

Ministry-wise Break-up of Projects Accepted by PMG

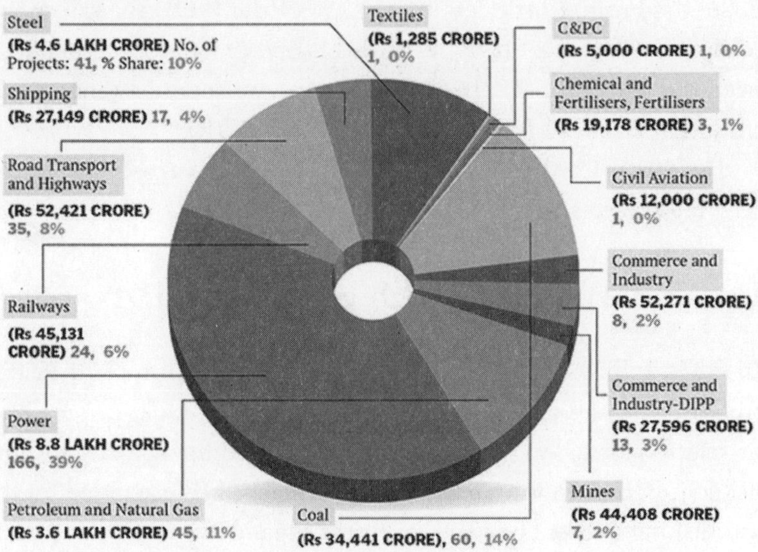

Source: Seetha, 'Project Monitoring Group: The Breaker of Deadlocks', *Forbes India*, 10 June 2014, https://www.forbesindia.com/article/real-issue/project-monitoring-group-the-breaker-of-deadlocks/37924/1.

So, Jayanthi Natarajan had single-handedly held back India's progress by holding back 350 files and ₹10 trillion of projects. And we are facing the consequences of those delayed and deferred decisions to date.

The numbers corroborate this. According to the 2014 version of *Infrastructure Statistics*, India's investment in infrastructure as well as private-sector investment rose from 2005–06 onwards. India's investment was barely 4–5% of the GDP in the years 1999–2000 and 2005–06. As the GDP itself was small in absolute value terms, this translated into an infrastructure investment of ₹1–2 trillion per annum. In 2005–06, it exceeded 5% of the GDP and subsequently 6% in 2007–08 and 8% in 2010–11. In rupee terms, we were spending ₹2 trillion on infrastructure in 2005–06, ₹3 trillion in 2007–08, ₹4 trillion in 2008–09 and ₹6 trillion in 2010–11. Between 2005–06 and 2010–11, investment had gone up three times. Private investment in infrastructure took off from 2006–07. From a little less than 1.5% of the GDP then, it grew to almost 4% of the GDP by 2010–11. Investments started falling from the year 2011–12. In absolute terms, we spent less than ₹5.5 trillion in 2011–12 (or less than 7% of the GDP).[40]

By 2011–12, the Environment Ministry was already red-flagging projects and destroying the momentum.

How Real Was India's High-growth Period?

In 2004, India's GDP stood at $721 billion, which rose to $2.03 trillion in 2014—an increase of 182%. While this looks impressive, in relative terms, we were laggards if one compares this to our peers in BRIC. In the same period, China's GDP expanded by an astonishing 440%. The GDP of Brazil expanded by 267% and that of Russia by 223%. This made India the worst performing BRIC economy during the period.

The rise of China in the early 2000s was unparalleled. In 2004, it was the sixth largest economy. Just six years later, it became the second largest. Here are some other facts. From 16th in 2004, Russia made it to 9th in 2014. Brazil jumped all the way from 13th in 2004 to 7th in 2014. But India's rank proved to be a disappointment, going from 12th in 2004 to only 10th in 2014. In other words, India went from being the second-biggest BRIC economy in 2004 to the smallest by 2014.

Inflation, too, rose geometrically during this period. Beginning from just 3.9% in 2004, inflation spiked almost continuously, reaching 11% in 2009. From there, it climbed even higher to 12% in 2010. From 2010 to 2013, India's inflation was the highest among all BRIC economies. This led to severe problems with the rupee.

The current account deficit widened. Fears of another balance-of-payments crisis emerged. Worried about inflation, the RBI under Governor Raghuram Rajan recommended to the Public Accounts Committee that as the value of the ₹1,000 note had been depleted owing to high inflation, it ought to consider printing ₹5,000 and ₹10,000 currency notes.[41]

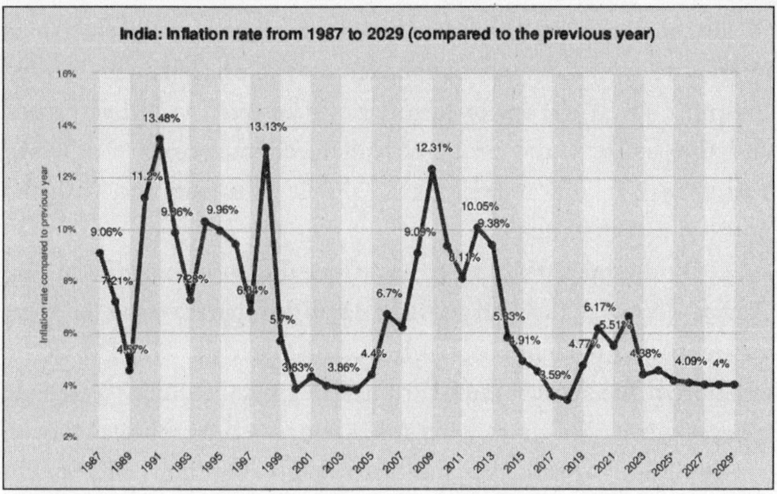

Source: 'India: Inflation rate from 1987 to 2029', *Statista*, 4 July 2024, https://www.statista.com/statistics/271322/inflation-rate-in-india/.

All considered, infrastructure companies saw little progress from 2007 to 2013. The events during 2011, 2012 and 2013 sequentially led to a crumbling economy, weakened leadership, unstable policy regime and, therefore, an unattractive investment destination for international investors. The government remained inactive and confused. It lacked a unified voice, and its bureaucracy called the shots.

The Anna Hazare Movement (2011–12)

The scam-filled atmosphere between 2011 and 2014 gave rise to the anti-corruption movement led by social activist Anna Hazare, which culminated in substantial political developments.

The movement began in April 2011 when Anna Hazare, inspired by Mahatma Gandhi's principles of non-violence, initiated a hunger strike to demand the enactment of the Jan Lokpal Bill, an anti-corruption legislation aimed at establishing an independent body to investigate corruption cases. The movement quickly gained nationwide support, with thousands of people participating in protests and demonstrations across the country.

The movement was marked by its use of social media and mass mobilisation, making it one of the largest protests in Indian history. Despite several rounds of negotiations between the government and the activists, the proposed bill faced numerous hurdles in Parliament, leading to widespread public dissatisfaction with the political establishment.

In November 2012, key figures from the movement, including Arvind Kejriwal, decided to form a political party to pursue their anti-corruption agenda through electoral politics. This led to the creation of the Aam Aadmi Party (AAP), which aimed to provide a clean and accountable alternative to the existing political parties.

The AAP made its political debut in the 2013 Delhi Legislative Assembly election. The party's campaign focused on corruption, transparency and good governance. Its success was unprecedented—it won twenty-eight out of seventy seats, emerging as the second-largest party in the assembly. This performance led to the formation of a minority government with outside support from the Congress.

Buoyed by its success in Delhi, the AAP decided to contest the 2014 general elections on a national scale. The party fielded candidates in several states, aiming to replicate its anti-corruption agenda on a larger platform. Although it did not achieve significant success, AAP's impact on Indian politics proved undeniable, as it continued to advocate for greater accountability and transparency in government.

The People's Mandate in 2014

During the same period, the BJP capitalised on the widespread discontent with corruption and governance issues. Under the leadership of Narendra Modi, the party ran a highly effective campaign that promised development, good governance and a corruption-free administration. Modi's reputation as a decisive and efficient leader, built during his tenure as chief minister of Gujarat, resonated with a large section of the Indian electorate. The failure of the UPA government to implement reforms and manage the economy effectively became apparent, setting the stage for potential political changes and hopes pinned on the incoming BJP-led NDA government to steer India back towards reformative growth.

The BJP's strategic campaign, combined with the momentum created by the anti-corruption movement, helped it secure a significant mandate in the 2014 general elections. The party won 282 out of 543 seats in the Lok Sabha, marking the first time in thirty years that a single party had achieved a majority. This victory underscored the public's desire for change and effective governance.

The period from 2011 to 2014 was thus marked by a significant shift in Indian politics, driven by the public's demand for cleaner governance and the rise of new political forces like the AAP and the resurgence of the BJP under Narendra Modi's leadership.

CHAPTER TWO

Annual Perspectives

2012

January

UP, as in Uttar Pradesh (not any positive sentiment!), was the buzzword at the beginning of the year, with elections in the state scheduled in March. Business sentiment was dismal, with policy paralysis having brought the economy to its knees. The mid-year review by the government showed that GDP growth had fallen to 6.9% in the second quarter; manufacturing had slowed down to 2.7% and construction to 4.3%, while sectors like mining showed negative growth. The annual growth forecast of about 7.3% presented by the finance minister appeared a pipedream, as did management of the projected fiscal deficit target of 4.6% of the GDP. While the RBI continuously raised interest thirteen times in the past twelve months to tame inflation, the National Rural Employment Guarantee Act (NREGA) scheme and food security bill were being announced on the back of a rising fiscal deficit and existing fertiliser and petroleum subsidies.

According to RBI data, year-on-year growth in non-food credit had decelerated to 17.4% as of November 2011, against a target of 18%. Similarly, year-on-year growth in M3 (money supply) had also fallen below the target of 15.5% growth. Stimuli, in the form of government spending, especially after 2008, had tapered off. During April–September 2011, the expenditure of the central government rose by 9.9% per annum versus an average growth of close to 20% per annum over the three years ending March 2011. The one reform that would have seen the initiation of supply-side reforms through agri-infrastructure was shot down in the political one-upmanship game. Parliament evidently preferred to pass the Food Security Bill, which would cost the country ₹100,000 crore, rather than foreign direct investment (FDI) in retail, which would result in the creation of backend agri-infrastructure, protect foodgrains from rotting and enhance realisations for the farmers by cutting out middlemen and enhancing productivity.

As for the roads sector, in several states, rural roads under the Pradhan Mantri Gram Sadak Yojana (PMGSY) and the NABARD-financed schemes presented a new and inviting opportunity, with no toll imposed for use, relatively light traffic and many trucks using them as an alternative to highways as they offered a smoother ride.

The scenario for industry at the beginning of the new year was low government spending resulting in a deficit in project pipelines, high building material prices with a forex double-whammy, the rising cost of hard-to-find labour, high interest costs and low demand.

February

Inflation regulation was clearly choking growth; policy paralysis caused government expenditure to dwindle; the government was way behind all targets of growth. Forex volatility exaggerated our negative balance of trade, with our fiscal deficit set to overshoot the budgeted figure of 4.6% of the GDP by 2%.

There were some rays of hope, though. The Big Mac index declaring that the rupee was among the most undervalued currencies in the world would warrant an inflow of FDI and foreign institutional investor (FII) investment as currency downward risk was limited; inflation was tamed; and single-brand retail with 100% FDI was permitted, which was likely to bring in $15 billion in the next five years. The prime minister put Pulok Chatterji from the PMO in charge to fast-track issues with a review scheduled in ninety days. The monetary regime was likely to be eased with a reduction in interest rates, and the cumulative FDI flows of $22.83 billion for the April–November period crossed $19.43 billion, the figure for FY2010–11. Further, the finance minister urged cash-rich public-sector undertakings (PSUs) to step up spending in the fiscal and introduced a system of review of their investment commitment, which would have implications for their ratings and the performance appraisal of their executives.

A movement appeared to be building to shake off the inertia that had depressed business confidence. Severe challenges in the contracting sector made companies use the best technologies and enhance efficiencies to compete and grow despite thin margins. International majors like Hochtief were reportedly in talks with Indian construction companies. NHAI had raised enough funds for its plans until the end of 2013—it had recently raised ₹10,000 crore through the sale of bonds, of which the majority would be used to acquire land for various projects.

What's more, the 2G spectrum verdict on 2 February pronounced a cancellation of all 121 permits given after 10 January 2008 by the then telecom minister, A. Raja. There is a fundamental flaw in the first-come-first-served principle in the distribution of state-owned natural resources, the verdict said, citing Article 14 of the Indian Constitution. The verdict sent everyone into a tizzy, mainly because the impending rectification of the 2008 action to skip auctioning would send financial institutions into a spiral and have widespread ramifications for other sectors, notably infrastructure. The government would not financially support the losing companies, and this could be a trend for future cases, with lessons essentially in transparency and fairness.

For instance, while both land acquisition and other clearances were the bane of the mining sector, there was a Damocles' sword hanging over the coal industry. Although auctioning of coal blocks had already been mandated, it was selective. While the auctioning of coal blocks was supposed to be a reality by the end of 2011, the government continued to hem and haw over the processes. The first big decision came in August 2011, when the Coal Ministry announced that it would auction 54 blocks on upfront payment basis. But the caveat was that it might not offer mines to power companies directly but allot blocks to states who would, in turn, open them up for bidding.

March

The green shoots of business confidence seen in February were aided by a surge in FII investment of up to $5 billion, which saw the Sensex surge by over 15% until the third week of February. A mechanism to enable access to the Indian debt market through infrastructure debt funds was evolved, for regulated entities with a sustained long-term interest rate and long-horizon entities like pension, infrastructure and insurance funds. The extent of foreign participation, both through debt and equity, in the financing of India's infrastructure was in the order of 8–10% in the recent past; from 1 January 2012, India allowed qualified foreign investors to invest in Indian equity, buying stocks of Indian companies. Many infra stocks appreciated in the rally; for instance, the realty sector gained over 45% and power over 25%. However, results indicated debt stress on profits.

Some other positives included Coal India Ltd (CIL) signing fuel supply agreements (FSAs) with power companies for the full quantity of coal mentioned in letters of assurance for twenty years—a benefit to power plants with an estimated capacity of over 50,000 MW. This would release the embargo laid by banks on further funding of power plants, thereby easing liquidity.

Also, NHAI was projected to cross the award of over 6,000 km in the fiscal against its target of 7,300 km and continue taking up an award of a further 7,300 km in the forthcoming fiscal. The equipment sector was expected to witness a CAGR of 20% in FY2011–15—a robust growth of 18% was projected in 2011, tapering to 16% in 2012, and thereafter between 9% and 12% annually till the end of 2015. Further, to aid skill development, the Planning Commission suggested a levy on the private sector to act as a regular source of funding for such initiatives. The labour crunch that hit contractors badly in 2011 appeared to have levelled out. This could have been owing to the slowdown as well as disenchantment with the Mahatma Gandhi National Rural Employment Guarantee Scheme (MNREGS) itself, as money released for the scheme fell from ₹35,242 crore the previous year to ₹21,441 crore, while expenditure went down from ₹39,000 crore the previous year to ₹20,000 crore by the end of January 2012.

As for the aviation sector, there was a debate about airlines accepting a steep increase in airport tariffs, suggested by the Airports Economic Regulatory Authority (AERA). A counter suggestion from the aviation sector was to delink airport tariffs from user fees.

April

The Union Budget failed to meet expectations. The legend of Nero playing the fiddle while Rome burnt was replayed as the government proposed the National Food Security Bill to an economy still struggling to contain its fiscal deficit. The Budget projected a revised fiscal deficit estimate at 5.9% of GDP against a budgeted fiscal deficit of 4.6%—a slippage of the magnitude of ₹1,092 billion vis-a-vis budgeted FY2012 estimates. The implementation of the Food Security Bill alone was estimated to amount to a minimum of 0.7% of GDP, with a possible high of 1.5% of GDP. There was also a deafening silence on the lack of any smart catalysts for the economic engine. To maintain the momentum in the economy, an investment of over 10% of our GDP needed to be made into infrastructure. However, although we had been managing to double the spend and outlays over past five-year plans, the execution fell acutely short. The dismal state of clearances, land acquisition and other regulatory roadblocks remained an overarching concern, with delays in almost every government-initiated responsibility in PPP projects.

May

The 'road' to riches got a little less rough, with the reduction of a few bumps thanks to notifications from the government. The Union Budget had already announced a relaxation in overseas borrowings norms (external commercial borrowings or ECBs) for road projects. It was further announced that ECBs would also be allowed for capital expenditure on the maintenance and operation of toll systems, provided they were part of the original project. (ECBs have a minimum average maturity of three years. In 2011–12, Indian companies borrowed $35.9 billion through this route, up 45% from the year before). Further, the Finance Minister Pranab Mukherjee reduced the rate of withholding tax on interest payments on ECBs to 5% from 20%. This made the ride smoother for highway developers under the PPP route, as they could get loans for the entire contract period of twenty or twenty-five, or even up to thirty years, rather than taking fifteen-year loans from banks and financial institutions and then going in for higher-cost loans. Also, the full exemption from duty on specified equipment imported for road construction by contractors of the Ministry of Road Transport and Highways (MoRTH), NHAI and state governments provided in the Budget was further extended to contracts awarded by metropolitan development authorities. That said, factors plaguing the roads sector that required more attention and transparency were road maintenance, quality inspection and a high time lag.

As for the railways sector, it continued to lag behind roads despite its scope to grow more than any other transport sector. With a length of 71,000 km, its coverage was far below par for both passenger and freight traffic. With an envisaged addition of 25,000 km by 2020, the potential for private participation was estimated up to 12,500 km by that year. In addition to expansion, the need was felt for modernisation in terms of networking, infrastructure, technology and automation as expressed by the Sam Pitroda Committee for Modernisation of Indian Railways, which submitted its report in February 2012.

June

The Sensex slipped, the rupee slipped and business confidence was on a downslide. Consumer demand took a hit post-policy paralysis. While no country hands over the reins of its governance to its central bank, our Finance Ministry let the RBI have a field day. As a result, the central bank incessantly choked growth. Fiscal control can be achieved by fiscal measures, but sentiment requires physical action. The government's tinkering with tax laws also cost us dearly, with multinational companies having pulled money out of India at an accelerating rate, moving $10.7 billion out in 2011, up from $7.2 billion in 2010 against just $3.1 billion in 2009.

Meanwhile, the 'scam' stories continued. In its report on the Delhi airport modernisation project, the Comptroller and Auditor General of India (CAG) claimed that the government had given out prime land that would fetch ₹1.63 lakh crore to its private-sector partner, DIAL. This 'scam' value was calculated on the basis of the land made available to the lessee for the project. The extrapolation of this opportunity, which was made available by virtue of a project that invited open bids, appeared to be taking governance to another extreme, where every PPP project could be termed as a scam at some point in time—especially with the CAG not exercising discretion in airing its reports.

As for PPPs, the government's biggest role in such projects is undoubtedly acquisition of land, even though land is only a relatively small fraction of the cost, as the sweat, skill and resources involved are worth more than merely the financial cost of the land. Compensation remained the diciest of the factors with dynamic and volatile market prices. Land acquisition delays in as many as sixteen national highways worth ₹15,000 crore in West Bengal, Kerala, Goa and Tamil Nadu resulted in major cost overruns, and such delays were among the primary reasons for wariness on the part of international investors.

July

The horizon remained hazy for those waiting for property prices to recede, with neither the debt burden nor the slack in sale transactions pressuring builders to ease prices. Further, of the total FDI of $230 billion India received since 2000, real estate received only $10.8 billion despite the rules for investing having been eased in the previous years. The minimum size for housing estates built with foreign capital dropped from 100 acres (40 ha) to 25 acres (10 ha), and overseas firms could put up commercial buildings as long as the projects surpassed 50,000 sq. m (538,200 sq. ft) of floor space. Earlier in the year, the government had relaxed single-brand retail norms from 51% to 100%, as only $44.45 million worth of foreign investments had been received by the sector, constituting barely 0.03% of total FDI inflows. Swedish furniture retailer IKEA announced plans to invest about €1.5 billion (₹10,500 crore), which was likely to have a trickle-down effect on other single-brand retailers wishing to come to India.

Meanwhile, the urban shift continued to create demand within cities, depending upon the opportunities created by each state. Input costs hit the ceiling and land prices were soaring. For their part, realtors appeared to have embraced professionalism, becoming more tech-savvy and customer-centric instead of transaction-centric. The levels of accountability being envisaged in the real estate bill also augured well for the growth of the sector.

The RBI clearly disappointed the industry with the status quo on interest rates. Huge amounts were stuck with infrastructure projects, and developers were in both a liquidity squeeze and a debt trap. Indian companies raised over $17 billion for the fiscal year ending 31 March 2011, taking advantage of relatively low interest rates. The government said it would liberalise ECB norms to allow a higher limit of $750 million under the automatic window and to allow borrowings in renminbi, the Chinese currency, besides refinancing the rupee debt through foreign borrowings. For long, policymakers have used the cap on annual borrowings—which was $30 billion—and the price ceilings to contain debt at prudent levels. Despite the RBI choking inflation at the cost of killing growth, the results of FY2012 were not too bad, with over 15% topline growth and around 10% profits after tax (PAT) growth, and companies calibrating their budgets for FY2013.

With Prime Minister Manmohan Singh taking on his favourite role as finance minister, a slew of reform-directed statements came forth: the push for FDI in retail; the overruling of the report that recommended that the government should have no role in land acquisition; and the announcement that the government could agree to acquire land for private companies under a new bill. Expectations rose that he would focus on removing bottlenecks in existing projects, especially the snowballing financing blues in the highways sector.

August

The rainfall blessing, awaited as the last miracle in boosting economic sentiment, eluded the country. But the silver lining was its reduced impact on GDP, owing to the diminished importance of agriculture (from 52% of the GDP in 1950 to 14%) because of the growth in the service sector. In terms of foodgrain production, the total production of rice at 102.75 million tonnes (mt) was a record, as was the production of wheat at 88.31 million tonnes, also a new record in 2011–12. The total of 250.42 mt was higher than the target of 245 mt fixed for the year. In the Tenth Five-Year Plan, the allocation for irrigation was $30 billion, which further doubled to $60 billion in the Eleventh Plan, and was scheduled at $97 billion in the Twelfth Plan. However, according to international experts, despite being the second-largest irrigated country in the world, the efficiency of India's irrigation infrastructure was among the worst, most of it operating at an abysmally low level, some of it even at less than 20%.

This must be viewed against the backdrop of a political spat in Maharashtra, where the skeletons of a ₹26,000-crore scam tumbled out. In the prior ten years, the irrigated area went up by just 0.1% despite billions of dollars spent. Even as we stood at the brink of a drought, dams initiated as long ago as forty-five years earlier remained works in progress. Construction deadlines were postponed endlessly and costs inflated, sometimes leading to projects themselves getting drowned. Nearly 1,000 dams in Maharashtra lay incomplete. Some, like the Warna Irrigation Project, approved in January 1967, remained incomplete owing to land acquisition troubles and insufficient funds. Typically, a project was proposed, the World Bank involved for funding, a separate corporation set up with a 'friendly chairman', tenders issued, contracts awarded, advances issued and the project forgotten for a few years. Then, to create some accountability, directions were issued on 'change of alignment and design' and additional funding sought. Other tactics included increasing the height of the dam, giving rise to rehabilitation issues. In all, the project was not completed, as it then stopped generating money. For the contractor, too, the margin of profitability lay in keeping the contract incomplete as he collected 60% of the contract value despite being unable to complete it. Clearly, irrigation infrastructure sucked up huge funds but delivered only to Swiss bank accounts.

As for Indian ports, cargo growth was subdued in 2011–12 with total throughput registering a 5% year-on-year increase to 930 million tonnes, following a significant slump in volumes of iron ore due to mining restrictions and policy issues. In March 2011, the government had announced plans to establish a port finance corporation, a welcome decision. This came close on the heels of the Maritime Agenda 2020 targets that ambitiously projected a total traffic of 2,494.95 million tonnes for all major and non-major ports taken together and a capacity of 3,280.04 million tonnes. Investments in ports by 2020 were proposed to be in the range of ₹1.19 lakh crore for major ports, and ₹1.68 lakh crore for non-major ports. The Agenda 2020 took a holistic view of the requirement and envisaged the facilitation of infrastructure, including capacity-building and promotion of inland waterways and coastal shipping, to help achieve the targets.

Yet, the government's first attempt at raising bonds failed and the development of non-major ports did not progress as planned. In addition, tariffs were slashed for some of the most congested ports, including Jawaharlal Nehru Port Trust (JNPT)—a decision received with widespread disapproval. Operational, private-owned ports seemed to be attracting financiers convinced of their viability. The thrust on state-owned non-major ports was hardly visible, with the result that investors could not see revenues that could offset the costs in the case of most ports—except where the state itself was proactive enough to dish out figures for bank consortiums, such as for Vizhinjam Port in Kerala. While many states eagerly launched new, smaller port projects under PPP, many ports had yet to justify their existence.

September

Census 2011 indicated an increase in urban areas by about 54% from 5,161 towns in 2001 to 7,935 in 2011. The total urban population was about 377.1 million (31.16%) of the total of 1,210.19 million.

There were 468 cities with a population of over 100,000, of which 53 cities had a population over 1 million. Analysts predicted a demand for 3.94 million housing units from 2011–15, growing at a CAGR of 11%. The total housing demand across the top seven cities during this period was also expected to be around 2.36 million units. Of this, the mid-segment was expected to be around 45%. And the affordable housing segment was likely to register three times more demand than supply. The rural appetite, too, was whetted by rising incomes from better productivity in farmlands and the sharp rise in land prices owing to infrastructure projects.

Progress with the Jawaharlal Nehru National Urban Renewal Mission (JNNURM), which was commissioned to undertake urban renewal, was tardy. Of the 500 mega projects sanctioned under the scheme, only 120 were commissioned, with JNNURM II, a revised version, being in the final stages of preparation. This was expected to be a significant increase over the first phase at around $35–38 billion. Analysts predicted that by 2030, nearly 70% of the GDP would come from cities and the time for Tier-II and Tier-III cities appeared to be on the horizon. Meanwhile, growth figures were crumbling and the estimate for India's GDP kept falling a few notches every month.

In other news, the CAG's report estimated a deemed loss to the exchequer of ₹1.86 lakh crore because of non-competitive allotment of 149 coal blocks—it blamed the Screening Committee for the lapses, observing that both the Coal Ministry and the committee failed to flag the use of coal for purposes other than allotted, or simply not mining. As a majority of the mines remained unmined, what was the purpose of hastily allotting the blocks ostensibly to overcome a dire power crisis? In the Eleventh Five-Year Plan (2007–12), which largely coincided with the coal allotment period, five companies were under the spotlight, as the Central Bureau of Investigation (CBI) raided them based on misrepresentations and false claims in the applications, presentations and connivance or lack of due diligence on the part of public servants. Most issues concerned unmined blocks. As we had reported in *Infrastructure Today* in January, 'In the last 18 years, 193 blocks have been allotted to various companies for captive use. But only 28 are operational so far. As against an estimated target of 90 Mtpa from 193 blocks, only 38 Mtpa is being produced now.'[1] The problem lay in accountability. The opposition promptly demanded that 142 allotted coal blocks be cancelled. Since 2009, the government had been issuing warnings to companies for not mining. In May 2011, it cancelled fourteen mines for not developing them or dragging their feet. As many as eighty-eight coal block owners received 'show-cause' notices; even the biggest power and steel companies were issued warnings. Many were being investigated by an Inter-Ministerial Group and the government was said to be deciding on de-allotting the mines to fifty-nine of these 'non-serious' players.[2]

October

In the previous month, the government finally decided to act—it called the bluff of its allies to attempt to save the country's fiscal situation, hiking the price of diesel by ₹5 per litre and restricting the supply of subsidised LPG cylinders to six per year. It also relaxed norms on FDI in aviation and retail. After this, the Sensex scorched ahead, with confidence finding its way back in Mumbai, India's financial capital.

While the diesel price hike was a tough call that breached a sacred wall, FDI in retail remained a cosmetic measure to see some impact in the future. But the moves would help India get back into the foreign investors' circuit. The ground was prepared for the RBI to relax interest rates by demonstrating action on the fiscal front. Once interest rates softened and consumer confidence rose, the index was expected to spike and pave the way for revitalising growth. Also, the power industry received a pleasant surge in the form of a financial restructuring package designed for state electricity boards. This was aimed at reviving their ability to invest in equipment and make fresh efforts to reduce the transmission and distribution losses that had reached gargantuan proportions at ₹3 trillion, while their banks had a questionable exposure of a staggering ₹2 trillion.

The government was next expected to train its guns on coal and other fuel-related issues that had brought economic growth to a grinding halt, as well as land acquisition issues, which had afflicted more than half the projects abandoned or shelved by promoters in the preceding two years. In fact, projects worth ₹1.8 trillion were shelved from April–August 2012 on top of projects worth ₹4.5 trillion shelved in 2011–12. Renamed 'The Right to Fair Compensation, Resettlement, Rehabilitation and Transparency in Land Acquisition', a bill had been pending for long and had a group of ministers giving it the final touches.

Meanwhile, corporate India tightened its belt, with companies trying to sell off assets bleeding their balance sheets. This consolidation boded a win-win for all with an improving foreign investment sentiment. FDI in retail helped in this aspect most, as it managed to grab maximum media attention globally and let everyone know India was open for business. FY2011–12 was projected to turn out to be a year of record completion of investment projects—as in mid-May, ₹3.8 trillion worth of projects were commissioned during the year. Projects worth ₹9.3 trillion were scheduled to get completed in the fiscal, and projects worth ₹9.6 trillion in the next fiscal year.

November

The Commonwealth scam of Suresh Kalmadi was followed closely by the 2G scam, which was followed by the coal scam. The Arab Spring uprisings in Tunisia, Egypt, Yemen, Libya and Syria created an environment of protests, and in April 2011, Anna Hazare initiated a hunger strike to demand the enactment of the

Jan Lokpal Bill, an anti-corruption legislation aimed at establishing an independent body to investigate corruption cases. With the anti-corruption movement turning into a tsunami, the reputation index or stock prices took a beating. The market capitalisation of major companies plummeted; stocks crashed. Some settled charges of breaching securities laws with payments, while senior executives were charged for insider trading. Investigations have to establish three basic elements. First, you need evidence of action in the market, a buy or sell. This is the easier part. Then, one must prove that the insider had particular information others did not. Finally, the investigator must establish that one caused the other. However, typically, SEBI orders are challenged in the tribunal or courts where they either drag on for years or end up going against SEBI. Yet, institutional investors watch such cases closely and they can derail chances of investment in the company's stock. A probe was also ordered in the Karnataka Lokayukta Court against three former state chief ministers and others on a complaint alleging irregularities in the Bangalore–Mysore expressway project. Thus, scams and scandals continued to occupy the front pages of business newspapers.

Meanwhile, according to the 2013 edition of IFC's *Doing Business* study, which ranks countries on the ease of doing business, India retained its rank of 132, below Bangladesh at 129 as well as Sri Lanka (81), China (91) and Brazil (130). Further, India was not among the ten economies that improved the most. China was ranked 12th amongst the top improvers while India ranked 27th.

In other news, several banks were seen to hire infrastructure experts, reflecting a longer-term goal to get specialised. As with most other lessons in India's infrastructure sector, this solution could be seen as reactive, not proactive or innovative. The simple truth is that banks had been trying to grapple with risks after they encountered them. Banks that have invested in specialists understand the risks better and factor in the margins of error better.

December

Near the end of 2010, a can of worms had opened and scams worth billions had tumbled out; the following year was one of policy paralysis. By November 2011, the government was being urged to break its inertia by prominent industrialists and other stakeholders in the India story.

Despite a move to allow international brands and retailers up to 51% FDI in the multi-brand retail sector and 100% FDI in single-brand retail, Parliament remained in a logjam over FDI at the end of 2012. Inactivity and project paralysis caused contracting companies to resort to unhealthy debt, eroding the market capitalisation of listed construction companies. Debt had become a financial cancer, remaining fatal despite efforts at treatment.

Meanwhile, the media went to town reporting on 'differences' within the government when the Environment Minister Jayanthi Natarajan openly disagreed with Prime Minister Manmohan Singh regarding the proposed National Investment Board (NIB), which was conceptualised as something of a single window to expedite projects worth over ₹1,000 crore, bypassing various ministries if required.[3] (Stringent environmental norms and sometimes unrealistic forest rules were among the biggest reasons for delay in clearances.) The hastily prepared Cabinet Note citing NIB's function as taking over when there is 'failure to act' on the part of a ministry understandably ruffled feathers. The conflict between industry and environment was not a new one, and green activists also sharpened their swords, calling the NIB autocratic and anti-environment.

2013

January

The year began with some hope for renewed acceleration in projects becoming available for bidding; projects stuck in the web of permission got the green signal. The RBI finally reduced interest rates, with P. Chidambaram in the Ministry of Finance determined to reduce fiscal deficit; and the UPA government continued its drive towards policy reform. Foreign institutional investors pumped in $23 billion in 2012, with the last $3.5 billion coming in December, indicating some restoration of confidence in the government with the retail FDI booster.

With the public sector growing in terms of market capitalisation by ₹200,000 crore over the previous year and nine PSUs sitting on cash piles of ₹180,000 crore alone, the finance minister (FM) directed them to 'use it or lose it'—invest or pay dividend. The formation of the Cabinet Committee on Investment (CCI), earlier the NIB, to expedite projects of over ₹1,000 crore was another positive move, as was the idea of the Infrastructure Development Fund (IDF) as an effective financial mechanism. But it remained to be seen whether these measures would have 'teeth'.

February

With the first year of the Twelfth Five-Year Plan already underway and growth of 5.6% forecast for the year, the balance four years were expected to be under pressure to perform at nearly 9% to bring the average up over 8%. This necessitated a strong build-up of projects during the year. In addition to ensuring financial closure for 'top priority' projects over ₹1,000 crore, it was an imperative to pursue half- finished projects for completion, where resources have already been invested. Examples include the irrigation projects in Maharashtra, which were recently exposed, and hydro projects in Uttarakhand left in the lurch despite hundreds of crores having been spent.

But the dark clouds were already on the horizon. After every available rating and analyst from Nomura to Dun & Bradstreet and India Ratings had expressed a negative outlook for India's infrastructure, the inevitable happened when the advance estimates stated that the nation could only achieve 5% growth in the fiscal, the lowest in a decade. Infrastructure growth fell from 6.6% in 2011 to 4.4% in 2012, and was likely to fall further, with investors backing out of projects. Many highway projects were stuck because of delays in developers securing environmental approvals and problems in land acquisition. The delays led to high borrowings, which were denting all prospects of financial viability. This was being compounded by a funding crunch in the face of slowing economic growth. Resultantly, major players like Lanco, GMR, GVK and others decided to exit critical infrastructure domains, including roads and ports. NHAI, too, which had planned to award 9,000 km this year, largely on non-BOT (build-operate-transfer) models, had to hastily postpone much of its highway building activity.

It was also a period of discovery for restructuring loans, leading to a further spiral of caution and scepticism, particularly to state-owned power and transportation companies. Observers maintained that this trend of restructuring was here to stay at least till the next year.

March

Opinions varied whether the Union Budget 2013 was a hit or miss. As for the Budget, the investment allowance proposal was seen as a trigger for construction equipment manufacturers to step up investments in India and use it as a sourcing hub.

That said, the highways dream seemed to have soured with two principal actors—GVK and GMR—quitting the stage well before the play ended (leaving a hole of ₹10,700 crore) and NHAI at the crossroads, facing not just the possibility of a rebellion from other private-sector players but a challenge to its authority, as well as a slew of delays. (The two projects—GMR's ₹7,700-crore Kishangarh–Udaipur–Ahmedabad project for which it had bid to pay NHAI an annual premium of ₹636 crore (which would increase every year), and GVK's ₹3,000-crore Shivpuri–Dewas project in Madhya Pradesh—were among the biggest in the sector.)

In terms of awards, merely 837 km were awarded until January 2013, as against over 5,000 km in 2010–11 and nearly 6,500 km in 2011–12. Further, to date, close to 251 players had, at various points of time, initiated arbitration proceedings against NHAI with their collective claim running to ₹13,000 crore. All this had set the government into damage control mode. The proposal to establish a road regulator is expected to assuage the domestic investor's scepticism. For its part, NHAI proposed to compensate for delays in PPP projects beyond a contractor's control, such as clearances. A realisation (however reluctant), perhaps that the government agency should optimally act as a partner, not boss.

April

In the news: the ambitious Aerocity hospitality zone project, launched in 2006 on the periphery of the Indira Gandhi International Airport in the capital. This PPP exercise of the

Government of India and the GMR-led Delhi International Airport Ltd consortium, involving sixteen international hotel groups and a retail firm, with a collective investment of ₹12,000 crore) became mired in red tape, with the Delhi Police refusing security clearances. (This, despite approvals from various other branches of the government.) Another avoidable narrative of negativity in terms of ease of doing business.

Meanwhile, policy paralysis had taken its toll on the balance sheets of construction companies, with the cumulative market cap of the top twenty-four construction companies declining 6.48% between April 2012 and March 2013. If you remove L&T from these, the losses exacerbated to 8.46%. That said, the CCI continued to move towards removing gridlocks with the government, urging banks to highlight funded projects stuck owing to clearances. Finance Ministry estimates showed that there were 215 projects, each with a project size of ₹250 crore and above (totalling over ₹7 lakh crore), that were stalled. Of these, 106 were in the power sector, 79 in roads, 20 in iron and steel, and 5 each in cement and ports. These projects had been supported by public-sector banks and had disbursed ₹54,000 crore by the end of December 2012.

The BRICS bank proposal, first presented by India in 2012, came to the fore with a focus on infrastructure funding. The sticking point, inevitably, was expected to be the corpus needed: $10 billion for each nation.

May

The state of Maharashtra was in focus this month. Once regarded as the country's financial powerhouse, the state found itself increasingly losing favour with investors, both local and foreign, who shifted their attention to more industry and business-savvy states like Gujarat, Andhra Pradesh, Karnataka and Tamil Nadu. Even so-called 'ailing' states like Bihar, Madhya Pradesh and Rajasthan overtook the state in certain areas of development.

Clearly, administrative implementation and regulatory roadblocks played their part in this decline. Attempts at course correction included the announcement of the state's new industrial policy and the decision to market the state as 'Magnetic Maharashtra'. A cautionary tale for Indian states to shed their complacency and keep it real.

Also on our radar was the Indian Railways, which made a whopping ₹24,600 crore in losses and lagged the most in private participation. While the manufacturing and mining industries that depend on the railways for transportation were clamouring for efficiency in transactions and wagon use, the technology, albeit available, was not implemented well. All eyes were on the dedicated freight corridors to provide the light at the end of the proverbial tunnel. In terms of tech, while the Centre for Railway Information Systems (CRIS), the autonomous organisation under the Ministry of Railways, had systems ready to go in wagon and vendor management, implementation had been partial and shoddy. Indeed, despite sporadic attempts to implement new technology, not a single one had been standardised across the network. Take, for instance, the anti-collision device piloted on the Konkan Railway, which was never implemented on any other sectors until the Northeast Frontier Railway decided to pilot it again recently.

June

Finance Minister P. Chidambaram went on a sales pitch for India Inc. with investor meets in Hong Kong, Singapore, the UK, Germany, France, Japan, Qatar, Canada, the UAE and the US, and made aggressive parleys with oil billionaires and sovereign wealth funds on the opportunities for investment in infrastructure and corporate bonds. Within India, too, as many as twenty-one infrastructure projects in Karnataka, collectively worth ₹700,000 crore and faced with delays, came under his scanner. Other green shoots: research by Timetric suggesting the prospect of considerable revenue growth in 2013–14 than the previous year on the back of increased investments in IT, infrastructure and public and private construction projects; and a rally in Indian markets buoyed by global sentiments. In other good news, Siliguri-based PCM Group acquired European track specialist Rail.One; even more notable considering the ₹200,000 crore of investments lined up for metro development across the country.

Also in the limelight was the ₹132,000 crore PMGSY, which had sanctioned paving or strengthening more than 0.42 million km of roads in 1.1 lakh habitations. Ironically, even after the scheme's scheduled implementation period was completed in 2007, it continued to limp along in most states, with less than 72% of the sanctioned work completed. Now, in the Twelfth Five-Year Plan, the Planning Commission proposed a budgetary allocation of ₹200,000 crore for the Yojana's next stage of implementation, covering villages of a population of 250. Spanning 2.7 million km, rural roads comprise over 95% of the country's network, so the task was a daunting one with stumbling blocks aplenty. States like Andhra Pradesh and Madhya Pradesh took advantage of the scheme to dovetail it into their own development programmes. Proper and adequate training of state officials was a concern. The National Rural Roads Development Authority (NRRDA) and its state counterparts did not have the same level of expertise, particularly in hilly states. Local contractors in many states like Uttar Pradesh and Bihar were known to have executed the project poorly, often owing to misuse in connivance with local authorities.

July

The cloudburst in the previous month in Uttarakhand, causing devastating floods and landslides, became India's worst natural disaster since the 2004 tsunami, with over 5,500 dead. It also threw up valuable lessons in maintaining the environment, exposing the cavalier disdain for urban planning and construction norms by both the authorities and developers, particularly in the belt prone to seismic shifts. The need to embed a culture of preparedness, in which our National Disaster Management Authority has been sadly wanting, became apparent. The silver lining was the rescue and support effort by infrastructure firms like HCC, L&T and Jaiprakash.

It was also raining problems on the financial front, with the rupee shooting well past 60 against the dollar. In the previous year, to tackle debt stress, the government had liberalised ECB norms, which meant that Indian companies could access funds at a low cost. The rupee's negative gymnastics made this effort counterproductive. The decline in the rupee was also expected to impact infrastructure projects dependent on international market borrowings and imported equipment. The upside: with the depreciation of the rupee, India became more attractive for overseas equipment firms planning to invest as they could derive a better exchange rate.

August

Despite the above average monsoon rains, the rupee slid to a lifetime low of 61.21 to the dollar and there was more bad news with global steelmaking giants ArcelorMittal and Posco scrapping multibillion dollar plans to set up plants across India, thanks to concerns like red tape, land acquisition issues and local opposition, not to mention a weak steel market and poor infrastructure. Ratings agency Crisil assessed that stresses could increase in power, construction, engineering and steel, forecasting more bad loans on the books of commercial banks. It also sounded a note of alarm, saying that one-third of the 11,500 companies it rates might not be able to make their debt repayments owing to the recent tightening of central bank liquidity. India Ratings & Research, too, maintained a negative outlook on the Indian construction sector for the second half of 2013. EBITDA margins of construction companies were expected to remain under pressure thanks to volatile prices of key inputs such as cement and steel. Some glad tidings came in the form of the Reliance Industries Limited (RIL) expansion plan of investing ₹1.5 trillion in the next three years in energy, retail and telecom, among others—a move sure to ramp up construction and engineering order books.

JNNURM, launched seven years earlier, vowed to rejuvenate Indian cities, with funds allocated segment-wise. Transport and water infrastructure were the most visible of the changes witnessed in the funded sixty-five cities. Yet, of 2,815 projects approved in the first phase, only 253 were completed—small wonder, then, that the deadline was extended from March 2012 to March 2014.

Notwithstanding the now-familiar incomplete missions, time and cost overruns (the first phase had an allocation of ₹1 lakh crore for sixty-five cities; the second phase aims to allocate 1.5 times that for an unspecified number of cities and towns), cities saw a leap in environment-friendly and international technology. ULBs also picked up better project management skills. While the first phase included cities of population of 10 lakh and above, the targeted cities in Phase 2 will be half that size. It is commendable that the next phase pays more attention to integrated city development by galvanising internal strengths and adding governance and management skills: comprehensive development plans (CDPs) and detailed project reports (DPRs) have given way to a Development Plan (DP)—a ten-year vision document—encompassing project sequence, timelines, intended outcomes and monitorable milestones based on service-level benchmarks.

September

The Cabinet Committee on Infrastructure's most recent ₹200,000 crore push for the implementation of thirty-five crucial projects, and assigning a sixty-day clearance deadline for them, was a hugely welcome initiative at a time of policy paralysis. One sector needing a dramatic overhaul is roads and highways. Despite the economic downside, there was still some room for optimism with the country's hospitality sector looking to add more rooms to its existing portfolio.

The industry could have been disappointed with the Food Security and Land Acquisition Bills, perhaps seeing them as a step back into the era of subsidies and socialism. In many ways, however, they also signified protectionism of domestic businesses against the onslaught of Chinese power equipment manufacturers. Meanwhile, the US went as far as to file a complaint with the World Trade Organisation (WTO) against Indian 'protectionist' measures. Further, when we posted on LinkedIn regarding our inherent or solvable project issues, the clarion call from international players was the need to resolve corruption in India.

October

The upcoming assembly elections in four states—Rajasthan, Madhya Pradesh, Chhattisgarh and Delhi—at the end of the year, heralded good news for India Inc's development agenda. For instance, the Union Cabinet was set to clear a long pending ₹38,000 crore refinery-cum-petrochemical complex in Barmer district, followed by a rail coach factory in Bhilwara and an airport project in Ajmer, all in Rajasthan.

Further, the Ministry of Civil Aviation was expected to soon float request for qualification (RFQ) documents for Kolkata, Chennai, Guwahati, Jodhpur and Ahmedabad airports and was even open to offering 100% stake to private players.

November

The aviation industry in India saw hectic activity. The Jet-Etihad deal, followed by the clearance of the Tata-Singapore International Airlines (SIA) joint venture, was possible due to the change in

FDI guidelines in airlines. The previous month saw the launch of India's tallest air traffic control (ATC) tower in Mumbai.

New Delhi had been eyeing an investment of $12.1 billion in the airports sector during the Twelfth Five-Year Plan period, a large chunk of which—close to $9.3 billion—was expected to come from the private sector for the construction of new airports, expansion and modernisation. Encouragingly, the Ministry of Civil Aviation was looking to speed up the process of privatising six major airports—Chennai, Kolkata, Ahmedabad, Jaipur, Lucknow and Guwahati—ahead of the general elections due in 2014. In September 2013, the authorities introduced the process of permitting private operators to pick up 100% equity stake in the operation and management of the six airports under the PPP mode, whereby the successful bidder would enter into partnership with the Airports Authority of India (AAI) for a thirty-year period lease to operate, manage and develop both airside and cityside facilities.

Electricity consumption, which occupies the largest share among the eight core sectors, grew at a massive 12.6% in September, compared with 3.9% a year ago. Cement grew 11.5% against 13.8% in the same period last year and steel at 6.6%, against 1.3% in September 2012–13. Further fillip could be provided by infrastructure debt funds. The Finance Ministry was in talks with the RBI to liberalise the rules to allow newly created IDFs to take over more loans from banks without having to make provisions as part of restructured loan norms.

According to the procedure laid out for giving out captive coal mining rights then, the Ministry of Coal made a direct allocation of coal mines to government companies under the government dispensation route. For private companies, it used to conduct allocations based on the recommendations of an inter-ministerial screening committee. Former coal secretary P.C. Parakh was charged with alleged irregularities in the allotment of coal mine to Hindalco, part of the Aditya Birla Group. The revelations on the coal mine allotment to Hindalco created a setback in the executive functioning machinery, raising charges of 'lobbying' and 'influencing' and impelling the government to fight a battle to save its credibility.[4]

Indeed, while industry observers promptly branded the growth in some of the core sectors in the second quarter as 'encouraging' and 'the first signs of recovery' for the infrastructure sectors and banks and several private industries posting decent figures, this hardly presented the complete picture. While the issue was not so much about ongoing, already financed projects, it was about those that were in the post-approval, pre-financial closure stages. National road projects were down to a trickle. The Planning Commission and the Finance Ministry were seriously rethinking the Model Concession Agreement (MCA) that led to the 2011 euphoria; the revised MCA could provide a firmer and more structured way to avoid and resolve disputes, any leeway in the contract for re-amortisation of premium payments, and rethink the selection process of concessionaires in PPP projects.

December

Two years into the Twelfth Plan and the project pipeline was drying up. With three years to go, accelerating to 9–10% GDP growth appeared a near impossibility. The plan envisaged a 50% contribution from the private sector, which could effectively be ruled out. While everyone blamed the government for the energy mess, we would lay equal blame on the private sector. The government had allocated 218 captive coal blocks with reserves of 49 billion tonnes since 1993, of which 50% have been bagged by private companies. The ministry has cancelled the licences of fifty-one coal blocks in two years after reviews indicated lapse of development efforts by companies. While many would have invested and been affected by clearance hurdles, many others leveraged the asset to their benefit without developing the blocks.

FY2013–14 was expected to see a serious deficit in infrastructure investment, with a telling impact on GDP growth. To add to the woes, vigilance and CBI officials cast a pall of gloom over decision-making, with most bureaucrats hesitating from taking even routine decisions. A glimmer of hope came with an announcement that the Project Monitoring Group (PMG) of the CCI had given all clearances to 128 projects worth ₹4 lakh crore (most in the power sector), allowing them to be funded and move towards the implementation stage. Finance availability was made easier by easing norms for banks in relooking at debt owed by delayed projects. Further, relaxation in FDI norms saw India emerge as the most attractive investment destination, surpassing China and the US, according to a report, which added that the US, France and Japan had emerged as the 'top three investors likely to invest in India'.

While the roads sector sagged to a low of awarding only 1,300 km of the targeted 9,000 km for 2013–14, aviation took off. In addition to the Jet-Etihad and Tata-SIA deals, top US companies expressed eagerness to invest in security and building new airports. Policy changes in easing aircraft acquisition and simultaneous enhancement of 80% capacity for Indian carriers between the Gulf and South Asia was expected to enhance air traffic. Further, the prime minister announced 100 small airports to meet the needs of 33 crore passengers by 2020.

In other encouraging news, smaller-ticket projects in urban infrastructure and renewable energy drew developers; as many as sixteen metro rail projects were lined up and JNNURM II was about to roll on a more evolved and larger scale. Further, Gujarat, Rajasthan and Karnataka were poised to award solar projects at lucrative prices and wind and micro-hydro were also expected to make major inroads in 2014.

2014

January

While the year started with abysmal industrial growth, agriculture was the star performer. Construction contributed around 4.8% to the GDP, while mining and quarrying suffered with the bans in Karnataka and Goa. The bans, put in place by the government to clamp down on illegal mining, have cut the iron ore exports by around 85%, or 100 million tonnes, over the past two years. They have also reduced foreign exchange earnings by more than $17 billion in the same period, according to the Federation of Indian Mineral Industries (FIMI). Home finance, which was cruising at 30% per annum, contracted to a growth of 26%, according to market leaders like HDFC. But more importantly, prices of residences and homes built by local builders and investors in the metro cities have crashed by as much as 20–30% in the past one year, with no takers in a buyers' market and sellers desperate to exit.

Owing to the sub-5% performance of the GDP in the first two quarters, we needed growth figures higher than 5% for the next two quarters to close with over 5%. High inflation with low growth besieging our nation was the result of supply bottlenecks created due to scams and malfeasance. In the shorter term, the RBI had to resort to higher interest rates that strangled growth. That said, the weakening of the rupee strengthened exports.

February

While efforts were on at the Centre to break the long-standing logjam of projects, states were making their own strides—Narendra Modi in Gujarat, Chandrababu Naidu in Andhra Pradesh and Nitish Kumar in Bihar had already proven that within the framework of national policy, it was possible for states to drive their own GDP growth. In Maharashtra, Chief Minister Prithviraj Chavan ventured overseas for the first time during his tenure of over three years to promote Maharashtra as an investment destination, with the thrust being on attracting investments in the manufacturing, pharmaceutical and IT sectors.

Meanwhile, the Mumbai Metropolitan Region Development Authority (MMRDA) was set to inaugurate India's first monorail, to be operated between Chembur and Wadala, covering seven stations. Mumbai Metro, too, was likely to soon begin operations, while the Eastern Freeway in the city continued to move towards completion. Elsewhere, besides extension plans in Kolkata and Delhi, metro projects were at various stages of execution in Jaipur, Chennai, Kochi and Hyderabad and planned in about a dozen more cities, including Ahmedabad, Bhopal, Chandigarh, Indore, Kanpur, Lucknow, Ludhiana, Nagpur, Nashik, Patna and Pune. Most of these projects were expected to be funded by the state and Centre with the help of multilateral agencies.

With the lull before the national elections having set in, the fate of over 150 post-clearance projects remained undecided. For instance, work had not started on more than 80% of the BOT road projects awarded in FY2012–13, and those awarded earlier were barely half-way through to completion. Meanwhile, Moody's heralded Narendra Modi, the BJP's prime ministerial candidate, as the saviour for India Inc., with the party's manifesto promising 100 new smart cities, a high-speed rail network along the quadrilateral, an agri-rail network, a National Land Use Authority, a river interlinking plan and measures to develop and modernise ports.[5] On its part, the Congress manifesto included a $1 trillion budget for infrastructure, a National Environmental Appraisal and Monitoring Authority; a National Wind Energy Mission and a vague promise that cities with a population of over 1 million would be covered by high-speed rail.

March

'It's not simply fiscal deficit. There are governance, trust, security and moral deficits,' said Narendra Modi to a packed India Economic Convention in Delhi, summing up the deficit in the economic mood and throwing down the gauntlet.[6] While the 4.9% GDP figure was achieved due to a strong contribution from agriculture, Modi decoded his growth formula: growth cannot come only through investments in one particular sector, he emphasised. All segments of the economy—services, manufacturing and agriculture—should be encouraged to increase their share in the country's GDP. He also stressed upon the need to develop rural areas to mitigate the migration to urban centres.

The government's recent urgency in passing the food security, land acquisition, Lokpal and Telangana statehood legislations was driven by electoral compulsions, while a number of decisions were left to sail through the ordinance route, which didn't go down too well with observers of the macroeconomic front. Another point of discontent was the Central Electricity Regulatory Commissions (CERC) order in favour of Adani and Tata Power that set the stage for other power producers demanding a similar exemption. The regulator granted higher tariffs to private power producers for costly imported Indonesian coal. State utilities were upset with this regulatory order that squeezed the margins of firms such as the National Thermal Power Corporation (NTPC), National Hydroelectric Power Corporation (NHPC), Damodar Valley Corporation (DVC) and Satluj Jal Vidyut Nigam (SJVN).

There was some good news for stuck road projects—those projects awarded on premium could now apply to get their premium payments rescheduled, after the Finance Ministry cleared the suggestions made by the C. Rangarajan Committee. Premiums committed by developers were on the assumption that there would be no delays in clearances as regards environment and land acquisition. However, that was not to be in several cases; resultantly, the developers found their projects turning unviable. But now, given this decision, they could apply for a waiver of the premium to seek relief on cost escalation on account of delays in getting regulatory clearances that should not be at the developer's risk.

April

The hustle and bustle at the hustings put business on the back-burner, with six airport modernisation projects being deferred until after the elections owing to the election code. The gas price hike also got the short shrift.

In some better news, by 1 July, the entire forest and environment clearance process is expected be online, clearly indicating the status of files at each stage for the applicant to view. The Planning Commission's proposal of the establishment of a cabinet committee on transport for speedy decision making in the sector, on the lines of the CCI, was a welcome move. But the final decision can only be taken by the new Planning Commission constituted after the general elections. The government also suggested that investment in the transport sector needs to be scaled up from ₹10 trillion in the Eleventh Plan to ₹70 trillion by the end of the Fifteenth Plan period in 2032.

Further, the stock markets defied gravity, heading north, as inward remittances and foreign institutional investments made the rupee stronger. And core industries' output grew 4.5% in February, the highest in the past five months, fuelled by the robust growth in the electricity sector owing to the performance of thermal, hydel and nuclear power; steel, cement and refinery products also improved their performance.

May

Industrial production was at an abysmal low, GDP was struggling to regain lost ground, tax collections dropped, nonperforming assets mounted and, except for pharmaceuticals, textiles and IT, all industries were reporting sub-par results. We clearly wasted some serious good governance time before the government finally woke up and pushed the PMG into action. According to the Finance Ministry, issues had been resolved in 108 of the 169 projects considered by the CCI and fresh loans to the extent of ₹102,292 crore had been released to project promoters. The total cost of these 169 projects was ₹837,632 crore, and the loan sanctioned by banks to them was ₹292,658 crore.

The agenda for the new government will evidently require a review of administrative hurdles. For instance, despite the Supreme Court order lifting the nineteen-month ban on mining in Goa, the state was still seeking the withdrawal by the Ministry of Environment of its draft notifications on the Western Ghats, which were likely to impact mining in the long run. The Ministry of Environment and Forest (MoEF) issued a draft notification proposing a ban on mining in the 1 km buffer zone of wildlife sanctuaries with immediate effect once the final notification was enforced. A total of thirty-two mining leases coming under the eco-sensitive zone in the wildlife sanctuaries of Mhadei, Molem, Bondla and Netravali were likely to be affected by the order. Of the thirty-two, only twenty-two were working leases till the Supreme Court imposed a ban on mining activity in Goa in October 2012.[7]

Besides, over ₹25,000 crore remained stuck in arbitration with NHAI and other infrastructure government agencies. NHAI was reportedly planning to award about 2,000 km through cash contracts, or EPC mode (engineering, procurement and construction), and was ready with 3,000 km to be bid via PPP. Further, an invitation for bidders via a request for qualification, which has been kept in abeyance for the Chennai, Kolkata, Lucknow, Guwahati, Jaipur and Ahmedabad airports, would need to be executed as interested bidders were keenly awaiting the response.

The total investment in infrastructure sectors in the Twelfth Plan (2012–17) is estimated to be ₹55.7 lakh crore, which is roughly $1 trillion at prevailing exchange rates. The share of private investment in the total investment in infrastructure rose from 22% in the Tenth Plan to 36.61% in the Eleventh Plan. It will have to increase to about 48% during the Twelfth Plan if the infrastructure investment target is to be met. These projections have also been validated by the high-level committee on infrastructure set up under the chairmanship of Deepak Parekh. The committee has however qualified its projections as dependent on several policy initiatives that the government would need to take for ensuring this level of investment. Clearly, the agenda for any government, irrespective of the party, had to be the revival of the economy.[8] The IMF pointed out in its April report that for India, real GDP growth is projected to strengthen to 5.4% in 2014 and 6.4% in 2015, assuming that government efforts to revive investment growth succeed and export growth strengthens after the recent rupee depreciation.

Policymakers must also concentrate on structural reforms to support investment, which has slowed markedly. Priorities include market-based pricing of natural resources to boost investment, addressing delays in the implementation of infrastructure projects, improving policy frameworks in the power and mining sectors, reforming the extensive network of subsidies, and securing passage of the new goods and services tax to underpin medium term fiscal consolidation.[9]

June

India took a clear stand, and Narendra Damodardas Modi became our new prime minister. He was now helming a country that, by 2020, was set to become the world's youngest, with 64% of its population in the working age group. With the West, Japan and even China ageing, this demographic potential offered India and its growing economy an unprecedented edge that economists believed could add a significant 2% to the GDP growth rate.

That apart, the new government was faced with some pressing problems in the areas of inflation, infrastructure and manufacturing (IIM). In infrastructure, the need of the hour was to overcome project paralysis by easing land acquisition, clearances and arbitration issues and introducing transparency in the system. As for inflation, strengthening our currency was a great economic mission, with hidden inefficiencies owing to a lack of accountability or things that were not accounted for, such as subsidies, which are reflected in high inflation. And the manufacturing sector was languishing, with no absorption capacity. There seems to be no readiness for manufacturing to take on large-scale production to compete on a global scale. Only if we can help the country match global nations in terms of capital availability, investor-friendly policies, skilled labour and plug-and-play infrastructure can we consider that we have provided 'equal opportunity'. Otherwise, the demographic dividend can very easily turn into a demographic disaster.

Let's not forget poverty. About 92% of India's 470 million workers were informal workers, with job insecurity, poor compensation and no social security. There was also a substantial difference between the wages of regular workers and informal or contract workers. In fact, the latter constituted one-third of workers in the manufacturing sector. As for unemployment, it was the highest among women graduates, at about 60%. After ten years, 40% of all girls were expected to be matriculates, but India had the lowest female employment rate, along with Pakistan and

Middle Eastern countries. And according to government data, although growth averaged at 8.7% from 2005 to 2010, only 1 million jobs were created, leaving 59 million new entrants into the labour market with nothing. Further, a third of the unemployed were graduates and above.

As for opportunities, the service sector provided only 26% employment but contributed 58% of the GDP. We needed to increase the share of manufacturing in GDP, which stood at 16%, compared to countries like China, Korea and Indonesia, where it was 40–50%.

July

India ranked 134th in ease of doing business and, out of forty nations assessed by the OECD, the country has the thirty-third most complex regulatory environment, thirty-seventh most restrictive FDI policies and most restrictive tariffs on trade. Moreover, businesses in India need as many as seventy certifications to operate. As a result, despite being an attractive market, it has managed a sub-optimal inflow of FDI.

However, things looked set to change with the new government. Overseas funds began to rush to invest in India. In fact, at least three sovereign funds invested over $5 billion in the previous eight months. The Canada Pension Plan Investment Board (CPPIB) formed a joint venture with real estate developer Shapoorji Pallonji Group to invest in commercial real estate and formed an equal real estate finance company with Ajay Piramal group's Piramal Enterprises, to specialise in debt and structured finance. The fund committed $200 million in the first and $250 million in the second venture. Further, it subsequently agreed to invest over ₹2,000 crore in L&T's infrastructure arm, L&T IDPL.

Two other funds were scouting for investments among India's real estate and infrastructure developers. Abu Dhabi Investment Authority (ADIA), which had invested around $500 million over the past decade, purchased a 51% stake in Jaypee Group's thermal power projects for $1.5 billion jointly with a Canadian pension fund. Local PE IDFC Alternatives Fund through its power company Taqa, owned by Abu Dhabi Investment Authority (ADIA). And in February, a Chinese working group submitted a five-year trade and economic planning cooperation plan, offering to finance as much as 30% of the $1 trillion targeted investment in infrastructure during the Twelfth Five-Year Plan (2012–17) to the tune of about $300 billion.

The Union Budget 2014–15 presented by Finance Minister Arun Jaitley laid out an infra trampoline for the country to leapfrog to growth. An eBiz integrated portal for all ministries was announced to facilitate business. A booster shot was given to manufacturing by protectionism against imports. This would lead to enhancement of industrial capacities for large as well as medium and small companies due to the extension of investment allowance benefits for small companies. Further, FDI was eased to 49% for manufacturing in the defence sector, finance was eased for the SME and MSME sectors; nearly $8 billion was allocated to kick off the road sector and another $8 billion was allocated for the urban infrastructure sector. Another 15,000 km of gas pipelines, housing for all by 2022, water and irrigation, education and rural infra were part of the whole infra push. Smart cities were allocated ₹7,060 crore and master planning and urban renewal took centre stage. Restrictions were lifted for FDI on size and investment amount if 30% of the project was reserved for low-cost housing. The introduction of real-estate investment trusts (REITs) for real estate and InvITs for infrastructure, integrated initiatives (such as renewable energy, particularly solar, etched in each initiative) and vitalisation of industrial corridors and SEZs were other highlights.

India's economy grew at 7.4% as per the new series released by Central Statistical Office. Given that sovereign funds like CPPIB and ADIA have invested over $5 billion in the last eight months, the government seems to be getting ready to use the Union

Budget as a platform to invite a surge in FDI across the board into India—a dollar tsunami. According to an UNCTAD report, the largest recipient of FDI in the subregion, India, experienced a 17% increase in FDI inflows to $28 billion. UNCTAD projects that global FDI flows could rise to $1.6 trillion in 2014, $1.75 trillion in 2015 and $1.85 trillion in 2016. The rise will benefit India too.[10]

August

By announcing 100 smart cities as part of its manifesto and then in the Union Budget, the NDA staked its claim on the second big idea after its first, which was the Golden Quadrilateral Project. While the GQ project trotted along during the previous NDA regime, it broke into a canter during UPA 1, fell into a slumber by UPA 2 and was finally completed in 2012. Just as the need to connect commercially vibrant cities, which then led to connecting the hinterland through the PMGSY, was an idea with great payback as it fuelled trade, the smart cities project was supported by strong economic reasons.

According to a McKinsey Global Institute (MGI) report, in 2014, 70% of India's GDP came from urban areas, while the investment for urban development was only 0.70%.[11] India's urban population was projected to increase from ₹34 crore in 2008 to ₹59 crore in 2030. With already fifty-three cities having a population of over 1 million—slated to grow to sixty-eight in 2030—the need to plan and manage services to take care of a density of 12,000 people per square kilometre was daunting. Further, according to a High-Powered Expert Committee (HPEC) report in 2012, the estimates for urban infrastructure in the eight core services of water supply, sewerage, solid waste management, stormwater drains, urban roads, urban transport, street lighting and traffic support infrastructure amounted to ₹39.2 lakh crore over twenty years. In addition, the HPEC estimated ₹19.9 lakh crore towards operation and maintenance over the twenty-year period.[12]

Thus, the planning of future cities in India had to be made a priority. And with a mission of maximum efficiency of resources, technology would become a natural partner. Although the Ministry of Urban Development was yet to give out details of the planned 100 smart cities, seven were being planned under the 1,483 km Delhi–Mumbai Industrial Corridor (DMIC). Others, like Naya Raipur, GIFT City, Kochi City and Palava, were also moving in tandem.

September

The Supreme Court confirmed the penalty imposed by the Competition Commission of India (CCI) on DLF and ordered it to pay ₹630 crore in three months. CCI had imposed the penalty on the developer (carrying a debt of over ₹19,000 crore) in August 2011 for using its dominant position to engage in unfair trade practices, such as making consumers sign inequitable agreements. Indeed, the high-handed attitude of some developers had kindled consumer activism, which, backed by recent judgements in favour of consumers, was on a high. Developers, therefore, began to modify buyers' agreements to protect themselves, including longer delivery deadlines of up to five years from the earlier three to four. Supertech started giving live feeds to buyers on construction updates. On the other hand, Raheja Developers added a clause in its buyers' agreement barring customers from posting derogatory comments about the company online.

In the aviation sector, a revised policy for regional and remote area connectivity was set to be announced with the Directorate General of Civil Aviation expected to be replaced by an industry-friendly Civil Aviation Authority. Unfortunately, the privatisation of Air India did not appear to be on the cards. In fact, the Indian airline behemoth was reportedly considering a REIT issue to get itself out of its financial mess. While the regulatory environment and market sentiments were right for the launch of REITs, a few players asked the government for greater clarity on the tax breaks proposed for this investment vehicle. Assets included in REITs had the potential to reach $20 billion by 2020, according to a few reports.

As for coal, it was heartening to note that the government started to take some commonsensical decisions like rationalising coal linkages. In simple terms, this meant that coal would no longer be transported across the length and breadth of the country; allocations would be amended and swapped to ensure mines were not far away from power plants.

In other news, in a poll conducted by a financial daily of fifty leading industrialists and CEOs, investment bankers and managers of large PE funds on the impact of Prime Minister Narendra Modi on business and economy after 100 days of forming the government, 74% of CEOs said they were already seeing a demand pick up; 80% made new investment decisions or were likely to do so; and two-thirds were stepping up hiring. What's more, the PM's tour to Japan yielded rich dividends. Japanese FDI was set to double over the next five years to $35 billion, with investments in the various industrial corridors and the proposed bullet train.

October

The report card for the new government was in—and it was a good one across the board.

The government administration appeared to be working, with ministers, bureaucrats and government officers being pulled up for dragging their feet. Crony capitalism was out, with touts barred at ministries, ministers hesitating to meet businessmen unnecessarily and most processes being laid out transparently. All processes started to go up on websites, and online updates of information were encouraged. Even tracking files for clearances was just a click away. Further, core issues were being dealt with head on. Efforts were on to enhance coal production and resolve fuel-starved plants.

Women's safety was being addressed by increasing the availability of toilets. Railway productivity was being improved by upping the speed of trains from 50 kmph to over 160 kmph for express trains and from 25 kmph to 100 kmph for goods trains.

The Jan Dhan scheme was launched to provide social security and financial inclusion—to date, banks had opened 40 million accounts and mobilised about ₹3,700 crore as deposits in these accounts. Under the scheme, account holders get an overdraft facility of ₹5,000. They are also provided RuPay debit cards and ₹1 lakh accident insurance cover. Further, the PMG was tasked with expediting projects with timelines set for ministries and states and the Department of Industrial Policy and Promotion set up an eight-member expert panel for quick grievance redressal and to answer queries to improve ease of doing business.

While pushing for creation of new infrastructure capacities, the PM tasked all core sector ministries with boosting the efficiency of India's existing infrastructure such as power, ports, roads, coal mines and telecom by at least 10% by March 2015. He earmarked clear measurable outcomes to determine if the country got concrete results from its infrastructure spend by the end of the financial year. And after three sluggish growth years, the outlook of most core sectors began to witness a positive change. Between April and August, power generation capacity increased by 8,400 MW, nearly 47% of what was achieved in the entire previous year. Port projects worth ₹4,200 crore were awarded under the new government, while five ongoing projects were completed, boosting India's export-import capacity for goods by over 30 Mtpa. What's more, India's infrastructure market was expected to touch $6.6 trillion by 2025, according to PwC estimates.[13]

Significantly, the government began to target investment in nearly two dozen sectors, including electronics, automobiles, civil aviation, defence, railways, tourism, hospitality and wellness. Special emphasis was given to FDI, manufacturing policy, industrial corridors and intellectual property rights. Indeed, armed with the 'Make in India' war cry, there was an expansive attempt to revive the manufacturing sector in the country and the mission set its sights on increasing the share of manufacturing to 25% by 2022. According to this new initiative, the increase in manufacturing output was expected to result in the creation of 100 million new jobs.

Further, the prime minister's visits to Bhutan, South America, Japan and the US, not to mention the visit by the Chinese president, went far in enhancing India's image and standing in the minds of international investors. He offered US industry lead partnership in developing three smart cities, having offered similar cooperation to Japan, China and Singapore. Both countries pledged to establish an Infrastructure Collaboration Platform to enhance participation of US companies in infrastructure projects in India. And rather than gloat over indications of Chinese interests in investing, President Xi Jinping was asked to prioritise the resolution of the border dispute—a sign of the country's growing stature.

November

The latest Cabinet approval permitting FDI in construction reduced the minimum built area requirement for projects in which foreign investment is allowed to 20,000 sq. m from 50,000 sq. m and the minimum capital investment by foreign companies was cut to $5 million from $10 million. The investor would be allowed to expatriate the investment on completion of the project or three years after the final investment is made, provided the trunk infrastructure was complete for those plots. The new rules were expected to encourage development of smaller plots in urban areas, where availability of land is limited. This would also complement the initiative to build 100 smart cities. In fact, India received $1.2 billion of FDI (in real estate) in the financial year ending 31 March, compared to $1.3 billion the previous year. Between

April and August 2014, it received foreign investment worth $446 million. This move was a further shot in the arm.

In the forthcoming winter session of Parliament, sixty-seven pending bills awaiting clearance were expected to help ward off the lag effect of the turnaround. The Real Estate Regulation & Development Bill, Coal Mines Amendment Bill, Prevention of Corruption Act, revised Goods and Services Tax (GST) Constitution Amendment Bill, Land Acquisition Bill and Motor Vehicles Bill were just some important initiatives awaiting clearance. Also, the proposed new Motor Vehicles Bill laid great emphasis on road safety and traffic management through new agencies specifically dedicated to forming and implementing new laws. It also proposed to create a National Road Transport and Multimodal Coordination Authority for coordination on road and other transport issues.

Although the roads sector had lost much of its interest for Indian bidders, the Construction Industry Development Board (CIDB) of Malaysia offered to bid for five such projects costing over ₹9,000 crore, giving PPP a new lease of life. New investors such as NGI and Tata Realty bucked the trend by entering the sector.

Another development that would boost industrial production by simplifying the need for regulation and administration for SMEs, which accounted for over 30% of industrial production, was the Small Factories Bill, in line with the amendments to the Factories Act. This act would reduce the number of forms required for compliance with rules, allow SMEs to employ women in night shifts based on the fulfilment of certain conditions and change the inspection system to one based on self-certification and inspections based on computer lots.

Other positive moves included diesel deregulation and allowing private participation in coal mining. A noteworthy opportunity was also provided by the Swachh Bharat programme, which aimed to cover 4,041 towns by 2019, for startups working in the fields of water purification, sanitation and solid-liquid waste management.

All considered, the government's stringent review and result-oriented approach was expected to push growth across the infrastructure sector. A new civil aviation policy in the works was expected to bring in much-needed reforms, including promotion of regional and remote area air connectivity. The Highways Ministry, too, showcased the revival of thirty-four projects worth over ₹26,000 crore in its presentation on infrastructure targets. Projects spanning over 4,084 km were being restructured or converted from PPP to EPC mode to get them going.

December

Debt remained a major concern, with several companies furiously flailing their arms and legs to stay afloat. Most companies got into project development buoyed by the infrastructure boom, but delay in projects, issues related to land acquisition, lack of fuel for power and environment clearances, among others, bled the companies dry. The need of the hour was a huge infusion of capital just to reach a stage of sustainability.

HCC used the Lavasa IPO to bring debt into control; Gammon India planned to sell 58.67% of its holdings in Gammon Infrastructure; Jaiprakash was selling its power and cement plants and raised nearly ₹15,000 crore from the sale of assets until March and ₹1,500 crore via qualified institutional placements; GMR Group sold 40% stake in Istanbul's international airport and another firm providing airline services for $305 million and Welspun sold its stake in a construction joint venture for $99 million. More than $10 billion worth of assets had already been sold, and another $5–7 billion were in the pipeline, as per CLSA brokerage research.

Positives included the government having moved speedily on the coal block auction issue after the Supreme Court diktat.

Further, Credit Suisse predicted that India would witness the fastest dollar nominal growth in 2015. Falling oil prices proved to be a major windfall for the country—its knock-off effects from the fall were helping the Centre cut subsidies, pare inflation and handle the fiscal deficit.

2015

January

An informal assessment of the performance of the Modi government was already taking place. While many from the opposition had already begun raising their voices about the 'feel-good' factor not translating into better bottom lines, even supporters—holding up the 'it-requires-time-to-resuscitate-a-sick-economy' line—were beginning to feel the need for answers.

The cumulative decline in global oil prices between June and December 2014 alone was 44% (or $49), and the slide of the oil price has continued into January 2015.[14] Despite the bonanza on the oil front, where the oil import bill had shrunk owing to falling prices, the Indian government was staring at a potential revenue shortfall of over ₹1 lakh crore for the fiscal year.[15] In the roads sector, the contracts awarded were struggling to reach the 5,500-km target. The UPA government had awarded just 3,169 km in 2013–14 and about 2,300 km in 2012–13. In fact, the average time overrun had increased from about twenty months in 2008–09 to about fifty months in 2013–14. Construction per year ranged in the region of 14 km/day from 2009 to 2013. The lag in awards in the past two to three years had cast a long shadow on a pickup in activity. Hence, it was important to expedite awards to reflect construction of at least 20 km/day as against Road Minister Nitin

Gadkari's target of 30 km/day. Despite low awards, projects were seeing better clearance timelines. Of the sixteen projects awarded in 2013–14, work had already begun on twelve (or 75%), an improvement from the previous two years. This, and the savings on land and environment clearances that accounted for up to ₹200 crore per project, would help better ROI.

Notably, the government had one monetary arsenal at its disposal to kickstart the economic growth engine. Though saddled with a few ageing behemoths and lumbering white elephants, India's public sector had a few battle-scarred organisations that had managed to hold their own through thick and thin. And these companies were sitting on a huge cash pile—of over ₹2 lakh crore, according to some estimates. And accounting for the prime real estate that a few PSUs had at their disposal, the kitty looked very promising indeed. Unfortunately, governments in the past had missed the bus on raising funds through divestment of PSU shares. The new government was nowhere close to meeting its ₹43,425 crore divestment target for the ongoing financial year, either.

February

One of the highlights of US President Barack Obama's recently concluded Indian visit was his recognition of PM Modi's focus in upping the ease-of-doing-business quotient. India ranked a dismal 142nd out of 189 countries in ease of doing business and, further, 184th in 'dealing with construction permits'. India further ranked 186th in 'enforcing construction contracts'.

With such a poor business environment, it was no wonder that Indian developers were laden with crushing debt while they struggled with permissions or were awaiting arbitration awards. Banks, too, were saddled with a massive ₹8.5 lakh crore in stressed assets, forming about 14% of their total loan book. This made it difficult for them to take any initiative in providing relief. While paucity of finance was a major hurdle, many infrastructure projects were also languishing because of missing periodic reviews of progress, lack of long-term planning and vision and political opposition. While the various stakeholders involved were at loggerheads with each other, the country suffered—reports suggested a loss of ₹1.77 lakh crore because of delayed infrastructure projects.

That said, the economy was showing signs of consistent improvement, as evidenced from the HSBC PM (Purchase Manager) indices. The Purchasing Managers' Index (PMI) is an indicator of the prevailing direction of economic trends in the manufacturing and service sectors. The headline HSBC Composite Output Index—that maps manufacturing as well as services sectors output—rose from 52.9 in December to 53.3 in January, signalling further growth of private sector output in January.[16] Rail freight by volume improved by 5% over the previous year. On 15 January, the RBI cut the policy rate by 25 bps to 7.75%, the first cut since May 2013, before the monetary policy meeting scheduled on 3 February. According to a report, the medium and heavy commercial vehicle segment, which signals improvement in the economy, was scheduled to see a volume growth of 13–17% in the next fiscal year and accelerate the commercial vehicle (CV) sector, while LCVs would see only a marginal growth of up to 3%.

March

The Union Budget was a much-awaited event, which needed to kickstart the economy by boosting public spending. An overall increase of ₹70,000 crore in infrastructure investment in FY2015–16 over the current year, with an increase in the allocation for roads and railways by ₹14,031 crore and ₹10,050 crore, respectively, was definitely a trigger.

Finance Minister Arun Jaitley made further provision for an infusion of ₹80,844 crore of additional CAPEX of the PSUs, taking it to a total of ₹317,889 crore. Considering that the cash-rich PSUs would inject adrenaline into the economy made this a credible proposition. Clearly, the recognition of the PPP proposition turning weak brought in the wisdom of depending on public spending rather than private. The minister also announced the formation of an investment and infrastructure fund and tax-free bonds for raising funds for investment in rail, road and irrigation infrastructure. Other highlights included a proposal to set up five new mega power projects, each of 4,000 MW, in the plug-and-play mode. With all clearances in place, this reformed investment magnet had the potential to draw ₹1 lakh crore, provided the distribution end was fixed.

In 'Housing for All' by 2022, the plan was to build 2 crore houses in rural India and 4 crore in urban India. For roads, the vision was to complete the 100,000 km under construction and build another 100,000 km. The DMIC corridors, especially the Ahmedabad–Dholera Investment Region in Gujarat and the Shendra–Bidkin Industrial Park near Aurangabad, were in a position to start work on basic infrastructure and had an outlay of ₹1,200 crore.

The most transformational idea of the budget, though, was the Fourteenth Finance Commission, which increased the share of states in central taxes to 42% from 32%, giving them more funds and making them more accountable for enhancing their civic infrastructure and their attractiveness as an investment destination. When Narendra Modi was the chief minister of Gujarat, he had to request the Centre time and again to issue funds for the state, based on local requirements. But the mandarins in Delhi in previous dispensations preferred the one-size-fits-all approach. Now, states had the power to design, implement and package their finance programmes tailored to their specific needs. Panchayats, too, stood to receive around ₹2 lakh crore (for a five-year period, till 2020) so as to provide basic amenities like sewage, sanitation and water supplies. Municipalities also stood to gain a substantial sum. The Public Procurement Bill, the Dispute Resolution Bill and the introduction of a bankruptcy law were other strong moves inviting investment in the infrastructure sector.

April

'There's no action on the ground!' That was the refrain heard in corners of corporate boardrooms about the slow pickup of the economy. Countering this at a private gathering, Minister of Power Piyush Goyal narrated that when the NDA set about seeking a tender for street lighting using energy-efficient LED lights in place of incandescent bulbs, the lowest offer it received was ₹315. (According to him, the use of LED lights would slash electricity demand by 10,000 MW and lead to savings to the tune of ₹12,500 crore.) He claimed that the price per LED bulb had come down to ₹81.93 over the past few bids compared to ₹315 in February 2014 owing to the transparent bidding process.[17] Shekhar Bajaj of Bajaj Electricals confirmed to me personally that 75% of inputs for LED lights are imported to achieve such cost savings. Reputed local companies like Usha and Crompton Greaves were among those bidding—such large-scale orders would also help the Make in India initiative, confirming quality was not being compromised in the quest for a lower price. Indeed, while such actions would not 'show on the ground' immediately, such solutions—including recovering the best price for natural resources like coal, which won a commitment of over ₹2 lakh crore during the transparent bidding for mines—were expected to show results on the ground eventually.

Also, SEBI, in consultation with the RBI, relaxed norms for converting the debt of distressed listed companies into equity by banks and other financial institutions, to help ease recovery in non-performing assets (NPAs). Although this could not be the only solution, the bankruptcy laws announced by the FM in combination with this had the potential to be effective, as there would then be a choice between converting into equity if the interest coverage ratio turned positive and liquidating the company. As in December 2014, total gross NPAs at banks had swelled to over 5% of all advances, and a more dynamic approach to resolve them was the need of the hour. The growth rate in bank lending had also plummeted to 8.41% by 31 December 2014, as against 16.05% in December 2013.

Further, the latest figures compiled by the Ministry of Finance in March 2015 indicated that 299 mega projects involving an outlay of ₹18.13 lakh crore still remained stalled with the PMG. As on 25 February 2015, 504 projects worth ₹25.38 lakh crore were reported with the PMG for resolution of pending issues.

That apart, there was more 'minister speak' to report. At the recently held annual general meeting of the CII, Finance Minister Arun Jaitley expressed that the land law (of 2013) was detrimental to rural India, not leaving any space for rural infrastructure, including irrigation, PMGSY and rural electrification.[18] He further warned that industrial corridor projects would be stuck and 300 million landless people looking for employment emanating from these projects would be denied opportunities. For his part, Minister of Roads & Shipping Nitin Gadkari said the cost of the land was much too small in the overall project cost and it was delays that were making projects unviable. Minister of State for Finance Jayant Sinha voiced the need to improve the tax-to-GDP ratio from the current 16% to well over 20%. He also indicated that the sizes of banks need to quadruple in tune with the GDP, which was set to grow from $2 trillion to $4 trillion. Power Minister Piyush Goyal asserted that the rise in output at Coal India by 8% was a landmark achievement and that he expected the import of coal to drop to a negligible number in years to come, while solar power tariff would dive to under ₹4.50 per unit. And Minister of Urban Development Venkaiah Naidu summed up the missions of the government as 'MISIDICI': Make in India, Skilling India, Digital India and Cleaning India. Meanwhile, Amitabh Kant, Secretary, DIPP, announced that there would be a rating exercise of the states where the top and bottom three would be named and shamed. He also shared how Maharashtra had been able to reduce the number of days required for electricity permissions from sixty-seven to fifteen, which was further reduced to five.

May

As urban migration gained momentum, it was projected that India was likely to add another equivalent of the existing urban population of around 400 million to its cities by 2050. With the lives and investment at stake even higher, the issue of building codes (and their abuse) came into sharper focus against the backdrop of the devastating earthquake in Nepal in April, which also affected parts of India, China and Bangladesh. In 2014, the Ministry of Urban Development (MoUD), Ministry of Finance and the Prime Minister's Office (PMO) approved, through an ordinance, the regularisation of 895 unauthorised colonies in Delhi benefitting 6 million people. The Delhi government had also suggested that regularisation of unauthorised colonies would bring in planned construction under existing building bylaws and other applicable rules that, in turn, would result in more orderly development of these colonies. This was all fine—but when disaster strikes, the 'house of cards' can truly crumble.

The economic ills India was facing clearly owed much to the complete shutdown of all new investments planned in 2012 and 2013. As a result, projects completed between September 2014 and March 2015 came down by 50% in comparison with the period September 2011–March 2012.

The highest value of projects stalled was seen in September 2013–March 2014, when elected representatives in government were probably more interested in re-election than governance. While the whole pipeline of projects was boosted during September 2014–March 2015, this was likely to yield results only in 2016–17 and 2017–18. Real estate, housing and commercial complexes, which took a sharp dive in terms of new investments planned between 2013–14 and 2014–15, began to pick up, except in the case of commercial construction. Electricity, roads, aviation and shipping stepped up the project pipeline steeply and looked healthy.

That said, the railways was yet to show whether it was on track. Despite being the largest rail network in Asia and the second largest in the world, the productivity of Indian Railways doesn't match up to that of many other countries. The prime culprit, of course, is severe underinvestment. A bad safety record, poor customer service and delays over the years have led to an erosion of the railways' share in national freight and passenger traffic. This in turn has slowed down expansion and modernisation. While delivering the Rail Budget for 2015, Rail Minister Suresh Prabhu said an investment of ₹8.5 lakh crore was required over the next five years.[19] Further, a white paper on Indian Railways released by the ministry a few months earlier estimated that there is a large shelf of pending projects which is estimated at ₹491,510 crore on the basis of originally estimated costs. Of these, fund requirement for the prioritised works such as doubling, new lines, gauge conversion, traffic facilities, signal and telecom works, workshops and electrification is estimated at ₹208,054 crore.[20]

That said, there were some encouraging developments in the infrastructure sector. The Union Cabinet gave its green signal for the Smart Cities Mission and Atal Mission for Rejuvenation and Urban Transformation (AMRUT). The cabinet also approved ₹48,000 crore and ₹50,000 crore over the next five years for the AMRUT project and the Smart Cities Mission, respectively. Apart from this, private developers can also explore the emerging opportunities under the PPP model. As a part of AMRUT, apparently the new avatar of the JNNURM, the government would execute projects in 500 cities.

Further, Finance Minister Arun Jaitley exempted units of business trusts in REITs from minimum alternate tax (MAT), thus paving the way for alternate ways of financing urban housing and commercial infrastructure projects.

June

While the government's momentum was strong, the lag in process was holding back impact on the ground. Results for the year ending March 2015 conclusively proved that the corporate sector was reeling under an almost negative demand and virtually nil margins with a debt overhang. The consumer sector, which was buoyant, was also not likely to throw up good numbers going ahead. The fall in inflation was expected to see improvement in demand, albeit gradually, over the next six months. The roads sector was likely to be the first to get into higher gear, with many EPC projects being awarded in the second quarter of the fiscal.

This sector had been the most visible statement on infrastructure with a solid track record—over 12 km constructed per day for the past seven years. While many attempted to ridicule the previous regime's quest to build 20 km/day, the fact remained that we were doing close to 16 km/day in 2012–13. If the NDA government was to award 10,000 km this year as intended and follow it up with a similar figure for 2016–17, we could move very close to 30 km/day, as stated by Minister Nitin Gadkari.[21]

Railways, too, was likely to see activity with 94,000 km of doubling and third line on choked routes receiving sanctions to decongest the network. To overcome the cycle of chronic underinvestment, the railways was approaching the markets to finance revenue generating projects. Further, metro projects were on track and the energy was upbeat, with an increase of 8.4% in electricity generation, the highest in the past twenty years. The country added 22,566 MW of generation capacity in the past year, with some contribution from enhanced coal production, which was up by 12%.

Also, the Supreme Court breathed new life into the renewable sector with a landmark judgment and reinforced the nation's renewable energy mandates by upholding the validity of Renewable Purchase Obligations (RPOs). These obligations require electricity distribution companies, open-access consumers and captive power producers to source a certain percentage of their energy from renewable sources. The case arose when several industries challenged the mandatory nature of RPOs, arguing that they should have more flexibility in meeting their energy needs.

The Supreme Court's decision was crucial as it underscored the importance of RPOs in achieving India's ambitious renewable energy targets, which aim for 175 GW of renewable energy capacity by 2022 and a longer-term goal of 450 GW by 2030. The ruling also emphasised the role of RPOs in reducing India's dependence on fossil fuels, mitigating climate change and promoting sustainable development. And the RBI gave some much-needed medicine, albeit in a very small dose, to the real estate sector by reducing the policy repo rate by 25 basis points, from 7.5% to 7.25%. The rate cut, when passed on by the banks to borrowers, was expected to act as a catalyst for the housing market.

That said, there was a fall in the number of tenders issued in FY2014–15 for infrastructure projects across the board—roads and highways, railways, mining, water supply systems, power plants, real estate—compared to FY2013–14.

July

A major development was the much-awaited launch of three mission programmes with a huge spend: Smart Cities, AMRUT and Housing for All by 2022. These initiatives were set to open up huge opportunities for investments and generating employment.

Smart Cities, along with AMRUT, Housing for All, Digital India, Swachh Bharat and HRIDAY, would see a total spend of ₹4 lakh crore over the next five years. All these missions were integrated and interrelated. The essential change over the past was that the Centre had passed down the responsibilities of city improvement to the state. Introducing a challenge added an element of competition. Once the 'smarter' states won funding for their cities, private-sector money, aka builders, would flow in, leaving other cities that did not qualify in the lurch. Once money started taking sides, city leaders would compete. This would open up opportunities for PPP as nearly 50% of the money for the cities would have to be generated by attracting the interest of private developers. Housing for All was expected to accelerate 'in-situ' slum redevelopment projects as it offered an incentive of ₹1 lakh per 30 sq. m flat built to developers. Housing loans of up to ₹6 lakh for a fifteen-year period at an interest rate of just 6.5% were being issued to the economically weaker segments of society to acquire a home.

Meanwhile, the ports sector was likely to gain traction with the thrust on 'Make in India'. The fillip to the manufacturing sector was expected, in turn, to lead to the improvement of all those infrastructural facilities that support manufacture—such as ports, which handled 90% by volume and 70% by value of our merchandise export-import (EXIM) trade. The Maritime Agenda 2020 also envisaged a capacity creation of 3,200 MMT. Further, the government revived the Sagarmala Project, which aimed at a string of port-led developments.

August

The manufacturing indices, which appeared to be positive until the previous month, turned negative. Loans continued to pile up. The RBI maintained its stance. And interest rates didn't ease off enough to make an impact in a debt-burdened commercial sector. The government was still struggling to get its Land Bill and GST Bill through Parliament. And corporate results reflected the pain.

Over a year into the new government's rule, and nothing much appeared to have changed on the ground. While there had been a rally in Indian equities since May 2014 owing to the optimism of investors, the BJP's lack of a majority in the 245-seat Rajya Sabha (forty-eight seats against the INC's sixty-eight) led to the derailment of the reform momentum. The real estate sector was holding an unsold inventory of 688,000 units, measuring 919 million sq. ft. While commercial real estate had been languishing for long, the residential sector also lost steam. This was likely to have a cascading effect on the building material sectors. Steel was already suffering on account of large Chinese imports, and cement was waiting for housing demand to rise. Poor demand was causing unemployment among labourers, and they were returning to their villages, where an even bleaker scenario awaited them. The budget of the MNREGA scheme had been slashed, agriculture yields were soft and rural infrastructure schemes were still struggling with environment clearances and land acquisition problems.

Despite Team Modi's tireless work to improve structural lacunae and to launch new schemes to digitise, smarten, skill, house, power and connect India, 23% believed that the performance was 'moderately to substantially' worsening for industry against previous month's FICCI's Business Confidence Survey at 3%. Also, the percentage of respondents expecting the situation to get 'moderately to substantially better' in the next six months dropped from 87% to 71%.[22]

September

The global gloom turned into panic as the Chinese stock markets tumbled 8.5% on 24 August, paving way for speculation that China was heading for a major slowdown. The Indian stock markets, too, caught the cold, as the Chinese markets sneezed. Luckily, it turned out to be a minor ailment and the markets began recovering their losses. The progress of the monsoon, movement of the rupee against the dollar, crude oil prices and auto sales numbers were expected to be key factors determining the trend on the bourses.

Realising that private capital was shy, the government took it upon itself to provide the triggers. It had already spent nearly a quarter of plan funds in the first three months of the fiscal year, the highest pace of spending since 2008–09. Finance Minister Arun Jaitley said capital expenditure increased by about 17.8% in the first quarter as the government looked to target 8% growth for the year. The government has proposed an additional ₹25,500 crore in spending, with nearly half allocated for capital support to banks. This is expected to enhance their lending capacity, potentially driving a growth cycle. As per FM Jaitley, achieving 8% growth could be possible if banks are recapitalized, GST is implemented, stalled projects are revived, and infrastructure spending increases. The government plans to inject ₹70,000 crore into state-run banks over four years, with banks raising an additional ₹1.10 lakh crore from the market. With private sector investment lagging, public investment needs to rise, Jaitley confirmed.[23]

The finance minister cited a pickup in indirect taxes as evidence for the green shoots of recovery. Calling this an 'enabling situation', the FM said the government would spend ₹70,000 crore, raised from additional revenue mobilisation measures, towards infrastructure.

What's more, the MoUD recently released the list of ninety-eight nominated smart cities, with two cities yet to apply. Although the impact of this mission was likely to be felt only in 2016–17, it addressed a compelling need to fortify our cities. The return on this investment was expected to be high, as cities generate 60% of the GDP and take only 0.6%. Indeed, the Smart Cities Mission would lead to opportunities in water, waste, security, HVAC and mobility management, power-efficient equipment and solar power generation systems, and much more.

October

The economy was not out of the woods yet. Eight core sectors—coal, crude oil, natural gas, refinery products, fertiliser, steel, cement and electricity—slowed to 1.1% in July after a growth of 3% in June, mainly on account of low expansion in coal output and contraction in steel, crude oil and natural gas production, all hinting at weakness in industrial recovery.

However, the roads sector definitely rebounded, to about 13 km a day from just 3 km when the NDA took over. The government planned to sanction 20,000 km of projects in the coming three years and the target for the year to March 2016 was set at 8,000 km. Seven top road builders raised ₹10,700 crore by way of bonds, paving the way for finance to the debt-stressed sector. Bonds come at a cost of 11% and can be serviced, provided tolls commence within the timeline. Recent easing of policies, including allowing companies to exit projects and getting environmental clearances in time, have helped improve the climate.

Raising finance overseas has been the route many companies followed.

The global scenario, though, was not too smooth, with companies like Caterpillar and JCB cutting jobs, the Chinese residential property market remaining under pressure and the award of new construction projects having slowed down in the Middle East, with the pressure on oil prices rubbing off on public-sector spending.

In light of this global upheaval, India remained an attractive option. During PM Modi's visit to the US, American CEOs implored him to step up the pace of reforms.[24] Equally important was seeing through infrastructural initiatives. For instance, the logic to accelerate connectivity of the hinterland through all means of transportation and communication, was unquestionable. The plan to build fifty non-frill regional airports had been revived. And as roads take their own time and a larger investment, one solution would have been to deploy air taxis on economically run airports, creating 'air corridors' that could accelerate economic growth. For his part, Minister for Roads, Highways and Shipping Nitin Gadkari was advocating the use of inland waterways. A bill was in the works and there was a proposal to offer 850 ports along major rivers to transport coal to the private sector. This would create new opportunities in logistics and was likely to bring in ₹4,000 crore of private investment, apart from saving sizeable freight costs.

More positive news: nearly two dozen countries were reported to be showing interest in the Smart Cities Mission. And addressing the rapid depletion of groundwater (India had 17% of the global population, with just 4% of the world's freshwater sources), a number of government tenders for the management of water resources and subsequent treatment of wastewater, were coming up. Serious players with technological know-how and execution capabilities were being encouraged to bid for these projects.

November

The ease of doing business rankings released by the World Bank indicated a minuscule improvement for India to a rank of 130, owing primarily to better points in 'starting a business' and 'getting an electricity connection'. However, there was no change in our abysmal ranking as far as 'obtaining construction permits', 'enforcing contracts' and 'registering property', highlighting the morass real estate entrepreneurs had to navigate to survive. If one had to secure over fifty-five permits over a two-year period before starting a simple building project, how long would it take to realise the dream of smart cities? The multiplicity of authorised departments working in silos had made it difficult even for a chief minister to ensure the creation of single-window clearance.

States seeking investments were actively wooing companies from overseas and corporate giants from other states to set up their factories. Telangana was wooing Foxconn and Microsoft while Andhra Pradesh was touring Silicon Valley to attract investment to Amaravati, its new capital, while the Singapore and Japanese governments were funding its master plan. Maharashtra had sought funding from Japan, and Tamil Nadu recently held a Global Investor Summit, which was to be followed by Rajasthan. It begged the question: why would you neglect your state's regular investors, its entrepreneurs?

December

As the year drew to a close, the roads sector was a source of optimism, closely followed by contract mining, irrigation and power. Minister Nitin Gadkari proved to be a dependable ally for the construction sector owing to his dogged determination in resolving issues affecting progress. The task ahead in roads remained huge, though. The country needed to increase its national highways network from about 96,000 km to at least 150,000 km. Moreover, of the existing 96,000 km, less than 25% were four-laned and there was significant room for improvement. State highways and other roads had been neglected and needed urgent attention.

Meanwhile, India began to emerge as a sourcing hub for construction equipment. With a current size of $2.8 billion, the Indian construction equipment industry was expected to grow to $5 billion by 2019–20. Even the after-sales spares market was about $800 million.

The rest of the picture wasn't so rosy. Aggregate sales, operating profit and net profit of over 300 companies from core sectors (including capital goods, cement, construction, metals, mining and power) fell in the September 2015 quarter, making it the third consecutive dismal performance. Half the operating profit was spent on servicing debt, indicating pressured balance sheets. This indicated that the decline had not been arrested conclusively and a turnaround in the economy may take longer than expected.

Companies were weighed down under a $640-billion debt burden, which was more than 30% of India's GDP. The strain lay in the stressed debt of over $50 billion in the banks and a rise in bond defaults. Gammon India was the sixth company where bankers decided to take majority control by converting debt into equity. Previously, lenders to Electrosteel Steels Ltd, Lanco Teesta Hydro Power Pvt. Ltd, VISA Steel Ltd, Jyoti Structures Ltd and Monnet Ispat and Energy Ltd had invoked conversion of debt into equity, giving them majority control. Gammon's T&D and EPC businesses had already been scheduled to change hands by incorporating them into separate Special Purpose Vehicles (SPVs).

2016

January

The United Nations declared 2016 as 'The Year of Pulses'. And it appeared safe to forecast that all infrastructure segments would set our 'pulses' racing! The numbers did tell a story of improvement and growth, whether it was the pace of road construction per day, numbers of stalled projects cleared, investments in renewable energy or addressing the woes of the mining and power sectors (DISCOMs in particular), ports or railways.

The year began with the big-bang announcement of the ₹40,000 crore National Investment and Infrastructure Fund (NIIF), conceived as a sovereign wealth fund with a mandate to maximise economic impact through infrastructure development in commercially viable projects. This was a major step to fix India's infrastructure financing issues. The sector was saddled with most of the country's stalled projects to the tune of ₹8.8 lakh crore and bad loans of about ₹600,000 crore. In addition to the woes of the past, it was estimated that an investment of ₹26 lakh crore would be needed in the sector till 2020. In the Union Budget 2015–16, Finance Minister Arun Jaitley had announced that the PPP mode of infrastructure development has to be revisited and revitalised. In pursuance of this announcement, a Committee on Revisiting & Revitalising the PPP model of Infrastructure Development was set up and was chaired by Dr Vijay Kelkar. The recommendations of the Vijay Kelkar Committee also seemed to be a step in the right direction with respect to setting up a more viable framework for PPPs.[25]

Meanwhile, the courts came to the rescue of the automobile industry after punishing it for its contribution to pollution. A notification to come into effect sought to retire roughly 3.4 million commercial vehicles (CVs) older than fifteen years from the Indian roads. Vehicular pollution contributed to 20–25% of the pollution in cities, and CVs contributed to nearly 74% of the air pollution caused by all vehicles. This was a win-win for both the residents of the cities and the CV sector. Further, the advent of commercial mining with the Coal Ministry identifying about six coal blocks for allotment to PSUs was more good news for the CV industry.

That said, FDI in construction development projects fell by over 38% during the year ending March 2015 to $758 million compared to $1,226 million in FY2014. FDI flow remained weak, with just $34 million of investments in the April–June quarter of the fiscal year. The poor pick-up in the inflow was because of the slow approval process. Environment Ministry approvals had not improved and remained contentious; for example, the ministry had given final forest clearance to only 6% of the 598 proposals it received for road and highways projects across India in the sixteen months starting January 2015.[26]

February

While the global outlook was disconcerting, it brought good tidings in the form of nearly $60 billion of savings owing to sub $30 oil prices. However, the Indian stock markets indicated that the near-term outlook was yet to see a revival. The Sensex was at the same level as when the government assumed office. Manufacturing indices slipped below levels that would have indicated a positive trend.

In real estate, sales volumes dropped and new launches plunged. Amid large-scale delivery defaults, slow sales and huge unsold inventory, residential real estate remained in the slow lane, as in the previous year. While luxury real estate was badly hit, the affordable housing segment gained some ground with sales of residential units from ₹50 lakh to ₹1 crore seeing maximum traction. The infusion of private equity into e-commerce led the boost of office space absorption to 3.5 million sq. ft, the second highest after 2011, with rise in rents across cities, especially in certain segments in Tier-I cities. This year was expected to see a continuation of the increase in demand driven by IT and ITES.

Around a third of over 25 lakh apartments launched between 2008 and 2014 were delayed by at least a year, according to property research firm Liases Foras. Of the total space of 3.2 billion sq. ft under construction across twenty-five cities, about 34% of the space valued at ₹165,064 crore (1.32% of GDP) was delayed by over a year. But consumers were being empowered. Their ire recently saw the courts order the promoters of the Unitech Group to be put behind bars. The Unitech directors—Chairman Ramesh Chandra, Managing Directors Sanjay Chandra and Ajay Chandra and Director Minoti Bahri—were hauled to court by two complainants on charges of cheating after they were allegedly not given timely possession of flats in Greater Noida. The directors also stood accused of flouting court orders directing them to refund the money taken from the complainants along with 11% interest, altogether over ₹1 crore. Home buyers complained to the National Consumer Disputes Redressal Commission of India (NCDRC), state-level consumer commissions, the Competition Commission of India (CCI) and even filed first information reports with the police where fraud was involved. Although the real estate sector was provided a foreign equity bonanza, waiver of entry and exit barriers, raising of approval limit for the Foreign Investment Promotion Board from ₹3,000 crore to ₹5,000 crore, doing away with area restrictions of 20,000 sq. m and capitalisation of $5 million, besides allowing investment repatriation before project completion with a three-year lock-in, the sector clearly lacked governance. The real estate bill was expected to provide some correction on this account.[27]

On the infrastructure front, Minister Nitin Gadkari announced that the pace of roadbuilding, which was at 18 km a day, would reach 30 km a day by March and projects worth ₹1.5 lakh crore would begin by March. He also set about finding solutions to nineteen stuck highway projects that had been grounded owing to various problems, including cost escalation, non-viability and rows between bankers and concessionaires. The cost of these stalled projects, which were threatening to increase bank NPAs, stood at least at ₹30,000 crore, with some having a cost escalation of up to 30%.

March

The 'leap' expected from the Union Budget turned out to be more of a 'hop, skip and jump'. The corporate sector was in severe pain. Profitability of business shrunk by ₹20,000 crore in the public sector and over ₹30,000 crore in the private sector (as per a survey of 3,000 companies that excluded banks, finance and broking houses). In fact, the year 2015–16 was the worst corporate India has seen in the post-liberalisation era in terms of growth in sales revenue. Sales during that year grew at a mere 1.6%, shows data from the Centre for Monitoring Indian Economy (CMIE), an independent agency that tracks economic and business data. The data, which collates information for over 21,000 companies, shows that other indicators like profitability and growth in employee compensation during 2015–16 were also among the worst in the last twenty-six years. In 2015–16, PAT for 21,588 companies for which CMIE compiled data fell by more than 19%, the third-largest year-on-year decline since 1990–91. The worst was in 2011–12 when profits had shrunk by over 20%.

Given a long period of stagnant sales and declining profits with policy paralysis caused by multiple scams and the fallout of these malfeasances, the results were now deep in red and not black and white anymore.

The proportion of corporate debt owed by stressed companies, defined as those whose earnings were insufficient to cover their interest obligations, increased to 41% in December 2015 compared to 35% in December 2014. Yet, the GDP was estimated to grow by 7–7.75% on the back of the three demand drivers: the infusion of the Seventh Pay Commission payout (estimated ₹1.02 lakh crore), the One Rank One Pension (OROP) payout (₹10,000 crore) and the public spending envisaged under the budget.

Indeed, public spending was clearly the engine of revival, with the private sector badly bruised. Finance Minister Arun Jaitley proposed an outlay of ₹221,728 crore for infrastructure. Of this, the Rail Budget proposed to spend ₹121,000 crore—the budget to electrify 2,000 km witnessed an increase by 50%, and it targeted commissioning 2,500 km of broad-gauge lines at 7 km/day, almost 30% higher than the previous year. Further, LIC agreed to invest ₹1.5 lakh crore to fund railway projects. In the roads sector, the budget accorded a higher allocation of ₹97,000 crore and included an accelerated PMGSY, with an outlay of ₹27,000 crore.

Coal production was the highest ever at 550 Mt, while imports were sliding. Last fiscal year, India had spent ₹1 lakh crore in importing coal; the country had already saved ₹22,000 crore this year. Coal India was directed to double production from the present level to 1,000 Mt by 2019–20. Most of this increase was expected to happen via the surface mining segment; to achieve this, the volume of overburden to be removed would shoot up from 1,000 million cubic metres to 2,500 million cubic metres. This would result in greater utilisation of existing deployed equipment while upping the need to invest in additional mining equipment.

That said, other than roads and highways, the budget disappointed other infrastructure segments, like ports, airports and urban infrastructure. For instance, a provision of only ₹3,200 crore was made for Smart Cities against a requirement of ₹10,000 crore. Only ₹4,000 crore were provided for AMRUT against an estimated requirement of ₹15,000 crore, and only ₹10,000 crore was allocated for metros all over the country against a demand of ₹33,000 crore.

All things considered, rural development was the true winner of the budget, as ₹87,765 crore was provided for irrigation, transport, electrification, sanitation and welfare. The proposals included money (and efforts) earmarked for the panchayats, MNREGA, interest subvention on agricultural loans, the Crop Insurance Scheme, rural LPG connections for poor women, direct benefit transfer for fertilisers, Provision of Urban Amenities to Rural Areas (PURA) and much more.

The change in the complexion of state budgets, like those of Bihar, Uttar Pradesh, Madhya Pradesh and Gujarat, were proof that federal empowerment would be the true opportunity in the years ahead. The Fourteenth Finance Commission's largesse to states would see an amount of ₹287,000 crore, which was expected to have a greater thrust on infrastructure and social welfare.

April

According to a World Bank report titled 'Dealing with Construction Permits', India was languishing at the 183rd position in this parameter, rubbing shoulders with the likes of Afghanistan (185th).[28] But the government appeared to be attacking this in earnest.

Indeed, the previous month was a watershed of sorts for construction. The budget announcement on allowing 100% deduction for profits to projects building homes up to 30 sq. m in the four metros and 60 sq. m in other cities was likely to spur the supply of affordable homes. This was followed by the passing of the Real Estate Regulatory Act (RERA), which created a robust structure for protecting homebuyers. Further, the Model Building Bye-Laws (MBBL) 2016 were recently proposed, providing a structural framework for a single-window, integrated building plan approval process and setting the maximum time limit for all kinds of building approvals at thirty days, after which the approval could be considered 'deemed'.

Our cities were in definite need for resuscitation. As per a twenty-one-city survey conducted by Janaagraha, our cities continued to score poorly in comparison with the likes of London and New York. The lowest-ranked city among all was surprisingly Chandigarh, having the dubious distinction of coming last among twenty-one for the second time in a row. Further, our cities were grossly underprepared to deliver a high quality of life that would be sustainable in the long term.[29]

This was particularly worrisome, given the rapid pace of urbanisation in India and the huge backlog in public service delivery. Cities faced governance challenges on multiple levels. Most failed to disclose audited accounts. They had no evaluation mechanism for the plans implemented by the municipal corporations. They had extremely weak finances and no city among the twenty-one reviewed had an effective system in place to monitor and prevent violations or mechanisms to undertake punitive or corrective action. City leaders didn't really have the power to formulate a long-term vision or the length of tenure to execute the same. For instance, how was it possible for Bengaluru and Jaipur to become smart cities unless they provided some stability to their commissioners? Both cities had six commissioners in the past five years while Raipur had eight!

Meanwhile, the Swachh Bharat mission ranked the 'cleanest cities' in India with Mysuru, Chandigarh and Tiruchirappalli securing the top three honours. The Smart Cities Challenge launched by the MoUD, too, saw a race among cities and their leaders, including chief ministers. This was being taken up on a war footing. Good news, indeed, for urban renewal.

May

The tide appeared to be turning with some good news on the economic front. Projects commissioned in the country reached a record high of ₹5.68 lakh crore in FY2016, according to CMIE.[30] This was the highest-ever commissioning of projects in a year and represented a 12% increase over ₹4.03 lakh crore in FY2015. The stock of projects on hand was also huge—total outstanding projects were worth ₹159 lakh crore. Of these, ₹92 lakh crore worth of projects were estimated to be under implementation.

FDI increased by 27.5% to $42 billion during April–February FY2016 as against $32.96 billion during the corresponding period of the previous year. Indirect tax collections moved up by 31.1% to ₹7.11 lakh crore in FY2016 over FY2015, indicating an improvement in demand. Transmission companies were recording a 20–25% surge in their order books. And initiatives like UDAY and DISCOM reforms were firing the power sector.

Other patches that started to see green shoots included the solar sector, railways and coal production. CV sales, which were languishing till a few quarters ago, veered into positive territory, especially in the medium and heavy segment. In FY2015–16, the overall CV industry posted 11.51% year-on-year growth, with sales of 685,704 units. Even the consumption of products used for construction or industrial purposes indicated an uptick: bitumen (up by 16.9%), petroleum coke (up by 42.9%) and furnace oil (up by 39.4%). Further indicators include sales of medium and heavy commercial vehicles (up 29.9% in 2015–16), cement production (13.5% increase year-on-year in February) and electricity generation (9.2% growth in February).

Government spending contributed to this spurt. In 2015–16, a total of 6,029 km of national highways were built—not just an all-time high but a substantial jump over the 4,340 km, 3,950 km and 5,732 km constructed in the preceding three fiscal years. In the past three to four months of 2016, construction equipment, too, was witnessing growth over the previous corresponding years.

A revival in PPP also indicated an improvement in the confidence of the business sector. A total of about 1,200 projects in different segments of the infrastructure sector, with investments worth about ₹7 lakh crore, were being carried out under the PPP mode throughout India, according to an ASSOCHAM study.[31] Of these, there were about 650 projects worth over ₹4.5 lakh crore, with about 67% share in roads and bridges; followed by over 100 projects in the ports sector (12%) with an investment worth over ₹80,700 crore; over 150 projects in energy (6%) with investments worth over ₹41,000 crore; investments worth over ₹30,000 crore in special economic zones (SEZ) (5%); as well as projects in water sanitation (2.6%) and others. Almost 73% of total investments worth over ₹3.3 lakh crore (the rest were either terminated or information was not available on them) attracted by the infrastructure sector in various segments under construction in the PPP mode were concentrated in roads and bridges. There were about 480 investment projects under construction in the PPP mode in various other segments: SEZ, ports, energy, water sanitation, airports, tourism, healthcare, cold chain and others.

June

Never before did the rains matter so much for the corporate sector as this year—despite all the efforts of a hardworking government that just completed two years. There was no doubt that in these two years, wastage had been targeted and reduced (₹36,000 crore saved in leakages). Natural resources like coal and gas had been protected and leveraged in a transparent and efficient manner (the reduction in imports in coal the previous year saved the country ₹24,000 crore in foreign exchange). The rightful recipients were provided the subsidies meant for them. Corruption was checked and faith in the administration began to be restored.

Considering that ₹205,000 crore was budgeted for food and fertiliser schemes for FY2017, plus pending bills of over ₹100,000 crore, the direct benefit transfer schemes would save crores of resources. While there were plenty of welfare schemes monitored both by the PM's PRAGATI mechanism (an ICT-based, multimodal platform for 'Pro-Active Governance and Timely Implementation') and the opposition, the infrastructure projects initiated by the Centre and states too were under observation.

Road projects took the lead, with 90% of 380 delayed projects worth ₹3.50 lakh crore taking off. Port projects worth ₹70,000 crore had been planned and inland water projects were likely to see some traction with the ₹4,000-crore Haldia waterway project getting the green signal. Railways stepped up the budget by 100% to ₹93,975 crore, and decision making was accelerated while political exploitation of this ministry ended. The Ministry of Power put the sale of LED on fire (LED sales increased from ₹6 lakh annually to ₹6 lakh per day). Several states joined the UDAY scheme, which aimed to restore financial viability to the DISCOM sector, which was sitting on a loss of ₹3.20 crore. Under 'Unnat Jyoti by Affordable LEDs for All' (UJALA) programme, as on July 2016, about 13.15 crore LED bulbs had been distributed to domestic consumers by Energy Efficiency Services Ltd. (EESL). Under 'Street Lighting National Programme' (SLNP), about 10.84 lakh LED streetlights had been installed.

The programme, voluntary in nature, without any budgetary support from Government of India was based on a sustainable business model where the cost was repaid by consumer/urban local body (ULB) from savings in energy and maintenance expenditure over a period of time through savings in electricity bill.

Then, there was RERA, the Smart Cities Mission and the AMRUT mission initiating urban renewal reform. The missions were on track and likely to see tenders being issued by the third quarter of the financial year. The Bankruptcy Code had been passed and ease of doing business had gained momentum, with states working on overdrive to reduce the number of formalities hindering quicker registration processes.

Further, the prime minister's overseas travel helped the renewed India brand get recognised at a time when we were the bright spot in economic growth among all countries and a record FDI of $55.4 billion was received during FY2015–16.

That said, the entire effort to reduce leakages and corruption and get the government administration to work efficiently to deliver results had yet to yield clearly visible results. The economy continued to be under strain, and the banking sector was heavily stressed despite the godsent savings in our oil import bill.

Meanwhile, according to a May 2016 World Bank report, 82% of the population in India did not have internet access as in 2014.[32] (The corresponding number for China was 51% and just 8% for the UK.) For quality of connectivity. Akamai's report on the state of the internet of 2015 compared the average speeds enjoyed by broadband users in various countries; India's average speed in 2015 stood at a paltry 2.5 Mbps, with only 7% of broadband users above the 4 Mbps threshold.[33] In contrast, take South Korea, which got average broadband speeds of 20.5 Mbps, with 96% of the citizens above the 4 Mbps level. A possible gamechanger was the BharatNet Project launched by the government on PPP basis, estimated (revised) at ₹74,000 crore, which was scheduled to be completed by 2020. BharatNet was not only expected to be India's new broadband backbone but had the potential to be a GDP multiplier. The acceleration of this project could be seen in the statistics released recently by the government: fibre-optic cables of 115,783 km were laid between July 2014 and May 2016, compared to only 358 km laid between 2011 and 2014. However, there remained some thorny issues to iron out, like right of way and a cost escalation of over three times.

July

Last month, exactly a year after the Smart Cities Mission was launched, PM Modi launched eighty-four projects from twenty selected cities that collectively aggregated to ₹2,000 crore. He lauded the efforts of the winning cities and thanked their citizens for their participation in the challenge that led to their selection. The PM had not just launched several schemes for the long-term development of the nation but ensured they were on track by periodically reviewing operations.

'Brexit' had heightened the volatility of global business even while PM Modi enhanced India's engagement with global leaders. Economic indicators, too, were turning positive. FDI in 2015–16 was a record $63 billion and nine more sectors were opened to additional liberalisation, with up to 100% under the automatic route, such as defence, pharma, cable networks, mobile phones, airport, air transport, broadcast carriage services and so on. Terms were eased for food processing and retail. This was the second major overhaul of FDI rules in seven months. In November, the government had eased norms in fifteen sectors. A ₹6,000-crore package was passed for the textile sector, aimed at generating 10 million jobs over the next three years and improving its global competitiveness.

To fill the huge infrastructure gap, India would require over $1.5 trillion in the next ten years. Acceleration in the construction of road projects had yielded twin benefits: injection of immediate liquidity into construction projects and the benefit of the multiplier effect caused by accelerating trade as a result of connectivity between cities, towns and villages. This was stepped up with a target of 10,000 km for 2016–17. Further, NHAI prepared a grid of twenty-seven horizontal and vertical national highway corridors at a distance of every 250 km crisscrossing the country. All these stretches would be of four lanes. The total length of these corridors, including ones such as Kanyakumari to Srinagar, Porbandar to Kolkata, Surat to Paradip Port, Rameswaram to Dehradun and Mangalore Port to Chennai Port, was about 36,600 km. Out of this, about 30,100 km were already national highways but only 18,800 km of them had four lanes. In addition to improved connectivity, the proposed National Highway Grid would provide a highway link to twelve major ports, forty-five out of fifty cities with a million-plus inhabitants and twenty-six state capitals.

The recently announced aviation policy also planned to increase the number of airports as part of the 'Regional Connectivity Scheme' servicing commercial flights from the current 77 to 127 by 2019.

August

Twenty-five years after Manmohan Singh's reform budget opened up the economy in 1991, India became the world's fastest-growing major economy. The time appeared nigh to leverage the demographic dividend and move into superpower status.

As mentioned earlier, projects commissioned reached a record high of ₹5.6 lakh crore in FY2016, according to CMIE.[34] The stock of projects on hand was also huge, with total outstanding projects worth ₹159 lakh crore. However, a low addition to the stock of investment projects contributed to a fall in the total outstanding projects from ₹171 trillion at the beginning of the quarter to ₹170 trillion at the end of the quarter of June 2016. This was the largest fall in outstanding investments during a quarter since June 2002 and the first since June 2014.

Meanwhile, Minister Nitin Gadkari was seeking FDI from the US and Asian countries to explore business opportunities in India, including Bharatmala projects, projects under the toll, operate, transfer (TOT) model, tunnel projects and intelligent transport systems (ITS). Further, the NIIF, with a mandate of ₹40,000 crore, identified the first eight projects it planned to invest in, including the Konkan Railways project, a power transmission project in the northern region and a few road projects.

Meanwhile, the spotlight turned again on quality (or lack thereof) in construction. Down came the rain and the roads in Mumbai caved—yet again. And six contractors—KR Construction, J Kumar, RPS Infraprojects, RK Madhani, Mahavir Infraprojects and Relcon Infraprojects—were named in an FIR filed by the state government as perpetrators of a scam.

Indeed, quality is an intrinsic part of building sustainable infrastructure, which in turn is essential to nation-building. According to an August 2016 study by S&P Global Ratings, the country's poor infrastructure was the biggest hurdle to the government's Make in India programme, with the infrastructure deficit costing the nation up to 5% of GDP.[35] (Apparently, every rupee invested in infrastructure has a ripple effect on the economy and generates value of ₹2 for the GDP.) According to Finance Minister Arun Jaitley, we need $1.5 trillion over the next decade to close this infra gap.[36] Alternatively, a study by CRISIL determined that we need ₹31 lakh crore to build up our infrastructure in the next five years.[37]

September

NITI Aayog, the body that replaced the Planning Commission in the new regime, was finally attempting to fix the loose ends with the construction matrix to allow the multiplier effect to breathe its magical effect across the economy. It put together a policy to remove hurdles for projects in which contractors were locked in arbitration with government agencies, so that 75% of the funds would be released to banks in cases where there was a unanimous award in favour of a contractor. This would help release funds and revive stalled projects. Close to ₹3.6 lakh crore were locked up in such cases and banks would see their performance improve even if a part of the funds were released.

According to a survey by research agency Daksh, if one had a case pending in any of the subordinate courts in the country, the average time for a decision to be made was nearly six years.[38] Even assuming a case did not go to the Supreme Court, an average litigant who appeals to at least one higher court was likely to spend more than ten years in court. Now, an underlying informal rule existed within government departments that was causing a huge bottleneck in judgments and awards. A large portion of the 'pending cases backlog' originated from the fact that all judgments issued against government departments were appealed against, as a standard practice. This was so much of a hard rule that if a government officer did not follow suit, he feared that the Vigilance Commission would come after him. This not only delayed justice, even in genuine cases, but unnecessarily clogged the judiciary system. Arbitration awards were also the victim of this informal 'standard rule'.

The new arbitration act came into effect on 23 October 2015, which allowed the awardee the fruits of the award after three months even though an application had been filed objecting to the award, unless the court issued a stay on the award. Considering the amount stuck in disputes and arbitration (as per ASSOCHAM), it was closer to ₹5 lakh crore; the amount stuck in arbitration and disputes with NHAI alone was ₹23,000 crore), the new act was expected to help resolve conflicts swiftly.[39]

Another factor strangulating growth was the escalating cost of land and delays caused in land acquisition. Data by MoRTH showed that in 2015–16, NHAI paid ₹19,020 crore to acquire 9,285 ha. This was the most it had paid out by way of compensation in one year compared to disbursements in the past five years. In the last fiscal year, it paid an average of ₹2 crore per hectare compared to ₹1.35 crore per hectare in 2014–15.

That said, the roads sector continued to bring cheer. The speed of construction of highways markedly went up from 11.6 km/day in 2013–14 to 22 km/day (extrapolated/projected) in the current year. Owing to the failure of the erstwhile PPP model, the government had inherited a very tough situation in the sector. Taking off with the help of plain vanilla EPC contracts to gain initial momentum, the ministry followed through with several well-meaning initiatives like the tweaked hybrid annuity model (HAM), relaxations for divestments of private players in completed projects and improvements in dispute resolution mechanisms. Other than improving the models and processes, it moved in parallel to conceptualise and announce newer road projects and hike investments in this sector.

Other than the impressive National Highway Grid, several projects were taken up under the Sagarmala Project for the improvement of ports and hinterland infrastructure for DPR preparation, which include fifty-eight road projects and twenty-three rail connectivity projects. And let us not forget PMGSY, running since 2000—since inception, it has provided connectivity of over 466,044 km (including upgradation of 167,977 km of existing roads), at an aggregate cost of ₹141,822 crore as in January 2016.

October

The NITI Aayog prepared a cabinet note which proposed that in case of a dispute and the order of the arbitration panel going in the company's favour, no appeals should be made against the order and the government should clear the payment due to the company. The note also suggested that infrastructure related ministries should ease arbitration norms and release stalled payments of infra companies.[40] Acting upon the note the government, in a swift move, reduced the misery of construction and infrastructure companies. Its ruling provided that the company in question was not squeezed to death of its finances and left to dry, though the core attitudinal problem causing the legal pileup was not addressed. Thanks to this much needed liquidity restored finances to the companies stuck in the legal quagmire.[41]

That said, the ruling led to the rerating of construction and infrastructure stocks at the bourses. Companies planning infrastructure investment trusts (InvITs) would see better valuations and huge funds were likely to come back into the system to infrastructure companies like HCC, Patel Engineering, Sadbhav, IRB, etc. While this augured well for equipment companies, there was also likely to be a shift in the list of bidders for EPC and HAM contracts issued by MoRTH and NHAI.

Meanwhile, real estate companies were experiencing rough weather as the consumer protection movement gained momentum. Several companies like Unitech, Supertech and Parsvanath were instructed by courts to return the money invested by those who booked flats where either the companies had not presented a 'true and fair' picture of the offering or violated deadlines for delivery. RERA sent a shiver down the spines of developers, as rulings began to send developer after developer behind bars for violations and misrepresentations, non-delivery and unfair practices. Consolidation was already in progress as several stressed developers made alliances with financially stronger partners to bail them out. Ajay Piramal's real estate fund initiatives rescued many. New money started coming in under changed conditions seeking fresh rules for play.

Meanwhile, the Smart Cities Mission released the names of twenty-seven additional cities, taking the total number to sixty. The new cities were from twelve states and proposed to invest a total of ₹66,883 crore under their respective city development plans. The amount included ₹42,524 crore in area-based development (79% of the total) and ₹11,379 crore (21%) in technology-based, pan-city solutions. With this, the total investment proposed for the sixty cities selected went up to ₹144,742 crore. Several of these cities were readying DPRs; requests for proposal (RFPs) for some projects had already been readied and launched (such as Pune, Jaipur, Ahmedabad, etc). Another ₹45,935 crore were approved under AMRUT. In addition to sixty-eight projects launched in fourteen smart cities in June, another 134 projects were identified, of which 114 were under bidding.

The pace of urban renewal was stepped up and growth initiated by eliminating bottlenecks and making structural changes. Liquidity released through the Pay Commission, OROP and government spending was expected to add to the buoyancy of the above-normal monsoon.

Meanwhile, the country got closer to the implementation of GST with the unified tax regime being passed by both houses of Parliament and a strong likelihood of it being introduced by early to mid-2017. Experts and industry bodies estimated that its implementation would incrementally bump up GDP growth by 1–3%. Further spinoffs expected from GST include improvements in turnaround times, cycle times, transparency, paperwork, ease of compliances, cash flows, inventories and service levels.

In other (good) news, India climbed from an ignoble 71st to a respectable 16th position in the World Economic Forum's Global Competitiveness Index, all in the space of the past two years.

November

The balance between social good and infrastructural development is a delicate one. A citizen has a constitutional right to basic amenities but the nation has limited resources, further constrained by a poor administrative system of collection of revenues, making it necessary to depend upon private investment. Private investment must serve the profit motive, which in turn conflicts with the citizen's 'right to be served'.

In October 2016, a judgment by the Allahabad High Court split this wound wide open. It denied Noida Toll Bridge

Company, which had been awarded the contract of collecting toll from passengers for thirty years, the right to continue collecting toll as it claimed that the concessionaire had earned reasonable profits. Even the Supreme Court did not entertain the plea of the defendant.

This threw up many questions. Were contracts that provide a service to citizens but allow the company providing the service to make profits, void? If power companies, airport operators and port operators could make 16% return or more, why not toll concessionaires? Would this not have a retrograde effect, as was the case with retrospective tax, which drove foreign investors away? How would the government, then, fund such projects?

Only funds with a long payout date that are ultra conservative would invest in these projects, provided the government offered sovereign guarantees. Noida Toll Bridge Company was a public-listed entity, and its business plan comprised the returns from this project alone. By withdrawing its right to earn tolls, the courts made the government renege on its commitment and kill shareholder value, apart from scaring away potential investors in such projects. The fear was that this would set a trend as local leaders with political ambitions would join protests to derail user charges and win the favour of voters.

The bigger issue was one of investor sentiment. Private money was not exactly gushing into our infrastructure sector. In fact, the decline of private investment in infrastructure projects had been dramatic over the previous few years. According to a World Bank report, India recorded a ten-year low point in public private investments in 2015. Judgments like these, clearly, were not likely to help matters.[42]

Meanwhile, GMR won an arbitration order of $270 million against the Maldives government, which had arbitrarily cancelled its contract to run its airport. The compensation covered the debt and equity invested in the project along with a return of 17%, as well as termination payments and legal costs.

December

There are very few events etched in the memories of an entire generation. For the Americans, it was the 9/11 attack and the collapse of Lehman Brothers. For Indians, it was the Kargil skirmish, the 26/11 terror attack and, now, demonetisation. While some called it a 'surgical strike' against black and counterfeit money, the Supreme Court labelled it 'carpet bombing'.

This bold move by PM Modi came with its share of execution challenges and extensive collateral damage. Just about the time that the green shoots were appearing, the land beneath them was scorched. Real estate, consumer goods, jewellery and the informal business segment of the country were victims of a frontal attack. Businesses reported a loss of 30-40% in revenues. The momentum of money ground to a halt. Banks ran out of money to dispense.

The government began to course-correct rapidly. It geared up to launch an extension of the 'Voluntary Disclosure Income Scheme', where a tax of 50% would give unaccounted money a holy dip, with another 25% of the money being subject to a zero-interest bearing bond for four years, thus allowing the offender to circulate 25% of his declaration in an official form. This would effectively cost the declarer 57%. The challenge was that several 'start-up gangs' reinvented the art of conversion at a lower cost of 25%. So, although the money remained tainted, legal tender was received in place of obsolete notes, which dampened the response to such conversion.

As for counterfeit currency which was another reason given for demonetisation, it was estimated that ₹400 crore of counterfeit currency was in circulation, according to government-commissioned studies carried out by the Indian Statistical Institute.[43]

Demonetisation hit the infrastructure sector, like all others, hard. Moving on from transient and immediate issues like temporary stoppage of toll collections on roadways and parking fees in airports, there were major implications. Overall, GDP growth in the last two quarters of the fiscal year was sure to be adversely impacted. Also, as the construction industry traditionally transacted a lot in cash for payments of building materials, labour wages, service fees, etc., construction was bound to slow down. Further, according to a report by PropEquity, housing prices in forty-two major cities across India were expected to drop by up to 30% over six to twelve months, wiping out over ₹8 lakh crore worth of market value of residential properties sold and unsold by developers since 2008.[44]

On the brighter side, interest rates were set to come down and income tax rates to ease up. The cycle of low rents and high interest was likely to turn with interest rates softening up and rents hardening. It was also possible that the government would inject a lot of money from the expected 'extinguished liability' of the RBI into infrastructure projects, which would turn out to be a stimulus. Public spending was expected to continue to drive economic sentiment. Though the private sector would defer all spending plans, overseas investments with a stronger dollar could rise if the federal rates remained easy. But there was a fear that the Federal Reserve System could increase rates and just as $3.18 billion fled the country in November alone (the steepest selling in equity and bonds by foreign institutions in the past three years); such a trigger could depress our outlook.

All this apart, the country undoubtedly improved its image by portraying a robust financial system that was able to withstand such staggering logistics.

2017

January

The year began with demonetisation having dealt a body blow to the economy—it delayed an uptick by a minimum of several quarters. The informal economy was in tatters and the business outlook was glum. The formal economy, too, was low down in the global rankings and had barely moved up a notch despite fervent campaigns trying to create a favourable pitch for it. This was because the constituents—the legal system for enforcing contracts, resolving insolvency, obtaining construction permits—needed overhauling. The Insolvency and Bankruptcy Code 2016 just got notified and activated in the last quarter and would serve to make progress in this direction.

Roads needed to step up the acceleration. Until November 2016, the total length of road contracts awarded was 5,688 km and the length of roads constructed 4,021 km, which was 12 km/day. A huge development in the Northeast under the National Highways & Infrastructure Development Corporation Limited (NHIDCL) was underway, covering a length of 8,007 km to be executed at about ₹100,000 crore. And, in urban infrastructure, from January to December 2016, a total investment of ₹272,380 crore was approved for the smart city plans of sixty cities, AMRUT, Pradhan Mantri Awas Yojana (PMAY) (Urban), new metro projects, Swachh Bharat Mission (Urban) and redevelopment of seven central government residential colonies in New Delhi.

Refreshingly, non-traditional areas of infrastructure—one could call it 'soft' infrastructure—were begging for attention and investment. These included rooftop solar power plants, internet network, telecom network, banking services backbone, weather forecasting systems, digital payment gateways, biometric identity database, various e-governance facilities and other such new-age, technology-driven infrastructure key to doing business in the modern age.

February

The Union Budget set the tone for 2017 by accelerating the growth agenda. The allocation for infrastructure at ₹3.96 lakh crore, ₹47,000 crore more than the previous year, was expected to fuel the sector. Of the increase of ₹47,000 crore, transport itself would consume ₹24,000 crore. A separate amount was provided for metro projects to the tune of ₹18,000 crore and, similarly, among other schemes like Swachh Bharat, Bharatnet, Deen Dayal Jyoti Yojana, etc.

The railway budget was the largest-ever at ₹1.31 lakh crore—an 8.26% increase over the ₹1.21 lakh crore allocated in 2016–17. Railway lines of 3,500 km were to be commissioned in 2017–18 while at least twenty-five stations were expected to be awarded in 2017–18 for station redevelopment. Allocation for highways was increased from ₹57,976 crore in 2016–17 to ₹64,900 crore in 2017–18. Around 2,000 km of coastal connectivity roads were identified for construction and development. The dark horse in the transport sector, the PMGSY, gathered pace. The pace of construction of PMGSY roads accelerated to reach 133 km/day in 2016–17, as against an average of 73 km during 2011–14. And the budget provided ₹19,000 crore in 2017–18 for the scheme. Together with the contribution of states, an amount of ₹27,000 crore was expected to be spent on PMGSY in 2017–18.

March

It was increasingly evident that India was on a path of deep-rooted reform. Many initiatives were expected to see fruition this year: Implementation of RERA (with a deadline of 17 May), appointment of a real estate regulator, credit ratings of municipal corporations, issuance of municipal bonds by cities, introduction of GST, and much more. While these shifts would cause disruption in the regular flow of commerce and required systemic adjustment, India could afford this exercise as the growth numbers were robust enough to absorb the shocks of change.

The government's record during the previous year gave reason to believe that spending had gathered momentum as the chains of bureaucracy were being delinked through transparency and accountability. However, it was important that the urgency shown in preponing the dates for the budget crystallised into an early disbursal of funds for projects.

Renewable power prices, including solar and wind, seemed to have ushered in hope for improvement in production costs for India's manufacturing sector. Labour costs had risen geometrically for all industries. Also, with rural electrification being implemented on a war footing and BharatNet expected to make high-speed broadband on a fibreoptic network available by 2017–18 in more than 1.5 lakh gram panchayats, the aspirations of the population were expected to explode countrywide. Lag in power availability had stunted progress but states were resurrecting their power finances with UDAY.

Further, housing was likely to gallop as it was given infrastructure status and the central government was providing interest subvention for affordable housing. An additional interest subvention of about 3% offered by states could really skyrocket housing demand, stated the Union Minister of Urban Development and Housing. What's more, the Smart Cities Mission was quietly making progress with thirty of the sixty identified cities having organised SPVs and appointed CEOs. Tenders were being issued and over ninety projects were underway.

April

The construction sector had taken a hit in the December quarter. The average net revenue of 156 firms in the mid and large-sized category, excluding L&T, fell by 9% year on year. Road developers took a hit on account of toll collections, which were suspended for three weeks. Orders across the infrastructure sector slid several notches. The road sector itself had not been able to achieve its targets.

NHAI and MoRTH had awarded projects of about 3,200 km and 3,100 km, respectively, till mid-February. NHAI had watered down its forecast for FY2017 from 10,000 km to 6,700 km. In nine months of FY2017, NHAI awards dwindled by 8% year on year. While the new HAM had many takers owing to PPP, lenders were reluctant given the overhang of past record liabilities. As per reports, only fifteen of the thirty-five projects awarded under HAM achieved financial closure and some were even cancelled.

Meanwhile, according to Minister of MoRTH & Shipping Nitin Gadkari, a national perspective plan under the Sagarmala project had been prepared and projects worth ₹8 lakh crore identified. This could accelerate momentum in trade—with a 7,500-km coastline, India transported only 6% of its cargo through waterways compared to around 55% on roadways and 35% by the railways. As a result, logistic costs as a percentage of GDP were as high as 19% compared to 12.5% in China.

On the brighter side, the process to expedite government spending was in the works. With four more states—Uttar Pradesh, Uttarakhand, Manipur and Goa—falling with the ruling party, the agenda of development was expected to step up activity locally. State budgets and their policies reflected the urgency to transform. This was evident from efforts to create a better business environment in Gujarat, Haryana, Maharashtra, Andhra Pradesh and Telangana. The most notable among the reforms were related to land and its use. Unlocking land for commercial and industrial use would lead to increase in economic activity. Now, if bad bank loans could find a solution, return on capital would accelerate and private investors return.

May

NITI Aayog put forth a plan to turn India's economy to reach a size of $7.5 trillion (though targeting $10 trillion), or more than three times of what it was, at $2 trillion. Implementation of GST, tax reform and ease of doing business were all building blocks of this plan. And they all seemed to be moving on course. The change was not only limited to the economy and industry but was also being instituted in social behaviour and changing mindsets. The 'Three Year Action Agenda' plan for a better India included plans for creating an innovation ecosystem, education and skill development, health, on building a more inclusive society, environment and forests, sustainable management of water resources among others.[45]

As for housing, the recently announced affordable housing scheme and PMAY saw the launch of over 350 projects to build about 200,000 houses with a private-sector commitment of ₹38,000 crore. The cost of constructing these units was in the range of ₹15–30 lakh, with an average construction cost of ₹18 lakh per house. Under PMAY-U, central assistance was provided to each beneficiary in the range of ₹1–2.35 lakh. Of the 200,000 houses, over 100,000 were to be constructed in Maharashtra, followed by 41,921 houses in NCR; 28,465 in Gujarat; 7,037 in Karnataka; and 6,055 in Uttar Pradesh. Cement prices had already reached pre-demonetisation levels on the back of demand from infrastructure and were expected to firm further owing to these housing projects. GST was on track and was likely to cause another disruption for a quarter, but eventually bring great prosperity for the economy as a whole.

Distressed assets of around $6.8 trillion sitting on the books of banks were also likely to heave a sigh of relief as firms and funds like KKR, Lone Star, Kotak and Edelweiss were planning to mobilise their resurrection. It was estimated by experts that the capital required for the next four to five years to resolve distressed situations was about ₹30,000–40,000 crore, and it was already being provided for by non-banking financial companies (NBFCs), private equity and international funds.

Historically, infrastructure projects in India have been funded on a mix of debt and equity. In 2017, as many as three initial public offerings—IRB, HUDCO and PSP Projects—hit Dalal Street, raising over ₹6,000 crore, testament to the fact that the bond market was gaining pace after the 2008 turmoil. That said, with InvITs coming into existence, Indian infrastructure developers now had a third dimension to infrastructure funding.

In a major boost to increase production capacity by 2030, the Union Cabinet approved the much-awaited new National Steel Policy (NSP), which planned an investment of up to ₹10 lakh crore in the steel sector. The target for 2030–31 was crude steel capacity of 300 Mt and per-capita consumption of 158 kg of finished steel. For the struggling sector, the announcement brought fresh hope to keep pace with the growing steel demands of India, curbing imports from countries like China and Japan. According to the mandate of NSP 2017, all government tenders would give preference to domestically manufactured iron and steel products, which augured well for local steel manufacturers, steel users and the steel trade in general. The policy encouraged capacity additions, cost-efficient production and assured acquisition of raw materials, facilitating foreign investments and increasing domestic steel demand.

June

The inauguration of the 9.15-km Dhola–Sadiya Bridge, India's longest bridge above water, by PM Modi coincided with his completion of three years in office. Apart from underscoring the government's emphasis on infrastructure, the event also reaffirmed its resolve in improving connectivity to the Northeast. Built at ₹1,000 crore under PPP with Navayuga Engineering over the Brahmaputra and Lohit, the bridge cut down travel time to the Northeast by four hours.

In fact, the Nitin Gadkari ministry had awarded 16,800 km of highway contracts and constructed around 8,500 km for the year ending in March, taking the count up to 23 km/day. The 135-km Eastern Peripheral Expressway, being constructed to decongest Delhi, was scheduled for completion in the next few months. Similarly, other expressways to take off included Delhi–Meerut, Mumbai–Vadodara, Dwarka Expressway, Bengaluru–Chennai and Delhi–Jaipur. With the Hybrid Annuity Model (HAM) not yet too popular, the EPC model appeared the easier way to accelerate road development. The 43-km, twelve-lane Dedicated Freight Corridor costing ₹3,000 crore from JNPT (Navi Mumbai) to Panvel, being built to ease container traffic, was also under construction.

Further, the UDAN schemed envisaged forty-five new airports and seventy regional routes, and capped ticket fares at ₹2,500 for one-hour flights. Six new ports were being developed, with automobile and leather clusters planned alongside.

July

Nagpur had been in the news ever since the political capital shifted under the current regime. All roads now led to this 'orange' city that has always been a 'capital in waiting'. The 710-km road that recently invited controversy was the ₹46,000-crore

Mumbai–Nagpur Expressway, which revised its invitation for bids with a supplementary advertisement and caused much heartburn, as the riders imposed were allegedly introduced to outfox fair competition. The project, which was expected to be completed in two years, envisaged sixteen packages of construction ranging from contracts for 13 km stretches to up to 73 km stretches. High-speed corridors had proven to bring prosperity within the corridor zone, and this could pave the way for some political capital, as twenty-four new nodes would be developed in phases and were projected to generate employment for 25,000 people each across logistics, industry, IT, agro-industry, tourism, education, healthcare, auto, warehousing and food processing. Jobs would also be generated from social infrastructure development, including hotels, malls, petrol pumps, offices, hospitals and educational institutes.

Thirty more smart cities were added to the existing sixty, taking the tally to ninety cities selected under the Smart Cities Mission, upping the total budgeted spend over $31 billion. Of the ones selected, twenty-six had proposed affordable housing projects, twenty-six would be taking up school and hospital projects and twenty-nine would undertake to redesign and redevelop roads to enable walking and cycling.

The recently launched Energy Conservation Building Code 2017 (ECBC 2017) developed by the Ministry of Power and Bureau of Energy Efficiency (BEE) mandated a 25% saving in energy for compliance.

Meanwhile, the Pune Municipal Corporation (PMC) created history by raising ₹200 crore for its ₹2,800 crore water supply project via bonds. The bonds were listed on the stock exchanges. The PMC planned to raise ₹2,264 crore over the next five years and repay the debt by enhancing its revenues through water charges. The remarkable aspect of this issue was the appetite, as the issue elicited oversubscription to the extent of ₹1,200 crore. This set the stage for a new stream of funds for municipalities while ushering in an era of transparency.

The worst news for India's economy was the loan waivers the state governments conceded to at the altar of political capital. On the other hand, the GST juggernaut was ready to roll—it was time to brace for impact.

August

The previous month, a new tax regime, in the works for over fifteen years, designed as 'One Nation, One Tax', went live! The impact of GST on infrastructure was expected to resolve future litigation in this area. And although it would mean higher tax, it would also allow input tax credit in many categories. Contracts with no room for renegotiation or those that do not account for contingency factors would feel the pinch. Credit restrictions were causing worry and needed clarifications. Clearly, the quarter was likely to be affected as the country adjusted to the new regime.

The NPA disease, with over ₹8 lakh crore of public money stuck in debt defaults, also received much attention because of the implementation of the Insolvency and Bankruptcy Code, 2016 (IBC) and the National Company Law Tribunal (NCLT). The RBI stepped up the pressure on companies to pay up or face liquidation. Insolvency professionals were given time of 180 days to draw up a rescue plan. Several companies slipped into the hands of lenders as they wrested control and sought new buyers. Several companies sold unprofitable or non-core divisions, subsidiaries and assets to save their financial burden. Jaypee Group, DLF, Essar Steel, Bhushan Steel, Jyoti Structures and many more were on the verge of bankruptcy.

As for roads, to date, around forty-three projects worth ₹42,000 crore had been awarded under HAM by NHAI. With just 9% equity commitment from developers, the model appeared to be a great bet for contractors with reputation and experience. With several experienced ones under a debt trap, the order book was overflowing for more recent entrants like Dilip Buildcon, J

Kumar, Gayatri and Ashok Buildcon, and twenty-two HAM projects reached financial closure. As for smart cities, the mission had mandated credit rating of cities and nearly ninety-four of them had got rated. All considered, the underlying theme was clearly Swachh Bharat, in economic terms too, as GST and IBC were expected to drive more transparency and fair practices. There were benefits for those who managed to clean up their act. Stock market valuations and order books were surging, while money-raising exercises were easier for clean and ethical organisations.

Meanwhile, the World Bank projected that gross fixed capital formation (GFCF), which indicates investment demand in the economy, would grow by 6.8% in FY2018 and 8.8% in FY2019. However, the situation currently appeared suboptimal. According to CMIE, announcements of new industrial and infrastructural projects remained muted in the first quarter of 2017–18. Only 448 projects were announced during the quarter. This was the lowest quarterly project announcement since June 2014, the time when the last capex cycle bottomed out. Further, the completion of projects dipped over previous consecutive quarters.

Public spending was a saving grace that kept our engines sputtering, if not humming. Government spending grew by 13%, year on year, in April–May 2017 to touch ₹4.6 lakh crore against ₹2.9 lakh crore in April–May 2016. Capital expenditure for infrastructure creation and other assets rose 63% in April–May to ₹54,000 crore from ₹33,000 crore in the same two months a year earlier.

September

The Nikkei India Manufacturing Purchasing Managers' Index for July was at its lowest in the past eight years, and demand took a deep dive owing to GST adjustments. By the deadline of 25 August, over 36 lakh businesses had filed their GST returns. The overall impact was indicated to be an upswing of 16.6% on a comprehensive level, though some states needed compensation and others may have had a beneficial gain. The disruption of demand hurt the industry and was not likely to be compensated by the same quantum of the drop in rates. Demand needs momentum.

The 2017 Mumbai flood which occurred on 29 August 2017, following heavy rain reminded of a similar disaster that Mumbai city had faced in 2005. Mumbai recorded 468 mm of rainfall in twelve hours, the highest in a day in August since 1997. Transport systems were unavailable through parts of the city as trains and roadways were shut. Power was shut off from various parts of the city to prevent electrocution. The International Federation of Red Cross and Red Crescent Societies (IFRC) called the South Asian floods one of the worst regional humanitarian crises in years. This event can be compared with the 2005 floods in Mumbai, which recorded 944 mm (37.17 inches) of rainfall within 24 hours on 26 July. Although social media had updated everyone on the weather and office-goers left offices early, as the tracks were flooded, trains stopped, electricity got cut off and the Bandra–Worli Sea Link closed, leaving traffic in a complete jam. The usual areas prone to waterlogging caused several people to abandon their vehicles and walk home in the filth. Notably, the High Court had banned new construction in Mumbai and an appeal to reverse this in May 2017 had been thrown out by the courts.

October

The economy was huffing and puffing, its health report indicating a serious infection after two rounds of serious disruption: demonetisation and GST. Before the GDP numbers were recalibrated, they had turned in figures below even 6%. After adjustment, they looked rosier and then they came back even worse than before adjustment. Whether demonetisation broke the economy's back or whether GST would give it a fillip, all the problems looming—bank NPAs, high unemployment, low capital investment—were the same afflictions hurting the economy when the current regime came into power. Despite the new government improving national pride and our international image, laying down long-term vision statements and schemes, eliminating middlemen in the distribution of subsidies, disrupting corruption and strengthening accountability in the bureaucracy in the past forty months, it had not made the environment friendly enough for business. No private capital had broken ground, credit disbursals were at an all-time low, employment opportunities were dismal and retrenchment was the order of the day.

While GST was a significant reform, its timing, right after hitting the economy in the gut with demonetisation, caused it to convulse. The SME industry was hit badly and was still grappling with the increase in the cost of labour and regulation with a decline in business. The informal economy was in shambles. Organised players clearly had the advantage as the unorganised sector lost its key differentiator, the cost advantage. The increase in momentum owing to a seamless tax regime across states was expected to create the case for an improvement in the economy. However, that would take time.

November

As the GDP figures of 5.7% appeared in the press, the murmurs began. GST was already making lives difficult for traders and businesspersons and the ghosts of demonetisation had not completely vanished. The evidence of the economy sputtering emboldened the critics and turned loyalists into sceptics. The government responded quickly with the announcement of the establishment of the PM Economic Council and a massive infusion of reforms soon after.

The ₹6.92 trillion road network of 83,677 km, on the back of the GST reform, was expected to be a potent economic multiplier in times to come. The road construction push included the Bharatmala Pariyojana with an investment of ₹5.35 trillion to construct 34,800 km. In addition, ₹1.57 trillion was slated for the construction of 48,877 km by NHAI and MoRTH. NHAI was made the nodal body to ensure timely execution. Financing was innovatively being raised by monetising road assets worth ₹34,000 crore from eighty-two operating highways under the TOT model. Further, the bank recapitalisation plan of ₹2.11 trillion over the next two years, in a bid to clean banks' books and revive investment, was a timely move. With this, the projects that would be put to bid could be funded by banks giving a boost to credit disbursal, which had fallen abysmally low.

Besides roads, the next biggest business opportunity had become the metro rail. Over ₹2 trillion of business was up for grabs over the next few years, with the Mumbai Metropolitan Region (MMR) itself contributing ₹1.5 trillion. Metro projects with a total length of 370 km were operational in eight cities. Further, metro projects with a total length of 537 km were in progress in thirteen cities. New cities acquiring metro services included Hyderabad (71 km), Nagpur (38 km), Ahmedabad (36 km), Pune (31.25 km) and Lucknow (23 km). The previous month, the government introduced a New Metro Policy that focused on giving clarity on the development of projects, collaborations, participation, standardising norms, financing and creating a procurement mechanism to implement projects effectively.

December

The GST rate reduction from 28% to 18% provided a breather to the construction equipment industry. Although 15% of items would still be at 28%, the major grouse was addressed. As many as 42,710 units of construction equipment were sold between January and September 2017, against 37,346 units in the same period in the last financial year. This year, the number of units sold equalled the prior record of 70,000 units sold during 2011. The industry grew by 19% in Q1 and 22% in Q2, except for the 35% dip in July owing to GST implementation, according to Indian Construction Equipment Manufacturers' Association (ICEMA) reports.

Although real estate was tottering, initiatives like Bharatmala and metro-rail projects were fuelling the revival along with irrigation and urban rejuvenation projects. There was a move to bring real estate under the GST ambit. However, the present constitutional amendment did not cover real estate and stamp duty continued to be within the domain of state tax. Several states may not have been ready to part with stamp duty, and legalities were therefore being explored. Even currently, as land was an immovable asset, the industry was given 33% abatement on the 18% GST amount. Therefore, the effective charge on the sector, for property under construction, was now 12% as against the listed 18%. There was no GST on completed projects as they were considered immovable assets.

As another year ended, roads remained the beacon of hope as the government approved a plan to build thousands of kilometres of roads and highways over the next five years at a cost of about ₹7 lakh crore, a spending push that could help generate jobs and lift the economy. The plan involved constructing 83,677 km of roads, highways, greenfield expressways and bridges in phases. In a quest to boost demand, the government announced an investment-cum-finance stimulus where, under the first phase to be completed by 2022, around 34,800 km of highways would be built. This was to include 24,800 km of Bharatmala at a cost of ₹5.35 trillion. That apart, around 1,837 km of greenfield expressways would also be developed under the programme. Interestingly, half the money would be raised from the market and private investments while the rest would come from the Central Road Fund, highway toll and monetising completed highway stretches.

One largely unsung success was PMGSY, under which the highest-ever construction of 130 km rural roads per day was achieved, leading to an addition of 47,400 km of PMGSY roads in 2016–17. PM Modi planned to spend an additional $14 billion under this scheme by March 2020; about ₹1.4 lakh crore had already been spent under the programme. The cost was to be shared in a 60–40 ratio by the Centre and state governments.

Logistics had been provided infrastructure status, allowing the sector's growth and expansion at easier financial cost, which could help in distribution and access of goods across the country, complementing the GST rollout. Even though the second quarter of 2017–18 had insipid financial results, with the net profit of 1,300 BSE companies declining by 3.54% from the same quarter the previous year and net sales rising 7.39% during the same period, the periods ahead were likely to improve as the base effects of demonetisation and relaxation of the GST effect trickled in.

Meanwhile, the *Economic Intelligence Unit*, based on a report on the 'Safe Cities Index 2017', said the global economy was projected to grow at about 2.9% in 2017 as against 2.3% in 2016. The report also estimated that India would grow at over 7% over the next decade.[46]

There was more good news. India was the only country among South Asian and BRICS economies to feature as one of the most improved economies of the World Bank's 'Doing Business Report', which surveyed 190 countries.[47] It acknowledged India as a top improver with the highest jump in rank. The ten indicators for the ranking were: starting a business, dealing with construction permits, getting electricity, registering property, getting credit, protecting minority investors, paying taxes, trading across borders, enforcing contracts and resolving insolvency. India improved its standing in six of these ten indicators.

Hearteningly, the country improved its standing to 103 in terms of resolving insolvency; it was previously ranked 136th. Indeed, the ₹8 lakh crore of despondency owing to stressed loans could get a breather with the new act. Further, a state to be completed over the next two years was announced in a bid to clean the books.[48]

2018

January

'Disruption' was an oft-used word in 2017. Sometimes it was used when describing a phenomenon that turned an existing business model on its head, as Uber and Airbnb did. But more often than not, it was used when wishful thinking was allowed over logic, or when no clear solution was visible.

In essence, disruption represents a desire to change the status quo. Jio challenged the status quo, but it has deep pockets. Meanwhile, HAM tried to be a gamechanger but did not get the desired results. The Smart Cities Mission took on urban rejuvenation through inspiration, but it had achieved limited success thus far.

That said, land pooling by Andhra Pradesh where farmers pooled land to contribute to the building of Amaravati as a new capital of Andhra Pradesh in return for a mix of alternate land and compensation, proved to be an intelligent solution. And the IBC was a gamechanger by addressing the need to revive assets that had potential for productivity but needed some respite. Assets changing hands would ensure they did not lie idle and rot. Putting them to use would increase the GDP.

In the construction sector, too, consolidation was the name of the game. Stressed owners were selling prime assets and seeking a new lease of life. New buyers were seeking revenue earning assets at good value. This allowed a more liquid market in trading revenue-yielding assets such that the investor had an exit route and could free up capital in engaging with new opportunities.

The year ahead was expected to be a watershed one for the construction industry, for the following reasons:

- The GST effect had stabilised and demand was limping back.
- The wounds from demonetisation had healed.
- Ease of doing business had helped ease regulatory hurdles.
- The IBC had helped revive several projects.
- Credit disbursement had picked up and private-sector investment was likely to revive.
- Uttar Pradesh, Haryana and Gujarat were likely to expedite their projects.
- Maximum contracts were expected to be awarded in FY2018–19 so that they could be secured before the election code kicked in by the time of the next budget.

February

Aggregating infrastructure under a single umbrella, Finance Minister Arun Jaitley announced during his budget address that India needed massive investments in excess of ₹50 lakh crore in infrastructure to increase GDP growth, connect and integrate the nation with a network of roads, airports, railways, ports and inland waterways, and provide good quality services to the people. The budgetary expenditure on infrastructure for 2018–19 was increased by ₹1 lakh crore to ₹5.97 lakh crore against an estimated expenditure of ₹4.94 lakh crore in 2017–18.

The PM's PRAGATI initiative was established to fast-track projects worth ₹9.46 lakh crore. The budget provided for plans to complete over 9,000 km of national highways in 2017–18, which means 25 km/day of construction. The railways' capex was pegged at ₹148,528 crore; 4,000 km of the rail network was targeted for electrification, 600 stations were being developed, and elevators were being provided to all stations with a footfall of over 25,000.

As for smart cities, ninety-nine cities were selected with an outlay of ₹2.04 lakh crore, of which projects worth ₹2,350 crore had been completed and projects worth ₹20,852 crore were under progress. State-level plans of ₹77,640 crore for 500 cities were approved. Water supply contracts for 494 projects worth ₹19,428 crore and sewerage work contracts for 272 projects costing ₹12,429 crore were awarded.

Expectedly, rural India, too, drew funds in gigantic proportions with a collective amount of ₹14.34 lakh crore. The Namami Gange programme was on track, with 187 projects sanctioned for river surface cleaning, rural sanitation and other interventions at ₹16,713 crore; of this, forty-seven projects had been completed and the rest were at various stages of execution. Significantly, all 4,465 villages on the banks of the river were declared open defecation-free.

The seriousness of envisioning an inclusive society seemed apparent in the budget. The government identified 115 aspirational districts for improvement in social services like health, education, nutrition, skill upgrade, financial inclusion and infrastructure, like irrigation, rural electrification, potable drinking water and access to toilets, at an accelerated pace and in a time-bound manner.

Meanwhile, the prime minister made his second trip to the UAE in less than three years to accelerate the infrastructure thrust. The previous year, UAE investors announced nearly $2.5 billion worth of investments in India, including a $1 billion investment by ADIA, a $1 billion investment by NRI-Emirati Investor's Group, and a further $460 million investment by Lulu Group in Andhra Pradesh. The two countries set up a multi-billion-dollar fund under the NIIF to tap into investment opportunities in India's infrastructure sector. The fund planned to raise up to $75 billion to support investment in railways, ports, roads, airports, industrial corridors and parks. ADIA deployed its funds in real estate and private equity, and backed two of the largest renewable energy companies in India, investing over $400 million in ReNew Power and Greenko. DP World, the Dubai-based port operator, and NIIF planned to jointly invest up to $3 billion in ports, terminals, transportation and logistics businesses in India.

South Korea, too, pledged around $10 billion to extend $9 billion in credit and $1 billion for three mega projects: the Nagpur–Mumbai Supercommunication Expressway (NMSE), Kalyan–Dombivili Smart City and Bandra Government Colony Redevelopment. Further, the Japan International Cooperation Agency (JICA) had extended a total soft loan support amount of about ₹1.50 trillion over the past ten years.

March

A report by McKinsey conferred construction with the dubious honour of having the lowest productivity gains of any industry. The reasons attributed included continued use of labour instead of technology, lack of consolidation and the aversion of builders to using technology even though architects increasingly espoused it.

Indeed, technology was becoming increasingly significant, with MoRTH trying to escalate the pace of execution from 25 km to 40 km/day; the PM's PRAGATI initiative, where he reviewed projects worth ₹9 trillion, emphasising upon the speed of execution; and the race for implementing affordable housing projects in line with PMAY, for which incentives were being provided to developers and buyers.

In fact, L&T, Shapoorji Pallonji and NCC had qualified for a number of projects that were being executed using technologies like MIVAN. Design and engineering, too, were gaining importance as cities were considering master planning, which would not bring tools of urban planning into play. Pre-engineered buildings, prefab and shuttering systems were being deployed like never before. Roadbuilding companies were completing projects to earn bonuses by advancing completion deadlines. What's more, the Smart Cities Mission's advocacy of technology in planning, administering and maintaining assets encouraged the use of IoT devices, GPS systems, RFID, digital systems, advanced CCTV, Wi-Fi, waste-to-energy management, tracking devices, data management, e-governance and so on.

April

The previous month was notable for Indian architecture, as its crown jewel Balkrishna V. Doshi was honoured with the Pritzker Prize, the first Indian ever to receive this coveted award. Born in Pune on 26 August 1927, Doshi was one of the last living architects to have apprenticed with the famed Le Corbusier, regarded by many as the pioneer of 'modern architecture'. In his illustrious career, Doshi built low-cost housing and public institutions, such as the Centre for Environmental Planning and Technology (CEPT) and Tagore Memorial Hall in Ahmedabad, IIM Bangalore and the Aranya Low-Cost Housing Project. In fact, the Aranya project, located 6 kilometres from Indore, had won Doshi the Aga Khan Award for Architecture in 1996. Its master plan had taken several aspects of sustainable living into consideration in a balanced manner, which were unique to the design and relevant to the concerned income group. Further, Doshi was significantly involved in the design and planning of the city of Chandigarh.

Speaking of city planning, while the official phrase was 'Smart Cities Mission', a more appropriate name would have been 'Smart Area Mission'. No city under the initiative would turn 'smart' as per the funding provided; only an area would receive focused attention in its transformation. In the case of the project, an area of 50 acres for redevelopment, 250 acres in case of greenfield or 500 acres in case of retrofitting, as the case would be, was enhanced to showcase the value propositions, with the intent that the rest of the city would get inspired to make alterations in existing localities, areas and communities, allowing the entire city to evolve with smart practices.

That said, many cities planning 'Smart Areas' were facing an uphill task owing to the biggest stumbling blocks: mindsets and capacity building. Notwithstanding the challenges, there were cities on the move. Andhra Pradesh did a commendable job in the area of greenfield cities and was likely to reap rich dividends. Developing cities based on their economics lies at the core of sustainability. The state was master-planning cities with this foundation. Pune's success at mobilising funds for its water project indicated a healthy appetite among investors for such projects. Hyderabad followed suit by also successfully raising bonds to the tune of ₹2 billion. However, 'corruption' in civic corridors raised its ugly head and the tenders in Pune had to be cancelled, leading to a delay in the Pune water supply project.

Another challenge relating to siloism, where civic departments do not take an integrated view, came to the fore when the Pune commissioner had to cancel tenders for concretising the roads, as the project could only be undertaken after the water supply project was executed (or else it would have led to breaking the concrete roads for the execution of the water project). The then Pune commissioner, Kunal Kumar, demonstrated alacrity in cancelling the subsequent tenders. Incidentally, Pune topped a 2018 urban governance survey of twenty-three cities conducted by Janaagraha Centre for Citizenship & Democracy as part of its fifth edition of the Annual Survey of India's City-Systems (ASICS). Pune was followed by Kolkata, Thiruvananthapuram, Bhubaneswar and Surat.

May

Oil, the single biggest factor that helped the government manage the fiscal deficit, climbed from its advantageous position to well over $75. per barrel. Even as the GST was gaining stability, the E-way bill ruffled feathers again. Not only were small companies having to contend with compliance changes a bit too often, there were certain anomalies that required clarification. GST for government contracts was brought to 12%, while GST on private contracts was at 18%.

That apart, roads and highways were gathering pace with the construction target for 2018–19 laid at 45 km/day. The ministry also raised the award target to 20,000 km for the current fiscal year, up 25% over the previous year.

Mumbai's Development Plan (MDP) 2034 was released after revisions and hiked the floor space index (FSI) in the island city to 3 from 1.33 for residential, and 5 for commercial. In the suburbs, FSI was raised from 2 to 2.5 for residential and from 2.5 to 5 for commercial. MDP 2034 proposed to unlock 3,700 ha of public and private land currently tagged as a no-development zone (NDZ) for the construction of 1 million affordable homes. While the unlocking of the land would be from NDZs, FSI was enhanced in the landlocked island city. This was likely to put severe pressure on the infrastructure. While the metro-rail was expected to ease traffic congestion, bringing enhanced capacity to public transport, the lack of any buildup in capacity in water, sanitation and waste management was likely to throw the city into an accelerated pace of decay.

The ban on the construction of new buildings in Mumbai, too, was lifted by the Supreme Court for six months, with conditions. The ban, which held up construction projects worth ₹20 billion, had been granted as landfill sites were saturated and developers and contractors were dumping debris all over the city.

June

While no one was able to definitively capture the mood of the economy, many positives were visible. IBC brought all delinquent cases on the auction table and bids were at advanced stages. Having bidders indicated that the propositions were attractive. Take the case of Bhushan Steel, which had helped bankers redeem their loans by curtailing the losses that would resulted from the liquidation of the company. Bhushan Steel would have fetched only ₹140 billion if liquidated, but Tata Steel paid ₹325 billion for the five-million capacity plant 150 km away from its Kalinganagar plant. With most banks having already made provisions for 50% of the total ₹560 billion Bhushan owed them, proceeds from the sale were seen boosting their profitability.

What was remarkable in this case is that while the liquidation of the company would have fetched ₹140 billion, the transparent process of auctioning the company was able to realise nearly three times this value. Further, the asset was getting a bidder that would restore two-thirds of the funds lent to an active status. In the erstwhile BIFR regime, this asset would have gathered dust until the plant became inoperable and the workers would have lost their livelihood. If the IBC could similarly convert many stressed assets into earning assets despite a haircut, it would stem the loss of jobs and save assets from decimation.

On another note, earlier, subsidies to the poor in India would not reach the intended beneficiary and be diverted owing to poor governance. Now, direct benefit transfer and Aadhar linking helped save ₹830 billion. What's more, the housing shortage in urban areas was now settled at 10 million homes, while the government wanted to build another 10 million homes for the rural poor by the end of 2018. Houses were being constructed at breakneck speed, with L&T, Shapoorji and NCC being some of the companies picking up large contracts. Further, mega infrastructure projects like the metro, trans-harbour link, coastal road, airports, Bharatmala, Sagarmala, railway stations, freight corridors and bullet train, despite the execution challenges they would face, remained our biggest prospects.

Meanwhile, the Smart Cities Mission continued to gain ground. While most metro cities did not figure in smartening up, cities like Pune, Bhubaneswar, Bhopal and Jabalpur, to name a few, were making strides in their efforts to make the mission a success. In fact, a progress report by AmCham and PwC revealed that Bhopal was ranked second in the implementation of smart projects, with Pune taking the top slot.[49] The city recently launched India's first cloud-based Common Integrated Data Centre, Disaster Recovery Centre and Integrated Control and Command Centre (ICCC). Bhubaneswar, which ranked first in the initial batch, was famous for its PPP-based common payment system. Pune was managing the entire city's function through a command control centre (CCC). And Jabalpur had a collection of projects to make solid waste management more efficient by introducing GPS-enabled trucks and RFID-tagged garbage bins.

Further, the Smart Cities Mission had plenty of convergence with other missions like AMRUT and Housing for All, and some of the projects were implemented under PPPs. The mission had identified projects worth ₹2 trillion for all ninety-nine smart cities across the country, of which around 1,333 projects worth ₹506 billion had been completed or were under the tendering process. There were 329 projects worth over ₹1 billion each and seventy-three affordable housing projects worth ₹170 billion.

The progress report was quite extensive:

- Ninety-one cities had already incorporated SPVs.
- Sixty-nine cities had appointed PMCs.
- 5,500 town planners were working on the mission.
- ICCCs completed in nine cities; work under progress on fourteen ICCCs.

- Smart road projects worth ₹51 billion in the tendering stage in forty cities.
- Smart solar projects in the tendering stage in forty-nine cities.
- Smart water projects completed in six cities, under implementation in forty-three cities.
- Smart wastewater projects completed in forty-six cities.
- PPP projects worth ₹7 billion completed.
- Projects worth ₹77 billion under implementation in fifty-two cities.
- Apart from this, other impactful projects like heritage conservation, waterfront development and public space development completed in thirteen cities worth ₹1 billion; projects worth ₹58 billion under implementation.

July

The size of project execution appeared to have grown manifold. New projects worth ₹1.95 trillion were announced in the January–March quarter, up from ₹1.20 trillion in the previous quarter. The capacity of companies for delivering larger projects expanded. The launch of the ₹167 billion Navi Mumbai International Airport project; the finalisation of eighteen bidders for the ₹460 billion Mumbai–Nagpur Expressway, for which work was expected to commence in September; the launch of the ₹79-billion fourth container project at JNPT to be operated by Singapore ports—all raised the bar on value, scale and size. Other notable projects set to take off included the Chenab River Railway Bridge, Charanka Solar Park, the Bogibeel Bridge, Banihal–Qazigund tunnel and Sewri–Nhava–Sheva Sea-bridge.

The PMAY drive to build Housing for All by 2022 had ₹600 billion being deployed to build 12 million houses, with 0.3–0.5 million houses being built every month. And recently, the consortium of Tata Projects, Capacit'e Infraprojects and CITIC

Group was awarded a ₹117.44 billion project by the Maharashtra government for redevelopment in Mumbai.

In FY2018 alone, NHAI awarded 150 road projects of 7,397 km, a record. HAM projects formed the bulk of the total value of awards last year at 63%, followed by pure EPC contracts at 35% and BOT projects the remaining. As for the metro rail, the overall cost of expansion of operational and approved projects under implementation was over ₹2.5 trillion, and another ₹2 trillion worth of projects were in various stages of approval and likely to come up for bidding in the next five years. In total, about 440 km of new metro network development was approved and another ~800 km was in the proposal stage. In addition, the Bharatmala project was generating interest in logistics parks worth ₹2 trillion in twenty-four villages, and was supporting investment in forty-four economic corridors. The Centre was expected to start projects worth ₹3 trillion under Phase 1. What's more, under the Sagarmala programme, the government had already awarded over ₹1.80 trillion in the ports sector and commenced railway works and road connectivity projects too.

Further, work on the mammoth $100-billion Delhi–Mumbai Industrial Corridor was progressing. The project aimed to create a trade corridor between Delhi and Mumbai running through Delhi, Uttar Pradesh, Haryana, Rajasthan, Gujarat and Maharashtra. Additionally, of the eight planned smart cities for Phase 1 of the project, Dholera, AURIC, Vikram-Udyogpuri and IITGNL were in the implementation stages.

Despite all this, the construction sector's share in India's overall gross value declined to 7.4% in FY2017–18 from 9.6% in FY2012 owing to poor demand in the real estate sector and lower capital expenditure. Essentially, private-sector spending, which contributed a big chunk in infrastructure, remained shy and public spending purses opened to drive the momentum. The government appeared to have finally recognised this imbalance and the GST council was likely to reduce tariff from 28% to 18% for paints, cement, plywood, plaster, etc, later in the month to give a fillip to building materials.

With stepping up awarding of contracts and expediting execution, the results of construction companies were likely to improve. Non-clarity of tax laws was a major reason for litigation and corruption. This helped the legal profession but paralysed economic growth! While India's ranking in ease of doing business improved to the 100th position among 190 countries, the country was still ranked 119th in paying taxes, 164th in enforcing contracts and 181st in dealing with construction permits. Also, contractors were yet to be compensated by the Public Works Department (PWD) of various states for GST compensation on rates reduced from 18% to 12% for government contracts.

August

As India inched past France to become the sixth largest economy in the world with a GDP of $2.59 trillion, the country's growth numbers for FY2018 seemed to be within reach at 7.3%, and then onwards to a tough 7.6% in FY2019.

The Sensex was at an all-time high, having crossed 37,000 points for the first time ever, amid worries over oil and trade war escalation. The reason for this jubilation in the financial markets came from the defeat of the no-confidence motion, a strong monsoon season so far and a weak rupee spurring export growth. The corporate results of the consumer and IT sectors were strong. Banks were seeming to find a resolution, having found takers for their stressed assets such that they were put to work again very quickly.

Although capacity utilisation was above 70%, at the aggregate level, the announcement of new projects was lagging. The optimism reflected in the bourses could suffer a bout of correction as liquidity, which was driving the financial markets, began to ease as interest rates were set to rise.

States were determining their pace of growth, which was amply demonstrated during the no-confidence motion by Andhra Pradesh. Recently, it announced the building of 'Construction Cities' throughout the state to facilitate large-scale construction and promote modern and advanced construction techniques and technology. The aim was to make available all building materials and construction equipment and a supporting ecosystem under one roof. As mega projects require a consortium approach, integration had become a key component of successful bidding.

Indeed, India's infrastructure spending would have to accelerate to at least ₹50 lakh crore or ₹50 trillion between FY2018 and FY2022 to make a visible impact on service delivery and provide a foundation for rapid and inclusive economic growth. This projection factored an average annual GDP growth of 7%, infrastructure investments equal to approximately 5.5% of the GDP, and a pick-up in private-sector investments after FY2019. Experts saw the power, ports, railways, urban transport (metro rail) and urban sectors accounting for 78% of overall infrastructure spending.

September

Union Minister Nitin Gadkari was a man in a hurry. He announced the ₹1-trillion Mumbai–Delhi Expressway, which would connect India's two most backward districts, Mewat (Haryana) and Dahod (Gujarat). With this, travel time would be reduced from 24 hours to 12 hours. The first tender for the project worth ₹440 billion between Mumbai and Vadodara was floated. The expressway was scheduled for completion in three years.

Further, the Maharashtra and Madhya Pradesh governments were to sign an MoU to build the 339-km Indore–Manmad railway line, worth ₹100 billion. The Centre and six states of North India were to sign an MoU for the construction of the Lakhwar multipurpose project in the Upper Yamuna basin in

Uttarakhand, worth ₹40 billion. Work on five major river-linking projects, including the one that would transfer surplus water from the Godavari to the Cauvery, was expected to commence from December. According to Gadkari, a total of thirty-one river-linking projects were under consideration nationwide.

The value of new project announcements by the private sector rose for the first time in two years in the June 2018 quarter, as per analysis by CMIE.[50] However, the bulk of them were made by foreign companies.

October

Beginning its operations in 2002, the Delhi Metro Rail Corporation had a route length of 296 km in 2018, making it the twelfth longest and sixth largest in daily ridership. Its punctuality was 99.9% (any delay of over 59 seconds was considered a delay). After expansion, it would reach a length of 350 km.

In fact, as many as 425 km of metro lines were already in operation in ten cities across the country. Ongoing approvals would take India up to 700 km. The prime minister envisioned metro lines in fifty cities. With such colossal investments, our cities would be greatly served, as transportation was one of the biggest urban banes.

As the stance of governance was hardening, institutions standing on weak or corroded legs were stumbling and crumbling. After the case of corrosion of ethics in ICICI, IL&FS, too, seemed to have bloodied its nose by first becoming a messiah to Maytas Infra (the Satyam scam fallout) in 2009 and then several unrelated forays. Maytas Infra, then run by Tejas Raju, was hit by the Satyam scam and had to be rescued as part of the overall operation by IL&FS. To date, Maytas, now renamed IL&FS Engineering, wasn't able to script a turnaround and was running in losses. However, IL&FS's downfall was its aversion to the principles of transparency and governance by defending itself using the clout of its investors, which included HDFC, SBI and LIC, among others.

IL&FS was downgraded from 'Triple A' to 'D' in a matter of a few weeks by ICRA, CARE and India Ratings. Having defaulted on debt repayments, it was in the process of selling its 37,000 sq. m headquarters at Mumbai's Bandra-Kurla Complex, among other assets.

November

With the mother of all elections around the corner, the government was keen to showcase its achievements. By and large, the infrastructure sector gained momentum in the previous two years as the order book of developers were in line with the street's expectation. According to a report, the entire engineering and construction (E&C) order backlog increased by 12%, following adjusting for the effects of GST.[51] The total order backlog of E&C firms was ₹8.1 trillion at the end of FY2018. Of the whole order backlog, almost 62% was contributed by construction companies, followed by 24% from capital goods companies catering to the energy industry. Interestingly, the roads industry emerged as an important contributor to the entire order book in FY2018.

The number of national highways awarded and executed rose considerably in FY2016 because of the various government policies to remove bottlenecks and an increase in road cess to fund these projects. The execution numbers picked up in FY2017 and were expected to improve further in FY2018. HAM was introduced in FY2016, which picked up the pace by FY2017 onwards. The overall awarding was expected to reach new heights in FY2019. NHAI awarded 7,400 km in FY2018. More than 6,000 km were awarded in the last quarter of the fiscal year. Awarding in FY2019 was expected to be higher on account of an increased push prior to the Lok Sabha elections. Apart from NHAI, projects under various schemes were awarded by MoRTH through state PWDs or NHIDCL. In FY2019, MoRTH awarded 9,700 km and executed projects of 6,700 km.

The government's alacrity in making policy adjustments to reduce delays in project execution certainly revved up the roads sector. As in April 2018, 543 national highway projects were under execution, floated by NHAI and MoRTH, of which 378 projects had no scheduled completion date. Of the remaining 165 projects, thirty-two had reported time overruns. The average time overrun for these projects was thirty-two months. In comparison, in April 2017, time overruns were reported in 104 projects of 484 projects, with an average time overrun of thirty-five months. Also, worries linked to land acquisition dwindled. In the past, especially between FY2011 and FY2013, several projects had been stalled and even terminated owing to land acquisition issues. Projects were awarded without the central government having substantial land in possession. However, since then, NHAI was careful to ensure that at least 80% of the land was in its possession at the time of awarding in the case of BOT and HAM projects, and 90% of the land in the case of EPC projects.

December

The election buzz was on at the end of the year. Some collateral benefits or features of elections include rapid decision-making, rapid project execution, timely payments, brisk purchase of materials and equipment owing to release of liquidity, increase in cash transactions and so on.

While the construction of the Ram Mandir was expected to be the most-talked about project during this period, the towering 182-metre Statue of Unity recently emerged on the project horizon, making its mark with the brilliance of its project execution and timely delivery, both of which were world-class.

Indeed, great projects with super engineering add to a country's perception as an emerging power. The Navi Mumbai International Airport was expected to be a class apart, just as the Chhatrapati

Shivaji International Airport in Mumbai proved to be. And metro projects had so far delivered on execution.

Technology was beginning to make a difference. Maha Metro was using 5D building information modelling (BIM) technology. Nagpur Metro was progressing as per timelines and 10% of the cost had already been saved, as quoted in the DPR, which amounted to about ₹8 billion, thanks to the use of technology. While other metro projects were going ahead with a 10.5-metre viaduct, Nagpur Metro opted for an 8.5-metre viaduct, which helped save around ₹1,260 crore. In addition, MMRC saved around 8.5% on DPR of the project cost and around ₹4.2 million on Metro Bhavan HQ because of the early detection of a quantity overrun through the BIM mode and clash detection.

A report released by the Ministry of Statistics and Programme Implementation (MoSPI) in July 2018 revealed that as many as 296 infrastructure projects, each worth ₹1.5 billion or above, had shown cost overruns to the tune of over ₹3 trillion owing to delays. Reasons included delay in land acquisition, forest clearance, supply of equipment, fund constraint, Maoist incursions, legal cases and the law-and-order situations.[52]

Given the huge cost of projects at stake, their deferment could make or mar the fortunes of a city. The Bullet Train project, for instance, included sixty bridges to be built on the high-speed railway corridor between Gujarat and Mumbai. The ₹120-billion Coastal Road project would see the use of the New Austrian Tunnelling Method (NATM) for tunnelling work of over 3.45-km-long twin tunnels running from Mumbai's Princess Street flyover to Priyadarshini Park, under Girgaon Chowpatty and Malabar Hill.

Clearly, project management and use of technology needed to drive the next phase of building and rebuilding India.

2019

January

The previous year had shown resilience and helped bring back some of the mojo that had faced the onslaught of the demonetisation and GST interventions. Large projects were cleared and several initiatives like RERA and PMAY helped new projects accelerate.

Samsung India inaugurated its ₹50-billion factory of mobile phones in Noida, the world's largest, completed in twenty-four months from the date of announcement. This consumer goods project was one of Make in India's successes. In aviation, the much-delayed Pakyong-Sikkim airport was completed, which was developed at a cost of ₹6 billion with a cost overrun of ₹4.5 billion and a time overrun of eighty-one months. Further, there was a sudden spike in completion of irrigation projects, especially in Madhya Pradesh and Uttar Pradesh. And Chhattisgarh, Punjab, Tamil Nadu and Madhya Pradesh saw the largest completion of road projects in recent times.

Projects worth ₹4.4 trillion were scheduled to be completed in the quarter ending December 2018, and another ₹2.6 trillion worth were scheduled for completion in the quarter ending March 2019. The accelerated pace of implementation seen in recent quarters could yield a higher completion rate in the second half of the year. This could take the total commissioning of projects to over ₹5 trillion in the year, compared to ₹4.9 trillion in the previous year, according to CMIE.[53]

In fact, from April to September 2018, NHAI constructed, widened and strengthened 1,363 km of national highways to four, six or eight lanes, which was 11.84% lower than the target of 1,546 km for the period. But it recorded a growth of 22.79% over the 1,110 km achieved from April to September 2017. The pace of project execution was likely to remain hectic until the clouds of elections gathered on the horizon by March 2019. The Union Budget, to be declared on 1 February 2019, would be the last opportunity for the current finance minister to woo the voters with populist measures.

Whatever the power swing at the Centre, it appeared that states would lead growth from the front in times to come. Hitherto, Maharashtra and Gujarat had shown a strong ability to grow their economies. But Tamil Nadu trumped them all. Its top ranking among big states was recognised by *India Today* magazine; the state had the second highest gross state domestic product (GSDP) with a CAGR of 9% over the past decade. Similarly, Haryana and Kerala improved too, driven by the development agenda.[54]

February

With the elections around the corner, the billion-dollar question was not what the budget held for the country but what the voters held in their heart and mind. Would India continue under Narendra Modi, would a neutral PM be chosen by a united opposition or would we remain 'hung'?

To the prime minister's credit, he had revved up the spirit of the country, won us esteem oversees and led from the front. Whether it was responding to enemy incursions with surgical strikes, making bold moves at COP 21 or setting up renewable energy targets, he moved decisively. Yes, demonetisation was a failure, though he did not admit it. But GST, which was a call of the industry, was introduced and constantly seeing course corrections.

The PM had begun his term by implementing the Seventh Pay commission and One Rank One Pension (OROP) payouts. His campaigns like Swachh Bharat, Smart Cities, Digital India, Start-Up India, Beti Bachao, Beti Padhao, Ujala, Atal Pension Yojana, Direct Benefit Transfer, and so on, were all implemented and accounted for in terms of their percentage accomplishments. All the schemes had ambitious targets and achieved above average success.

The biggest lacuna under his administration was an underestimation of the banking problem when the NDA took over. Had he drawn up a white paper on the economy on assuming charge, we would have known the exact state of affairs. Despite a favourable oil price during most of his term, the NPA overhang was a drag on the economy.

The IBC was a gift under his regime to the corporate sector, as assets frozen under liquidation began to spring back to productive life. The pace of project launches was slow as, first, the NDA fought off the Land Acquisition Act issues and then as the economy was appearing to look ripe for private investment, throwing all caution to the winds, the PM made a scathing attack on black money through demonetisation. This was followed by GST, which was already scheduled, and the economy could never recover from this double whammy. Meanwhile, the NDA, in support of the religious spirit, brought in the Cow Slaughter Ban Bill, which not only began to affect the social and secular spirit but hurt the beef export and leather businesses and disrupted the farmers' model of sustainability.

So, while the middlemen in politics, black money dealers, hawala dealers and unscrupulous builders were miffed at having been given the short shrift by the PM's progressive policies, he also hurt the MSMEs and farmers through some of his ill-advised actions and inactions.

March

While the interim budget for FY2018–19 was comprehensive, albeit with an emphasis on farmers and taxpayers, it continued the emphasis on infrastructure development with an outlay of over $66 billion aiming to propel the nation into a $10 trillion economy. However, the current budget spoke about political economy. Political economy is purely governance by the appointed government that takes decision with economic consequences, always weighing the political significance of every decision. A smart government always runs a good political economy, and one which is not smart enough tends to struggle. So, where did the current government feature in this case?

Over the past four years, while the media was critical about the NDA government on many issues, there are a few areas where it did well on political economy. First was the IBC, which made it impossible for companies that default on bank loans over time to get away with it. In fact, the period of 2008–14 can be recognised as the period of aggressive credit growth, as the outstanding loans of public-sector banks ballooned from ₹18 trillion to ₹52 trillion. This happened because many projects that were started could either not be completed or had low-capacity utilisation. Considering, for instance, the powerful Reliance Communications filed for bankruptcy, it was clear that the government had become more vigilant and made it difficult for top industrialists to get a reprieve. And once it was clear that nobody was too big to fail, others fell in line. Banks were now reporting a recovery of ₹3 trillion through the IBC process.

Private empires built on crony capitalism and opaque governance mechanisms were flushed out into oblivion: Essar, Videocon, Jaiprakash Associates, Unitech, DS Kulkarni, IVRCL, all suffered and were facing bankruptcy proceedings. Even companies like ZEE, Jet Airways, IL&FS and Dewan Housing announced plans to seek 'white knights' to save their sinking ships.

Other positives included keeping inflation under check—the inflation rate of 8.3% that it inherited was down to 2.2%—and better tax compliance and collection, which improved tax-to-GDP ratio. This created the fiscal headroom to give away freebies promised for centrally monitored schemes and large investments in the infrastructure sector. GST, too, was settling down with the January 2019 figures showing an uptick beyond ₹1 trillion.

That said, the overall corporate performance of the private sector was suboptimal according to an analysis of 2,088 companies by *Mint* newspaper, which put net profit growth earnings at 5.29%, the lowest in five quarters.[55] Small and medium enterprises were struggling to survive as non-availability of finance strangled their liquidity. A new ordinance introduced to regulate unregulated chit funds and Ponzi schemes was likely to backfire on the finance of the last resort available to MSMEs as, according to the ordinance, no individual could lend money to another unless they were relatives.

The economy was receiving steroid shots through various schemes—the current direct benefit transfer of ₹250 billion as a first tranche was being sent under the PM-Kisan Samman Nidhi Scheme. This would be followed by another ₹500 billion during the year. Further, several states were trying to woo voters by offering loan waivers. All this was possible, of course, only on account of the ability of taxpayers to bear the burden!

April

From roads and highways, the growth magnet moved to water supply, irrigation, affordable housing and railways. EPC projects were increasingly finding favour over HAM projects.

A huge consolidation exercise was under way as the IBC paved the way for resolving management under debt stresses and new management was set to put these assets to productive use. Essar Steel was being taken over by Arcelor Mittal; NBCC was eyeing

Jaiprakash Associates along with Suraksha Group and Amrapali; JSW Steel had already taken over Monnet Ispat; Tata Steel had taken over Bhushan Steel; Vedanta had taken over Electrosteel Castings; UltraTech had taken over Binani; Brookfield had bought over Leela Hotels; Reliance had bought over Alok Textiles; Sharad Sanghi of Net Magic was set to buy over Jyoti Structures, thereby stalling its liquidation—all would contribute around ₹800 billion. Several construction companies could not sustain the debt shock and landed with the NCLT, such as Punj Lloyd, IVRCL, Hubtown, Unity Infraprojects and Gammon India.

Meanwhile, global construction equipment sales hit an all-time high of 1.1 million units in 2018, with a retail value of about $110 billion, according to Off-Highway Research. India, too, had a great year. Sales of construction equipment grew 35%, the third successive year of robust growth, generating sales of a record high of 98,204 units, 45% above the previous high seen in 2011.[56]

Elections would determine the pace of growth in 2019–20. In all likelihood, this momentum would continue. The government announced gross market borrowing of ₹7.1 trillion in 2019–20 as against FY2019, which stood at ₹5.71 trillion, indicating a provision for the largest borrowing plan in the past nine years. This would ensure that the programmes for development continued unabated.

May

As the new government assumed power, the primary question was whether it could revive project momentum and put the economy firmly on track. The pressure of elections had set the pace for delivery on the ground. Schemes announced and then monitored through PRAGATI and other mechanisms were planned to benefit all segments of society. In 2018–19, project completions would be close to peak levels of ₹6.4 trillion seen in 2016–17.

Roads and railways were the big drivers, followed by irrigation and real estate. According to CMIE, road projects worth ₹756 billion were completed in 2018–19, nearly double than the ₹381 billion worth of projects completed in 2017–18. For railways, project completions more than doubled from ₹292 billion in 2017–18 to ₹646 billion in 2018–19. In real estate, introduction of RERA and punitive judicial orders brought some order. Residential housing projects worth ₹652 billion were completed in 2018–19 compared to ₹341 billion in 2017–18. Besides, commercial complexes worth ₹134 billion were completed in 2018–19. Irrigation projects also saw a sharp jump in completion in 2018–19 with projects worth ₹306 billion completed compared to ₹22 billion the previous year.

Given the failure to encourage private capital, it is no surprise to learn that government-owned projects accounted for 53.8% of all completion during 2018–19. Even more worrisome was the fact that new investment proposals were at the lowest over the past fourteen years. The momentum that put India's economy in a high growth orbit in 2004–05, which led to a pipeline of investment proposals to the tune of ₹25 trillion a year from 2006–07 to 2011–12, was elusive. The decline of investment proposals beginning with the deep dive in 2013–14 at ₹10 trillion provided some hope in doubling to ₹20 trillion in 2014–15 with the new government; but if had since caved in, back to ₹10 trillion.

In the context of the corporatisation of the real estate sector, the REIT instrument proved to be a great new accomplishment as it set the tone for higher FDI flow into the sector. However, only an improvement in the economy was expected to lift the clouds over real estate momentum. Meanwhile, the rainbow continued to be affordable housing, for both building contractors and developers.

June

As a country, the first stage to providing a growth-led economy was set with the election verdict, allowing the current PM to continue the process of rebuilding India with the requisite authority in Parliament. The other ensuing benefit would be the acceleration of existing schemes and restoration of momentum to unfinished and ongoing contracts and projects.

The manifesto had outlined $1.44 trillion or ₹100 trillion investment in infrastructure in the next five years, by 2024: To build roads, railways and other infrastructure like 100 new airports, 50 metros and so on, a boost to manufacturing, and a doubling in exports. The economy needed stimulus. Consumer spending had been reduced to a dribble as the IL&FS crisis snowballed. Projects were at a fourteen-year low, investments had slowed and unofficial figures suggested that unemployment was looming. The government had already widened its budget deficit target for the year through March 2020 to 3.4% of the GDP.

According to the budget presented in February 2019, the government had planned to spend ₹27.84 trillion, which was 14% above last year's expenditure. Amid the trade war between China and the US and the oil price spike, there was external volatility that India still could not leverage to grab export market share. Internally, the banking mess had now hit the one factor that kept our engines running: demand.

Meanwhile, while PM Modi declared 2019–20 as the Construction–Technology year,[57] the sector faced tremendous hardship. For instance, according to the CGST Act, a refund of input credit was available only for ITC (input tax credit) on inputs (i.e. goods other than capital goods) used in providing output supplies. This was resulting in denial of ITC refund in case of inverted duty structure in the service sector, including construction services and works contract services providers. This resulted in a huge unutilised ITC balance in the hands of construction service and works contract service providers and led to a major cash flow and permanent loss in cases of SPVs formed as JVs or consortiums.

July

Our cities were sinking—at some places, we were dangerously close to breaking point; at others, we were skirting disaster. According to reports, the Karnataka government was contemplating a ban on the construction of new apartments in Bengaluru to resolve water scarcity. The deputy chief minister revealed that there was a gap between construction of new residential apartments and the amenities provided to these spaces. Similarly, the High Court had banned construction in Mumbai in March 2016 over the inability of the state government to provide landfills for the waste generated. The city had assured the court but could not fulfil this condition. After several pleas, the Supreme Court lifted the ban only in March 2018.

This is what is taking our cities to the brink of disaster. Few large cities in India are able to treat wastewater before dumping it in the closest lakes or the sea. Other fast-growing cities are also not paying much heed to this aspect of growth—infrastructure capacity measurement and account. Sand mining, not recharging groundwater, landfills, plastic waste, e-waste, untreated sewage water and effluent dumping are some other alarming time bombs.

Following the implementation of the green building movement in 2001, India is aspiring to a green building footprint of 10 billion sq. ft by 2022. As in March 2018, the country had already achieved 5.27 billion sq. ft, making us the second in the world in terms of the largest registered green building footprint. However, with flagrant abuse of the national building code guidelines, this green movement was seriously under threat. Though RERA's scope may not have covered this aspect, it was time for state urban planning authorities to take the onus.

August

The Union Budget signalled a new era of stability with a plan to deliver a $5 trillion economy in the next few years. The government focused on provision of electricity, LPG cylinders, toilets, housing access, direct benefit transfers and insurance to households in urban and rural India. With the JAM (Jan Dhan Yojana, Aadhaar and mobile number) combination, existing policies became more effective by lowering costs and reducing leakages. This budget affirmed Swachh Bharat's solid waste management extension, piped water to all rural households by 2024, affordable housing for 19.5 million eligible beneficiaries, new metro projects for 300 km, rural roads for 125,000 km for ₹800 billion, railway station redevelopment, gas and water grids, i-ways and regional airports.

The government also trained its eyes on FDI, overseas bonds, divestment, public partnership in railway projects, cess on petrol and taxing the rich to raise funds. Further, the maiden plan to issue sovereign bonds to the world to raise funds for a part of its overseas debt could be initiated in the second half of the borrowing calendar year. The macroeconomic situation was given attention by capitalising banks by ₹700 billion. By divesting its stake in PSUs, the government could hold them more accountable, making them more efficient and raising funds. A divestment target of over ₹100 billion was set during the year.

The government had been the main driver of capex in the past couple of years and the steady pace of investment is expected to continue—the intention was to spend ₹100 trillion on infrastructure in the next five years. Of this, the railways was given a huge boost. Also, tax rates of 25% available up to a ₹4 billion turnover limit was a significant move in leaving money on the table of over 99% of the corporate world.

Improvement in norms and acceleration in divestment, FDI, NCLT, the development of the bond market and taxes were sure to help. But the possible gamechanger was the FM's statement: 'More than ₹75 lakh crore is blocked in litigations in service tax and excise. There is a need to unload this baggage and allow business to move on. I, therefore, propose, a Legacy Dispute Resolution Scheme that will allow quick closure of these litigations.' If implemented expeditiously, this was expected to be a winner.[58]

September

The finance minister heard the cries of anguish and decided to act, with initiatives aimed at generating sales for the auto industry. The construction equipment industry, too, could heave a sigh of relief with BSIV vehicles registered before 31 March 2020 being allowed to operate till their registration expires.

This is the first time the government blinked—the FM's assurance of another two booster doses clearly held promise. Accelerating GST refunds would improve liquidity with MSMEs, but then this was just undoing the wrong caused by unnecessary delays. Similarly, the rollback of surcharge on long- and short-term capital gains arising from transfer of equity shares would correct an ill-advised move with regard to foreign portfolio investors.

October

The economy received a shot in the arm as contrary to its perceived stance, the government swung right. It took the bold and decisive step of cutting tax rates by 10–25% for domestic companies. For new manufacturing investments, companies could avail a tax rate of 17%, provided the new assets became operational before 31 March 2023. Old assets could not be shifted out of existing units to new units to avail this. Other reversals of the removal of surcharge on capital gains and connected with share buyback programmes were part of the offerings. The total booster shot was to the tune of ₹1.45 trillion.

This new tax rate regime put us in business in comparison with our Asian peers. Corporate profits had been trailing for the past three years, but this fresh dose would mean 10% to PAT for corporate India. Additions to the bottom line would play out in the form of fresh investments and were, therefore, expected to generate employment. However, this stimulus was not an 'instant voodoo'—it would pan out over the next six months and would set the direction for the future, affirming that India was welcoming and facilitating businesses.

Meanwhile, social improvement schemes began to show positive outcomes; for instance, Swachh Bharat. India had built 100 million toilets across 600,000 villages and another 6.3 million in cities. The results indicated, as per reports provided by IPE Global and Kantar, that 93% of people had access to toilets; people did not defecate in the open in 93% of villages; 96% of those who had access to toilets used them; all built toilets had been geo-tagged and could be verified; and, according to the WHO and UNICEF, there was a dramatic reduction in cases of malaria and diarrhoea among children in areas that were provided toilets.[59]

Ease of paying taxes, arbitration and stalled projects were the hurdles yet to be addressed in as bold a manner as the FM dealt with tax rates. Some beneficial announcements, like obviating the need for a bank guarantee by the private organisation when the arbitration award in its favour is being challenged, had helped.

Also, mining promised to be a new frontier—it was expected to grow four times in the next ten years.

November

While several scoffed at the government's avowed aspiration of targeting a $5 trillion economy, it was important to read between the lines and understand the statement as 'India will invest ₹100 trillion in infrastructure in the next five years'! The investment into infrastructure was planned as part of a National Infrastructure Pipeline (NIP), which was a project plan for each of the years with investment amounts across all segments of infrastructure from 2019–20 to 2024–25.

Without a doubt, our economy was in the doldrums with the project pipeline having slowed severely. One positive change was India's recent improvement in the ease of doing business rankings, where it moved up to 63rd place—a significant improvement considering we were at 142nd place in 2014. The Department of Investment and Public Asset Management (DIPAM) had a new secretary, and the government intended to stand by the divestment process, which was being readied for a real sale, unlike the intergovernmental transfers of shareholdings in the past.

December

Former Andhra Pradesh Chief Minister Chandrababu Naidu's ire was not unjustified as he raked up the issue of the cancellation of orders on projects relating to trunk infrastructure, to be built over land he had managed to obtain from farmers.

The Andhra Pradesh government had readied a plan to develop over 54,000 acres of land pooled for the construction of a new capital city at Amaravati—Naidu's pet project. Its master plan, consisting of nine theme cities and twenty-seven townships in 217 sq. km, aimed to connect Amaravati with six neighbouring towns, including Vijayawada and Guntur. However, in November, the new state government terminated its agreement with a Singapore consortium to build the city. Lulu Group, among others, decided to cancel its plan to invest ₹22 billion in the state after its land allotment was cancelled. It was estimated that projects valued at nearly ₹300 billion were put on hold, affecting the order book position of NCC, L&T and GMR, among others.

This was unfortunate at a time when the project pipeline was already at its lowest in fourteen years and private investment was at its lowest in sixteen years. According to CMIE, revised estimates for 2018–19 showed that new investment proposals declined by over 19% compared to the new investment proposals made in 2017–18—the fourth consecutive year of decline. Even the best performing sector, roads, saw a completion of construction of only 4,622 km by end-September against its target of 12,000 km for the year.

CRISIL estimated that India needed infrastructure spending of ₹2.35 trillion over the next decade, from 2021 till 2030, to be supported by an average GDP growth of 7.5% and infrastructure spending of above 6% of the GDP. States would have to contribute close to half this infrastructure outlay, or ₹110–125 trillion. States already accounted for 41% of the overall infrastructure spending of ₹77 trillion, including public and private spending in the current decade. Five sectors—transport, irrigation, energy, urban and housing, and water and sanitation—accounted for two-thirds of states' spending so far. However, with state finances under stress, capex plans had been hit. Populist measures and unproductive expenditure on the revenue account had depleted the ability of state governments to continue to drive the capex cycle. The value of new state government projects saw a 75% decline from a year earlier in the quarter ending in June 2019, and was the lowest in fifteen years.

The NIP announced that their intention to build a ₹10 trillion investment in infrastructure over the next five years was to include greenfield and brownfield projects costing above ₹1 billion each. The task force was to submit its report on the indicative pipeline for 2021–25 by 31 December 2019. How the government would fund all these ambitious plans seemed to be the trillion-dollar question.

Meanwhile, Indian Railways appeared to be on the move with an ambitious modernisation exercise, envisaging station redevelopment, private trains, high-speed train corridors, improving customer experience, additional streams of revenue, private participation, seamless connectivity and freight movement. An SPV was also being created to raise funds for the world's largest exercise in transit-oriented development (TOD) through the collection of a user development charge on tickets at redeveloped stations.

However, the reports of Maharashtra's contribution of ₹50 billion to the Mumbai–Ahmedabad corridor of the bullet train project being diverted to fund populist schemes in the name of farmers' welfare hit a sour note—not only would it derail the project and an important development scheme but it was likely to send out a very wrong signal to international investors.

Elsewhere, the delinquency issue at discoms continued to undermine attempts to infuse dynamism in the sector. It was hoped that the new framework for reforms proposed by the Ministry of Power and New & Renewable Energy would address this aspect.

2020

January

The year began with a reality check. Economic growth would at best touch 5%. Government spending would be tepid, and only a sharp decline in oil price could give the government more elbow room. Fundraising for critical infrastructure projects was another issue. Informing the nation about the central government's intent to spend ₹100 trillion on infrastructure over the next five years without sharing how this would happen only made the private sector wait and watch.

Commercial mining was the silver lining for 2020, as nearly 200 coal blocks were up for auctioning, constituting 400 million tonnes of coal at peak capacity over the next five years. The Coal Ministry was expected to issue bidding rules for commercial coal mine auctions and hold stakeholder consultations.

Although Minister Nitin Gadkari had indicated an expected spending of ₹2 trillion in the coming year, followed by ₹3 trillion in the following year and ₹17 trillion over the next five years on the roads sector alone, it was not clear how the government would have access to these funds. The only hope appeared to be FDI, which was currently slated to come from Saudi Arabia and Canada. However, the PM was expected to use his charisma to secure funds from Japan, the US, Korea and Germany as well.

That said, domestic institutional investors (DIIs) and foreign portfolio investors (FPI) together invested ₹1.43 trillion (around $20 billion) in 2019, the highest in any single year over the past fifteen years.

February

The UPA government had subjected the infrastructure sector to policy paralysis, environment clearance roadblocks and high-intensity red tape. The NDA government fought tooth and nail to bring about an ordinance when all other measures failed to get all parties onboard the Land Acquisition Act. This was necessitated as the methods for acquiring land under the dated Land Acquisition Act of 1894 hit a wall, because of the forced nature of acquisition at ridiculously low rates of compensation.

Finally, Parliament passed the Right to Fair Compensation and Transparency in Land Acquisition, Rehabilitation and Resettlement Act 2013, which relied upon five tenets: enhanced compensation, social impact assessment, informed consent, rehabilitation/resettlement and return of land. The land so acquired had to be purchased at four times the prevailing rates mentioned in the 'ready reckoner'. The desire to bring in the act quickly and defang all opposition led to the establishment of a very high compensation multiple. This caused NHAI's ballooning debt, as cost of land was contributing to nearly 40–50% of the cost of the road project. NHAI's debt servicing cost was projected to shoot up nearly four times by 2022–23—from ₹144.43 billion (including ₹42.81 billion principal repayment and ₹101.22 billion interest) in 2018–19 to over ₹610 billion. NHAI was forced to increasingly rely on market borrowings—up to ₹612.17 billion in 2018–19 from ₹33.43 billion in 2014–15, an increase of nearly 1,800%.

Under PM Modi, the government spent ₹11 trillion, of which nearly ₹3 trillion were estimated to have been spent on land acquisition alone. In January, Minister Nitin Gadkari reviewed 500 road projects where nearly ₹3 trillion of investment was involved; the biggest culprit for delays was land acquisition.

Ready reckoner rates had been kept artificially high as they provided stamp duty revenues to the city administration and also helped secure four times the rates for land acquisition, especially for those who had already bought land around the area of proposed acquisition on 'inside information'. Towns and cities so infused by cash from land acquisition were known to splurge the windfall gains in material comforts. Realty prices showed a spike in such areas as some of the gains also found their way into buying assets that were earlier out of reach. Soon, this temporary inflation in prices would diffuse and investors almost certainly had a hard landing.

While the Union Budget 2020 was expected to usher in new hopes of a ₹102 trillion infrastructure pipeline, the government would have factored in nearly 30% of this as funding land acquisition, which could have well been averted with an out-of-the-box approach.

March

The coronavirus put the brakes on growth in several industries. But it also pummelled the 'Make in China' story. China produced nine times the volume of steel that India did; 40% of this was used in construction. Over a third of Chinese steel mills were considering cutting production because of rising inventories. Owing to slow construction activities, the outlook for domestic rebar demand was negative. JCB UK had already cut its production as over 25% of its components and parts suppliers were affected, in turn disrupting its delivery and production schedules. Komatsu, which sources components from its own plants and outside partners in China, was shifting the production of metal parts used in the body of vehicles as well as wire harnesses to Japan and Vietnam. Japan's Daikin Industries was considering moving the assembly of commercial air-conditioners to Malaysia. Only about 30% of the nation's 183 auto assembly plants were online by the end of February, according to the China Association of Automobile Manufacturers.

The pandemic was truly a black swan event. And companies began scouting for alternate sources for supplies. Not having a fix on how long the situation would last, companies wanted to secure an alternate supply chain route. Even contractors from India expected to see a revision in tenders of some projects been awarded to Chinese contractors as it would have been extremely difficult for them to now provide Chinese workers and machines to undertake the task.

Meanwhile, the NIP had an interesting line-up. The FM had set aside ₹220 billion towards the NIIF. This would be leveraged to raise funds from pension and sovereign funds, which would now find the deal worthwhile, given that the impact of the dividend distribution tax had been muted. They had also been provided tax relief when investing in infrastructure. Cube Highways had been agile and was already looking at offloading its road assets at a premium through an InvIT. Stepping in after construction and then offloading after the asset had gained traction had the potential to bring smart returns for the courageous.

Maritime infrastructure was also in focus as master plans for twelve major ports were ready as well as ninety-five capacity expansion and port modernisation projects, identified since 2014 in a bid to enhance their capacity and efficiency. In September 2019, the Asian Development Bank (ADB) had shared an action plan for the development of coastal shipping with the government. Technology is also playing a part as the government unveiled a National Logistics Portal at the Revolutionising Ports Conference organised by the Indian Ports Association and FIRST Construction Council in Mumbai.

April

The construction industry employed 35 million people, more than the population of Australia or Malaysia, and contributed 8% of India's GDP. Unlike manufacturing, this sector takes months to mobilise the 4Ms—men, materials, machines and money—for projects. Owing to the COVID-19 pandemic, the supply chain was disrupted. Droves of workers boarded trains to the safety of their villages as sites downed shutters with the national lockdown. In the Mumbai Metropolitan Region alone, 10,200 projects, worth ₹5 trillion, were registered under RERA. The total area under construction was around 80 million sq. ft and the total value was ₹5 trillion. Total loans taken by developers to finance their projects amounted to around ₹2 trillion. As much as ₹2.5 trillion was raised through the home loan route.

PM Modi stated that the twenty-one-day lockdown could help us avoid getting pushed back twenty-one years. That said, the sooner we could get our construction projects up and running, the quicker we could serve the daily wage needs of 35 million households. In fact, China was speeding up construction on major infrastructure projects to mitigate the economic impact of the pandemic. The construction on 89.1% of 11,000 key projects (those in hard-hit Hubei Province not included) was restarted as on 20 March, as per the National Development and Reform Commission (NDRC), China. The country was fast-tracking fund allocations from the central budget and increasing special-purpose bonds for local governments to bolster infrastructure construction.

Finance Minister Nirmala Sitharaman recently announced a relief package of ₹1.7 trillion to help workers from the construction sector. Labour Minister Santosh Kumar Gangwar wrote to all states to dip into the ₹520 billion Construction Cess Fund to give financial and allied benefits to construction workers through DBT. According to data till 31 March 2019, released in response to a Lok Sabha query, cess collected in the welfare funds added up to

₹496.74 billion. Of this, only ₹193.79 billion had been spent; so, close to ₹300 billion was mired in administrative red tape.[60]

May

The RBI came out with a stimulus package for ₹1 trillion for MSMEs. However, there were reports that owing to the invocation of the Disaster Management Act 2005, MSME employers were being warned that they should continue to pay the wages of their staff and workers irrespective of the lockdown and lack of revenue. How could the government lock up our cities and then expect the expenses to be paid? How would this work and how was it fair?

If the government expected jobs to be retained and workers' wages to be paid, it had to enforce its own laws. For instance, as per the Ministry of MSME, the Government of India had enacted the Micro, Small and Medium Enterprises Development (MSMED) Act 2006, where payments made by large companies and PSUs to MSMEs after forty-five days were subject to interest equal to three times the RBI rate. This was also mandatorily to be reported in the annual report as per Section 16 and Section 22 of the MSMED Act. This was being abused because of the dominance of the buyer, vendors did not get compensated as decreed. In fact, even PSUs did not adhere to the rules. Even though complaints were filed on the portal, no authority addressed them. Further, PSUs were mandated to procure 25% of their purchases from MSMEs. However, this was never followed and procurement remained at around 10%.

June

According to a report by the ADB, the pandemic and subsequent lockdowns were likely to cost the global economy up to $8.8 trillion. An estimate by the Manila-based multilateral funding agency pegged the loss to the Indian economy at nearly $30 billion.[61]

Unprecedented times call for extraordinary measures. On 12 May, PM Modi announced a ₹20 trillion package to provide stimulus to growth. The largest economic package announced in post-independence India also sought to fast-track growth by strengthening critical pillars of the economy, such as infrastructure. The Cabinet Committee on Economic Affairs approved the methodology for auction of coal and lignite mines or blocks on a revenue-sharing basis.

A report by CRISIL indicated that the Indian economy would have to grow by 11% for three consecutive years to match the economic growth pre-COVID-19. In other words, we were not coming back to the economic growth levels of 5% prevalent from 2019–20 to 2024–25 at the earliest.

Further, unavailability of labour was a self-created blunder that hurt our country's ability to get back to work. Economies in Europe were getting back to work with even restaurants and movie theatres being opened. China was already at a near-normal capacity of work. But an inadequately planned lockdown with a scant eye on the details of the consequences did us in. This resulted in nearly 2.5 million migrant labourers returning to the state of Uttar Pradesh alone, of which 75% were from Maharashtra. In total, 9.1 million migrants were transported by trains and road transport in May. Several more walked their way home. The entire 'Make in India' workforce was disrupted, adding to the losses of businesses that were ready to commence operations.

The 'Atmanirbhar' package, too, did not address the immediate fiscal needs of businesses but chose to address long-pending reforms. Besides, the PM's claim that the package would infuse 10% of the GDP into the economy seemed hollow as the fiscal interventions were not over 1.5% of the GDP. This was an example of a well-intentioned but badly carried out exercise in communication and created a sense of disbelief in the intention itself. It became evident that only aggressive spending on the NIP could revive the economy.

July

The world economy was expected to contract by over 6% and the Indian economy, too, was in a mess with an unprecedented negative growth of 4.5% for the financial year. The GDP had slid from 6.1% in FY2018 to 4.2% in FY2019 to –4.5% in FY2020. Government resources were overburdened in handling the pandemic. Priorities changed and overstretched finances saw the fiscal deficit spiral to close to 10% of the GDP. In 2019–20, the central government ran a fiscal deficit of 4.6% of the GDP against the planned 3.5% as a result of the gross overestimation of its tax collections, which fell short by a gap of over ₹1.5 trillion. The government planned to bridge the fiscal deficit by borrowing more money. Initially, it had planned to borrow ₹7.8 trillion, but on 8 May, it said it would borrow ₹12 trillion.

There were arguments in favour of and against borrowing from overseas where money was available at historically low rates, and there were arguments in favour of and against printing money. But how did we get here? Was it only because of the pandemic? Herein lay the rub. The moribund economy was already in the ICU. The project pipeline had been drying up for the past eighteen months. It was amply clear that the malaise in the economy came before the pandemic and would continue to plague the recovery process. Labour began to return to cities under duress as our rural economies offered no opportunities. However, we now had to contend with a higher cost of labour and be prepared to train labour for better productivity.

The government acted wisely in using this crisis to introduce certain key reforms in agriculture and mining, as these would have otherwise found opposition in a normal scenario. Public-sector divestment, too, had the potential to benefit the economy.

HDFC Bank, established in 1994, was a shining example of how privatisation could build value. Another example was the unlocking of value by Vedanta Group, which acquired BALCO and Hindustan Zinc for an aggregate value of ₹10 billion for a 50% and a 25% stake. The balance government stake sale would fetch up to ₹250 billion—a growth of twenty-five times in twenty years! Our PSUs were indeed sitting on a goldmine. In 2019–20, a total of ₹500 billion was raised through divestment and targets were regularly underachieved (partly due to a reluctance to part with power).

Road construction, which sped our way to infrastructure growth in the recent past, with FY2019–20 clocking in contract awards of 10,676 km, hit a speed breaker. With financials under strain zooming 9.5 times to ₹2.28 trillion in five years, a monetisation programme of toll-yielding assets was initiated. As part of the NIP, the roads sector would elicit an expenditure of ₹3.24 trillion in FY2020 alone apart from its total allocation of nearly ₹19 trillion over five years until 2025. Despite its pre-eminent role in infrastructure, NHAI had been delaying filing its financial results for the past four years. It was finally fined by SEBI for a breach of regulations. Further, with costs of ₹200–250 million per sq. m, its costs were being driven by land prices that had been unnecessarily rising owing to the failings of the Land Acquisition Act.

August

India's disinvestment target for 2020–21 was ₹2.1 trillion against the previous year's achievement of ₹34.85 billion, against the 2019–20 target of ₹1.05 trillion. Divestment crossed ₹1 trillion only in 2017–18 in the past ten years; ₹37 billion from this was received by selling shares internally among PSUs; ONGC bought the government's 51% stake for cash. The second highest divestment was in 2018–19 of ₹80 billion.

Government shareholding in three blue chips that were part of the CPSE ETF—namely NTPC, BEL and PowerGrid—reached the 51% threshold, thus making further stake dilution impossible. It could have to replace these stocks with other blue chips, where government shareholding was comfortably above the 51% threshold. So, while FY2018 and FY2019 did send out a good signal for divestment, FY2020 slipped.

India's other means of raising economic spirits was possibly to engage high-level FDI. Here, the country managed to attract $20 billion during April–June 2020 through the lockdown. Google's parent Alphabet's CEO Sundar Pichai announced a $10 billion investment in Digital India in the next five to seven years. US-based Facebook said it would put in $5.7 billion in Reliance Jio platforms. Saudi Arabia's Public Investment Fund also announced plans to put in $1.6 billion in Jio. Another substantial investment of $1 billion was announced by Taiwanese electronics company Foxconn.

Besides these, chipmaker Qualcomm's investor arm Qualcomm Ventures, consumer electronics major Thomson, Japan's Hitachi, South Korea's Kia Motors and Samsung, auto parts company Hyundai Mobis, SGS (which partnered with Amazon to open its first accreditation testing lab in India) and Japanese electronics company Tsuzuki, which opened a brand-new plant at Reliance's Model Economic Township in Jhajjar in Haryana, were all in the fray in the final stages of negotiations to benefit from the Ministry of Electronics and Information Technology's (MeitY) ₹410 billion production-linked incentive (PLI) scheme to make mobile phones and certain other specified electronic components. This scheme, which offered incentives of 4–6%, would be active for five years, with FY2019–20 considered the base year for calculation of incentives. This meant all investments and incremental sales registered after FY2020 would be considered while computing the incentive to be given to each company. This was likely to set the stage for India to become a major production hub for exporting mobile phones. Initially, five global and five local companies would be selected to avail of the scheme.

GST collections for the April to June quarter stood at ₹1.86 trillion, a 41% drop compared to the ₹3.14-trillion collected in the same period last year, resulting in a shortfall. The Centre was unable to guarantee the shortfall for states as was originally decided. If revenue collections in FY2020–21 were projected at 65% of the revenues collected in FY2019–20, there would be a revenue gap of ₹2.67 trillion for states. This would create a huge setback for them in coming months in funding their projects.

Workers began returning to sites as large contracting firms like L&T and Shapoorji indicated. The projects expected to be quick on their feet included roads, metro rail, irrigation, mining and agri-infrastructure, among others. While there would be more innovation in cost engineering, revised plans, alternative materials and new technologies, one factor would not change: trust. It was evident that trusted brands would draw more business and unorganised products, services and organisations, not known to place great emphasis on quality, would feel the pinch.

September

After months of speculation on GDP numbers, the results confirmed our worst fears. Construction contracted by 50.3% (from ₹2.62 trillion to ₹1.30 trillion) as the sector worst hit during the quarter, contributing to the overall GDP contracting by 23.9% from ₹35.35 trillion in Q1 of 2019 to ₹26.90 trillion in Q1 of 2020. The rates of gross fixed capital formation (GFCF) to GDP, which had been falling ever since 2007 at its highest at 35.81%, plunged to 22.3%. GFCF itself halved to ₹5.99 trillion. The supply shock and COVID-19 fear traumatised demand.

The Atmanirbhar package mostly offered liquidity relief and did very little in terms of demand stimulation. India's MSMEs, which employed about 120 million, contributed to 33.4% of

India's manufacturing output and made up 45% of India's exports, were at the receiving end. Whether it was demonetisation, GST or COVID-19, this segment suffered the most. While agriculture was expected to show improvement this year, its contribution to GDP was marginal.

Demand stimulation was the challenge going forward. However, the government was strained for resources with the fiscal deficit already having exceeded budget estimates between April and July 2020. Against a revenue projection of ₹22.45 trillion, the government received only ₹2.32 trillion while expenditure remained at around the similar levels of last year during the same period at ₹10.54 trillion, leading to a deficit of ₹8.2 trillion.

The good news was the inauguration of two important infrastructure projects: the Atal Tunnel in Himachal Pradesh and the Kosi Rail Mahasetu in Bihar. The 9-km Atal Tunnel connects Manali to Lahaul-Spiti throughout the year. Earlier, the Spiti Valley would remain cut off for about six months in a year owing to heavy snowfall. The strategically important Kosi Rail Mahasetu was dedicated to the nation several decades after the original bridge was washed away by severe flooding and an earthquake in 1934 that left a large part of Bihar devastated. Despite independence thirteen years later, it took eighty-six years for the 1.5-km-long bridge to be rebuilt!

In other news, reports suggested that MoRTH was contemplating a change to HAM to address the issue of repayments to developers. This came amid speculation of MoRTH linking the interest rate on annuity payments to the rate of the country's largest lender, State Bank of India, instead of RBI's rate.

October

The states of India were beginning to wake up. They had realised that they could not depend on the Centre if they had to keep their promises to their electorate. The GST shortfall was estimated at

₹3 trillion, of which ₹970 billion was due to GST implementation and the balance was owing to COVID-19. With cess collection expected at ₹650 billion, states were likely to witness a shortfall of ₹2.35 trillion. The government claimed that eighteen states had agreed to go ahead with the option to use special dispensation from the RBI, for a sum of about ₹970 billion shortfall.

The need to attract investment into the states had never been greater. Some states had already got their act together, reformed their labour policies and were offering incentives for investments.

Uttar Pradesh, for one, went ahead and decided to tap private lenders to fund the 628-km Ganga Expressway project, which was estimated to cost over ₹360 billion. The mega project would be the world's longest access-controlled expressway, when completed. The UP Expressway Industrial Development Authority (UPEIDA) board also approved a proposal to raise ₹29 billion from HUDCO for the land acquisition costs of the Ganga Expressway, which entailed the acquisition of 6,556 ha. The state government sourced public-sector bank credit for its various ongoing and proposed expressway projects, including Ganga Expressway, Purvanchal Expressway, Bundelkhand Expressway and Gorakhpur Link Expressway. Further, from just two operational airports to seven, development work was being carried out at seventeen airports in Uttar Pradesh over the past forty-two months.

Uttarakhand also lined up six mega projects to be launched under the Namami Gange Mission, which included sewage treatment plants (STPs) and a museum, among others. Not to be left behind, the poll-going Bihar would also see a largesse of ₹160 billion worth of projects before the elections. An STP under the Namami Gange project, water supply schemes, riverfront development projects, a railway bridge electrification project, new railway lines and construction of highways and bridges were slated to be inaugurated.

Assam, too, announced infrastructure projects worth nearly ₹120 billion, which included the construction of colleges, flyovers and road corridors across the state. Besides government funds, the state had twelve other road projects worth ₹60 billion funded by the ADB and Asian Infrastructure Investment Bank to begin. Odisha had also cleared proposals worth ₹150 billion, which included investments in infrastructure, tourism, metals and cement.

As long as the SPVs created observed the discipline of land acquisition and project execution as scheduled, funds could be raised and repaid as construction risks were mitigated with the state government backing the projects. This was likely to be the infrastructure development model for coming years as states came into their own to build their future.

Meanwhile, the National High-Speed Rail Corporation also announced plans for seven new projects at an expected cost of around ₹10 trillion. It awarded tenders of ₹200 billion to three bidders comprising seven Indian companies. A tender for a 237-km corridor, part of the Gujarat section of the Mumbai–Ahmedabad project, was likely to consume 7.5 million Mt of cement, 2.1 million Mt of steel and 0.14 million Mt of structural steel during construction. Another tender for twenty-eight steel bridges, which would consume 70,000 Mt of steel, was underway.

The potential of such projects to provide employment to 90,000-odd people, apart from the benefit of not affecting our liquidity and bringing in long-term Japanese debt for infrastructure building, was good news for the country.

November

The 508-km Mumbai–Ahmedabad bullet train project may have seemed like a vanity project, but getting Japan to fund it under a fifty-year loan at 0.1% rate of interest, where the civil works and building material supplies were not restricted to Japanese companies, appeared to be a positive benefit. Getting overseas sovereign funds to invest in India's infrastructure was our best option to catch up with economic growth befitting our demographic dividend.

Such massive infrastructure projects were expected to restore employment generation. So, while we would need to pay for these after fifty years, we would have infused capital for growth. Both the Delhi metro rail and bullet train projects had the advantage of deploying long-term funds from overseas governments at negligible rates of interest where, owing to relaxation in terms, contracts were being awarded to Indian companies with the building material sourced from Indian companies.

Road construction was in the process of resetting its model to monetise its assets and reduce the debt load. This year, too, MoRTH planned to construct 11,000 km with an output of 30 km/day. The ministry had been accommodating with regard to liquidity issues by providing working capital loans to developers through executive agencies like NHAI and infusing funds with many more instalments at regular intervals. It was also likely to issue instructions to speed up the conciliation of differences between the contracting community and NHAI.

While order books were good and workers back, the worry was about the future—the project pipeline and the government's ability to focus on the economy. With a setback of a negative 10% GDP growth, the recovery was expected to be K-shaped, with some sectors gaining and others crumbling.

December

India had a leaking bucket. So even while the economy grew, it was unable to benefit from the growth as the resources added were not deployed efficiently. Our second quarter results indicated that the economy shrank by 7.5% as we unlocked our cities.

One of the holes in the bucket was created by the banking sector. Between FY2009 and FY2019, the government infused ₹3.15 trillion in public-sector banks. The Union Budget 2019 further provided for a ₹700 billion provision to recapitalise banks. As on 30 September 2019, the public-sector banks were carrying NPAs of ₹7.27 trillion. Every year, the taxpayers funded ₹2 trillion of NPAs of banks, according to some estimates. RBI data showed that Indian banks wrote off nearly $85 billion over FY2014–19, of which state-owned banks contributed nearly 80%.

The previous year, we completed fifty years of bank nationalisation; over the past six years, even the current NDA Government witnessed the decimation of wealth under its watch. PM Modi had already sought a reduction in the government stake from four banks: Punjab & Sind, UCO Bank, Bank of Maharashtra and IDBI Bank (LIC now owned 51% of it). But the pace of privatisation and of divestment had been too lackadaisical. A recent respite came in the form of the BPCL disinvestment, which would provide succour in the form of ₹400 billion and was not an eyewash, as PSUs were expressly forbidden from participating in the divestment process—but the response was tepid. Other than BPCL, there were nineteen more PSUs for which the government had given an in-principle approval for disinvestment, including the likes of Container Corporation of India, Bharat Earth Movers and Shipping Corporation of India.

Further, project delays continued to torment the infra sector. As per data shared by the Ministry of Statistics and Programme Implementation (MoSPI), 441 infrastructure projects incurred cost overruns of ₹4.35 trillion owing to various factors, but predominantly delay in implementation.[62] This resulted in projects being set back by a period ranging from one month to over five years. Minister Nitin Gadkari went on record to say that fixing these issues would save NHAI ₹1 trillion, yearly.[63]

Meanwhile, the sit-in by farmers' organisations at certain border crossings in the national capital put the focus on farm sector reforms.

2021

January

In December 2019, we were dangerously treading close to the lows in GDP and the project pipeline continued its downward spiral with only a quarter of projects completed at ₹764 billion, as against a target of ₹4 trillion worth of completions scheduled for the quarter ending in March 2020.

The private sector had mixed results. The topline of companies declined in both the first and second COVID-19 quarters, by 6.3% in Q2 FY2021 and 27% in Q1 FY2021. Of a sample of 3,095 companies, as per a *Business Today* study, aggregate profit (excluding extraordinary transactions and banks and financial services) rose to 37.6% compared to a 54% plunge in the previous quarter, on a yearly basis.[64] This was obviously a result of cost cuts, efficient utilisation of inventory and interest waivers, backed by the revival of pent-up demand. The fourth quarter of FY2021 was likely to be weighed down by inflationary pressures and flat demand.

Proposals worth ₹587 billion were made for investments in the creation of new capacities during the quarter ended September 2020. This was comparable to the ₹561 billion worth of investment proposals made initially in the previous quarter ended June 2020 where the lockdown brought activities to a grinding halt. Of this, ₹258 billion worth of investment proposals made by both the Centre and the states were the lowest made by them in any quarter in the past sixteen years, since June 2004. The private sector, too, at ₹328 billion, was the lowest since June 2004. New investment proposals fell from ₹15 trillion in 2017–18 to ₹14.6 trillion in 2018–19 and ₹14.2 trillion in 2019–20. Cumulative new investment proposals in 2020–21 were ₹1.3 trillion. According to CMIE, new investment proposals were unlikely to cross ₹5 trillion this year, the lowest since 2004–05.

The pandemic brought into focus the economic malaise in the country, and the government recognised that it needed to be fixed, finally. FM Nirmala Sitharaman announced Atmanirbhar stimulus packages to help the economy face the setback caused. It also used the opportunity to unleash some bold reforms like commercialising the mining sector, agriculture reforms, opening defence to domestic production by increasing FDI under the automatic route from 49% to 74%, consolidation of forty-four labour laws into four codes under the Wage Code Bill, the Industrial Relations Code 2020, initiating the central government's contribution of 24% of EPF wages (12% + 12%) for establishments with up to 1,000 employees and 12% (employee part) of the EPF for establishments with over 1,000 employees for two years, income tax relief to developers and homebuyers, etc. The Department for Promotion of Industry and Internal Trade identified twenty-four sectors that could add ₹20 trillion to manufacturing output when policies were fully implemented. These included food processing, toys, furniture, agro-chemicals, textiles, organic farming, iron, aluminium and copper, electronics, industrial machinery, furniture, leather, shoes and auto parts, among others. The government also started a pilot of a land bank where over 0.1 million ha of land was available for industry to start operations in India.

Going forward, India was already at or on the brink of 'stagflation', where we would see stagnation and inflation. The inflation was 'cost-push' led. We were also likely victims of 'salad bowl stagflation' where, even though pump-priming fiscal stimuli in one country failed to cure stagnation in that country, it could trigger inflation in other countries where excess liquidity would land up. However, several economists argued that we should not have an excessive obsession with 'inflation-targeting' and continue public spending to awaken India from its economic slumber.

February

Faced with adversities aplenty, FM Nirmala Sitharaman delivered a budget with a positive outlook to mend India's economy and nurse it back to health.

For rising NPAs, she proposed asset reconstruction that would take over existing stressed debt and manage and dispose of the assets to realise value. She also recapitalised public-sector banks by ₹200 billion. For the DISCOM distress in the energy sector, she proposed a revamped reforms-based, result-linked power distribution sector scheme that would be launched with an outlay of ₹3.06 trillion over five years. The scheme would assist DISCOMs in infrastructure creation, including prepaid smart metering and feeder separation and upgrade of systems well tied to financial improvements. Against a provision of ₹4.12 trillion for capital expenditure, an amount of ₹4.39 trillion seemed to have been spent during the year. Further, a provision of ₹5.54 trillion, which was 34.5% higher, plus a provision of ₹2 trillion for states and autonomous bodies for capex, was a great sign of the enhancement of infusion in the economy. For tending to the needs of long-term financing for infrastructure developers, a development finance institution with capital of ₹200 billion was proposed, which was to build a loan portfolio of ₹5 trillion over the next three years.

The FM reiterated her commitment to the NIP, updating that it was launched with 6,835 projects, but the project pipeline had expanded to 7,400 projects with around 217 projects worth ₹1.10 trillion completed. Apart from the higher capex, she also proposed an enhanced outlay of ₹1.18 trillion for MoRTH, of which ₹1.08 trillion was for capital, thereby strengthening its ability to leverage.

By March 2022, awards of 8,500 km and the completion of an additional 11,000 km of national highways was indicated. This meant a construction pace of 30 km/day. Similarly, a record sum of ₹1.10 trillion has been allotted to the railways, of which ₹1.07 trillion was for capital expenditure. Further, seven ports would be offered under PPP on a landlord model basis.

For revenue mobilisation, the FM relied upon disinvestment and an asset monetisation programme that would house assets under an asset monetisation company, including NHAI operational toll roads; transmission assets of PGCIL; oil and gas pipelines of GAIL, IOCL and HPCL; AAI airports in Tier II and III cities; other railway infrastructure assets; warehousing assets of CPSEs such as Central Warehousing Corporation and NAFED, among others; and sports stadiums. These would use the InvIT route for monetisation. Debt financing of InVITs and REITs by foreign portfolio investors was being enabled. Clearly, borrowing through off-book methods like these would help shore funding, while interest rates were at all-time lows.

At a strategic level, the PLI scheme envisioned the creation of manufacturing global champions for thirteen sectors with a commitment of nearly ₹1.97 trillion over five years, starting FY2021–22. This was expected to trigger a wave of manufacturing activity across manufacturing hubs.

March

The Union Budget delivered sweet music to our ears—from Atmanirbhar (self-reliant), we morphed to InfraNirbhar (infra-dependent)! The NIP, which was looking like a pipedream, catapulted back into the reckoning.

While Minister Nitin Gadkari was already setting his sights on achieving the 40-km/day target, Minister of State for Housing & Urban Affairs Hardeep Singh Puri was laying the ground for 1,700 km of metro rail in twenty-five cities by 2025. According to

Dr T.V. Somanathan, Secretary (Expenditure), additional funding towards meeting the enhanced infrastructure spending required for the NIP had been prioritised. The establishment of a development fund for infrastructure funding would provide long-term finance and leverage the low rates of interest trending owing to the sea of liquidity on global markets. He was candid that the NIIF could not accomplish its expectations in their entirety; hence, the need to set up this alternate institution.

Deepening the bond market, a perennial demand, was also made a priority. The asset monetisation programme for MoRTH was already underway, with InvITs set to raise funds on existing toll-yielding road assets. Minister Nitin Gadkari, not content with scaling up execution targets, urged the industry to create greenery, look at interventions like steel fibre as building material and crash barriers made of bamboo and other ways to improve sustainability.

Metro-rail plans were well funded with the need to increase the number of passengers to improve viability. Metro Neo Lite, a lighter version of the metro rail that also makes a smaller hole in the pocket, was seen as a possible answer for smaller cities that did not have enough numbers to support a larger investment. Metro-rail authorities in Andhra Pradesh and Nashik were exploring this.

Meanwhile, a sharp rebound in construction and manufacturing helped India's GDP record a marginal 0.4% growth in the October–December quarter, according to data released by the National Statistics Office (NSO). For the full year, the NSO forecast a steeper contraction of 8% than the 7.7% forecast earlier. For the quarter ending December, construction recorded a growth of 6.2% as against a contraction of 7.2% seen in the preceding quarter. Financial, real estate and professional services comprised another sector that saw a sharp revival, growing at 6.6% in the quarter as against a contraction of 9.5% in the previous quarter.

That said, while we may have been out of the recession, we were still not out of the woods.

April

When projects get stuck, costs soar. As many as 442 infrastructure projects, each worth ₹1.5 billion or more, were hit by cost overruns of over ₹4.34 trillion, according to MoSPI, meaning an average escalation of ₹10 billion per project. While the project pipeline was already at a record fourteen-year low even before the pandemic, real estate project launches also went into slowdown mode.

Property sales, however, proved to be outliers and witnessed a clear correlation to incentives. Registration of residential properties in Mumbai jumped fourfold in March to 12,696 units compared to March last year on account of a reduction in stamp duty by the Maharashtra government, according to Knight Frank India.[65] A combination of record low home loan rates, reduced property prices along with discounts and offerings with payment flexibility offered by developers helped provide a much-needed fillip to the sector. This also showed that a combination of multiple factors helps to create a momentum and that announcements in isolation do not necessarily work. Hyderabad and the Mumbai Metropolitan Region recorded the highest bump in sales over the same quarter last year, as per Anarock Research.[66]

It was a good ride for the roads sector, as we managed to cross the target set for FY2020–21 of 11,000 km at 30 km/day. Minister Nitin Gadkari announced that in 2020–21, MoRTH constructed 12,205 km of national highways with a construction rate of 34 km/day.[67] Divestment also gained traction with companies being prepared for IPOs. The Development Finance Institution was being set up at a rapid pace with a clear goal to serve up funds for infrastructure.

May

As an intense crisis hits the Centre, the central command often abdicates responsibility and decision-making ability to the states. This was witnessed during the COVID-19 crisis and now with the mounting disaster of its virulent second wave.

As stated before, states hold the key to India's economic growth. Dynamic chief ministers and their able finance ministers can do a *jugalbandi* like Narasimha Rao and Manmohan Singh and turn around the fortunes of their states.

In the past, we saw Nitish Kumar do this in Bihar as his government constructed roads in the state at breakneck speed and brought in prosperity. The state, which used to be notorious for its potholed roads or no roads in most areas, now boasted 27,000 km of state highways and district roads and 96,417 km of rural roads, all accomplished in the past fifteen years. Bridges had enabled better access for people all over the state. Bihar was now a power-surplus state and villages had electricity supply. There was hardly any area in the state that did not get over 20 hours' power supply. Har Ghar Nal Ka Jal, the piped water supply scheme, provided further convenience to its citizens.

In fact, Bihar was poised for double-digit growth had it not been for the pandemic, though as per the state's estimates, it was likely to increase its share in India's GDP. Maharashtra had the highest GSDP among the twenty-eight Indian states and eight union territories. It contributed 14.2% of India's GDP at current prices, followed by Uttar Pradesh, Tamil Nadu, Karnataka and Gujarat. Last fiscal, Tamil Nadu was second and Gujarat third, while Karnataka was at the fourth slot. The top five states shared 46.6% of India's total economy. Five southern states together accounted for close to 30%, while eight states of the Northeast shared 2.8%.

Although all states were staring at deficits, some states like Uttar Pradesh, West Bengal, Madhya Pradesh and Rajasthan indicated an expansion in FY2021. The speed with which a state could grapple with and then normalise its healthcare, business and commerce would decide its fate. States that deployed healthcare measures with determination and, at the same time, procured vaccines for their citizens, would restore normalcy sooner. Those in denial or who continued to host mass gatherings with low vaccination cover would push back growth.

Meanwhile, according to Care Ratings, in the capital goods segment, there was recovery and positive growth for tractors, agricultural equipment and power-generating equipment.[68] However, a sharp fall in production was witnessed in air-conditioning systems, cranes, construction machinery, electronic conductors and wires and firefighting equipment between April and February 2021 over the same period in the previous year.

All considered, the hard reality was that our economic trajectory had lost five years of momentum to demonetisation, state elections and COVID-19.

June

As we have done in the past, India would overcome the crisis caused by COVID-19; however, we would have paid a very high cost. One, we may have pushed the 273 million Indians who had overcome poverty between 2005 and 2015 back to misery. Two, we would have pushed our economic prowess back by a decade; this would be reflected in the strength of our currency, our ability to negotiate trade deals in time to come, our ratings, our ability to attract FDI, our ability to retain and attract innovative talent and, consequently, our future.

Meanwhile, as the country slowly emerged from the severe second wave, policymakers in the central government were actively implementing solutions for kickstarting the economy. More recently, the establishment of the National Bank for Infrastructure & Financing Development (NaBFID) would ensure long-term financing for major infrastructure projects in critical segments like railway, urban transportation, irrigation and roads and highways.

Further, with the losses accumulated by state power distribution companies continuing to go north, the central government set in motion a series of reforms to help mitigate cash flow stress in what is often perceived to be the weakest link in the country's power supply chain. However, the task was not expected to be easy, as the states were likely to play hardball because electricity was included in the Concurrent List.

July

Despite the devastation caused by the pandemic, the corporate results coming in belied any financial disaster. Of the Q4 results (January–March 2021) of 1,800 companies analysed, revenues from operations rose by 17% over the previous year, PAT grew by a tremendous 523% and operating profits grew by 64%. If we excluded banking, finance and oil, operational revenues rose by 22% and PAT by 180%.

GST collections, which touched ₹1.23 trillion in March, jumped to ₹1.41 trillion in April and clocked ₹1.02 trillion in May 2021, indicating a healthy trend so far. Advance collection of corporation tax and personal income tax in Q4 grew 146% over last year, while overall net direct taxes doubled during this period compared to 2020. According to ICRA Ratings, the jump in direct tax collection in Q1 FY2022 relative to Q1 FY2021 reflected healthy exports and a continuation of various industrial and construction activities, given the lower stringency of the staggered regional lockdowns in 2021 versus the nationwide lockdown in 2020.[69]

Exports did extremely well, with $156 billion from January to May 2021 being the highest figure ever during this period. Trade between China and India grew to over $48 billion between January and May 2021. Exports to China surged by 90.2%. China had overtaken the US to become India's largest trading partner in 2020, with total India–China trade in the financial year worth $86.4 billion.

These figures showed that corporate India was not as fragile as it seemed when the country imposed a national lockdown in Q1 FY2020–21. Having said that, business sentiment hung on a thread. Any major calamity could be the last straw that broke the camel's back. Areas that seemed to be attracting investments were 'green', 'automation' and 'digital'. Features that enabled these were finding favour with customers and investors alike. The steel sector was making abnormal profits and clearly could not only kickstart the investment cycle but also shed its investment shyness and leapfrog private capital contribution, which had been trailing for several years.

The GDP for this year was projected at 7.5% by the UN, 9.3% by Moody's and 9.5% by CRISIL. The number would be higher or lower depending on how hard we were hit by the expected 'third wave'. If the pace of vaccination was anything to go by, the hope was that the third wave wouldn't hit us as badly as the second.

The ₹6.3 trillion stimulus package announced by the finance minister, representing about 3% of the GDP, was mostly in the form of credit guarantees that did not need immediate spending. Direct fiscal measures were limited to the extended free food grains scheme, health infrastructure credit guarantee scheme and additional spending on BharatNet, amounting to ₹1.2 trillion. This would provide only token relief to the hard-hit sectors.

In April 2021, sales of passenger vehicles, including cars, SUVs and larger passenger vehicles, stood at the same level as in 2016. Electricity consumption during the second wave was equal to 2014, sale of two wheelers plunged to levels attained a decade ago and core industries slipped to levels attained in March 2017. In sum, we went back three to five years in terms of demand and output. We expected to come back to pre-COVID levels by 2023–24 for several consumption and production indicators. In construction, the gross value added (GVA) equalled the levels in 2018.

August

According to MoSPI, of the 1,737 projects of over ₹1.5 billion that it monitored, 470 reported a cost overrun of over ₹4.4 trillion till April 2021 and 525 projects reported a time overrun. The time overrun was attributed to a host of issues, including delay in land acquisition, forest or environment clearance, lack of infrastructure support and linkages, supply of equipment, fund constraints, geological surprises, change in scope, delay in tendering, shortage of labour, contractual issues, state-wise lockdown owing to COVID-19, legal cases and the law-and-order situation. Expenditure incurred on the 1,737 projects till April 2021 was around ₹13.2 trillion, which was 49.3% of the anticipated cost of the projects. So, having spent half the cost, we incurred an overrun of 16%.

Technology can make construction precise and timely. It can help plan well and save wastage. There was a need for cost control, which meant wastage had to be curbed. Timeliness was also being rewarded in infrastructure projects with bonuses and in realty projects by avoiding penalties. NITI Aayog recommended the use of BIM, estimating a 20% saving with it. According to an Autodesk IDC report released in August 2020, 66% of construction companies said digital transformation was a key priority in driving much-needed changes to processes, business models and ecosystems. While over 70% of construction companies in India were only starting their digital transformation journeys, large infrastructure projects had already embraced this technology at an advanced stage.[70]

The Delhi Metro Rail Corporation (DMRC) implemented custom-made software to monitor the progress of its Phase-4 corridors and the Patna Metro as part of a major initiative to digitise operations. The integrated project management software (IPMS) enables integration of other construction-related software such as Primavera schedules for project planning and 3D BIM and a mobile app, through which real-time, on-site progress can be uploaded.

Maha Metro was the first organisation in the country to implement 5D-BIM project visualisation. This digital project management concept integrates many software seamlessly and employs 5D BIM to accurately predict outcomes and timelines. This unique system enabled Maha Metro to tightly control quality, cost and time. Nagpur Metro achieved a saving of 10% over the estimated cost in the DPR using technology. Maha Metro geared up to replicate the 5D-BIM benefits in the Pune Metro project as well.

The contractor for the structural steel framework of the Statue of Unity extensively relied upon Tekla Structures' truly constructible technology to complete the statue in a record thirty-three months, a full two months ahead of schedule—the project holds the distinction of being among the fastest to be completed. Even the Samruddhi Expressway, the 701-km project that connects Mumbai and Nagpur, used BIM services for virtual monitoring of on-site construction activities. It also used 4D simulation services to assess accurate quantities and for cost estimation.

These technologies are more cost-effective when there is scale. Even prefab and precast technologies don't deliver results for small projects. Given that there was momentum in the construction of our road network, standard elements could use the advantages of precast.

When it comes to investment in BIM-based software, 47% of construction companies in India claimed they had already invested in BIM-based workflows. These were mostly used by private companies and utilised for overseas clients. So, the awareness existed, but it could only be deployed when developers took the onus of doing it.

September

A report by Cushman and Wakefield rated India as the second-most sought-after manufacturing destination in the world. It ranked second only to China and surpassed the US to bag the ranking. However, India slipped a rank in the cost scenario to the third rank, and was overtaken by Indonesia. The Cushman and Wakefield 2021 Global Manufacturing Risk Index stated that India could benefit from relocations from China to other parts of Asia, as it already had an established base in pharmaceuticals, chemicals and engineering—sectors that continued to be the focus of US–China trade tensions. It recommended reforms in land and labour laws, as these were critical to ensuring India's success as a global manufacturing hub.[71]

However, when it came to the risk scenario, which accounted for lower levels of economic and political risks, India lost its prime spots. The country was clubbed in the third quartile of the rankings along with Malaysia, Belgium, Indonesia, Bulgaria, Romania, Thailand, Hungary, Colombia, Italy, Peru and Vietnam, indicating high risk. On top of the first quartile was China, followed by Canada, the US, Finland and the Czech Republic. The second quartile had countries like Lithuania, France, Netherlands, Spain, Poland, Japan and the UK.

Exports crossed $35 billion in July and $34 billion in March 2021, and remained above $30 billion for the fifth consecutive month in July. PM Modi set an ambitious target of $400 billion for merchandise export in 2021–22, directing the Ministry of Commerce to work on a detailed roadmap that included finding products with export potential in virtually every district of the country, roping in industry bodies and involving Indian missions abroad. Exports of construction equipment like JCB, Schwing Stetter and ACE were also on an upswing. And the $1 trillion infrastructure plan launched by US President Joe Biden had a great opportunity for India's engineering back-office business.

Further, with an intent to push the Make in India and Atmanirbhar Bharat initiatives, the Cabinet approved a ₹26,058 crore PLI scheme for automobiles and ₹120 crore for the drone industry. This initiative was expected to boost the manufacturing capabilities of India, creating employment for over 7.6 lakh people. Moreover, it was likely to attract automobile giants like Tesla to manufacture in India. Recently, Tesla had demanded a reduction in import duties on electric vehicles (EVs) in India.

The PLI scheme was part of the announcement of the overall PLI schemes for thirteen sectors made during the Union Budget 2021–22, with a total outlay of ₹1.97 lakh crore. With such a massive boost from the Indian government, minimum additional production in India was expected to be around ₹37.5 lakh crore over five years, with additional employment of nearly ₹1 crore. The drone industry was picking up fast in India; with the encouraging PLI scheme for the drone industry, a turnover of ₹900 crore from drone manufacturing was expected in the next three years, according to Civil Aviation Minister Jyotiraditya Scindia.[72]

That apart, it was evident that the private and public sectors had to join hands by increasing the capital expenditure to bring back the Indian economy to a pre-pandemic level. So why did we need private participation? Within the GDP was the private final consumption expenditure (PFCE), which accounted for 55–56% of all national GDP in a year and was the biggest driver of economic growth. Another important driver was GFCF, a measure of the money spent by businesses when they make investments. PFCE and GFCF together accounted for 88–89% of all GDP in India. Unless this variable improved sharply, PLI schemes and other government initiatives could not offer any benefits to our economy.

Further, India could prosper if it started diversifying its investment. China Plus One, also known as Plus One, was the business strategy to avoid investing only in China and instead diversifying into other countries. The policy had started showing positive signs. As per available data, the export of ready-made garments of all textiles increased 67% during the first five months of the current fiscal year. Japan became the first country to offer subsidies to its companies to move production out of China into other South Asian countries. India received $64 billion in FDI in 2020, making it the fifth-largest inflow in the world, according to the World Investment Report 2021 by UNCTAD.[73]

October

Just when India was inching ahead to achieve higher rankings in the annual ease of doing business survey, the World Bank scrapped it in a shock announcement—an independent auditor found, among other things, that China had managed to successfully inflate its ranking in the 2018 report by putting pressure on top bank officials.

Among 190 countries, India earned the rank 63 in the survey in 2020, improving its ranking by 79 positions in the five years between 2014 and 2019. In a report, consultancy firm McKinsey stated that even as India rose from rank 130 overall in 2016 to 63 in 2020 in the business index, Indian companies still faced obstacles, ranging from delayed payments for public procurement to tedious processes for obtaining permits.[74] Even though the survey was abandoned, NITI Aayog took on the mantle and continued its drive to focus on streamlining forms, initiating single-window clearances, simplifying land acquisition, instituting labour reforms and rationalising the costs of power to industry.

Addressing the nation on India's seventy-fifth Independence Day, PM Modi had announced the launch of the Pradhan Mantri Gati Shakti National Master Plan to help local manufacturers become globally competitive and develop possibilities of future economic zones. Meanwhile, his visit to the US was another show of the government's intention to focus on the economy. The PLI scheme for thirteen sectors, the vehicle scrappage policy, the renewable energy policy, the withdrawal of retrospective tax, the mining policy, drone policy and the Model Tenancy Act were all steps towards strengthening the economy and making it attractive for foreign and domestic investors.

The launch of the National Asset Monetisation Pipeline (NAMP) to raise resources for the NIP was a good move. The government's track record in raising resources through divestment was so poor that it was bound to attract criticism. Our PSUs collectively contributed profits of ₹1.75 trillion in 2018 against ₹430 billion in 2003–04. However, the share of contribution of the profits declined from 2.1% of GDP in 2004 to 0.4% of GDP in 2018. It was clear that reducing government shareholding in PSUs would enhance their productive efficiency as they would become more accountable.

November

The NIP envisaged an average spend of ₹20 trillion per year over the next five years. However, reports from MoSPI were citing a regular overrun of an average of ₹4 trillion per annum on a base of half the size of the project outlay envisaged. This clearly meant that the project overrun was likely to cross ₹6 trillion in the coming year if the government managed to step up spending by 50% of the existing spend on infrastructure. Further, going forward, the project overrun was likely to hit ₹8 trillion in 2022–23 if the NIP got going full throttle.

The Centre issued a strict advisory to different ministries and departments to reduce delays and cost overruns that had reached a staggering ₹4.30 trillion in 1,670 central-sector projects. The 1,670 projects spanned twenty-five sectors, including roads, railways, petroleum, power, coal, telecom and fertiliser, among others. The original cost of implementation of these projects was about ₹21.66 trillion, while the present anticipated completion cost was around ₹26 trillion, reflecting a cost overrun that amounted to almost 78%

of capital expenditure proposed this fiscal. Further, one of every five infrastructure projects had a delay of over five years.

The PM Gati Shakti intended to save 5–6% of costs spent on logistics, amounting to savings of ₹20 trillion. Cost estimates were also not being reflected accurately as project agencies were not reporting the revised cost estimates and commissioning schedules for many projects. The report listed fifteen reasons for delays, which included lockdowns in states owing to COVID-19, law-and-order problems, land acquisition issues, obtaining forest/environment clearance, contractual issues and inadequate manpower. Gati Shakti was launched to create savings through greater coordination among various central ministries and departments and with state governments and local bodies.

The roads sector had already seen a lag in the award of contracts. A hope of overcoming such obstacles was seen in the award of highway projects, which though lower than FY2020–21 were more than double of those in the same period (April–September) in FY2019–20.

The stock market had been beating gains in all asset classes as the Sensex continued to move north. Notably, one of the most undervalued asset classes could have been the roads sector, which could fetch rich gains as part of the asset monetisation plan. The previous year, IRB had bagged the Mumbai–Pune Expressway tolling contract for ₹82.62 billion for ten years. The 94.5-km expressway was India's first six-lane, concrete, high-speed, access-controlled tolled expressway that significantly reduced the travel time between Mumbai and Pune. Earlier, in 2004, IRB had won a fifteen-year contract from MSRDC for toll collection to IRB Ltd for an upfront payment of ₹9.18 billion for fifteen years. The same road asset had appreciated about ten times in fifteen years! With the government greenlighting second airports in Mumbai and Bengaluru, the aviation space was also likely to see a build-up in valuations. However, the biggest contributors to the ₹6 trillion asset monetisation plan were roads, railways and the power sector.

December

PM Modi retreated and withdrew the proposed farm laws—a step back for progressive reforms for the sector, but a step forward for democracy. Meanwhile, critical reforms were silently underway that could have a cascading impact on our national assets on which we proposed to spend ₹110 trillion over the next five years under the NIP.

Public procurement policy norms were tweaked to allow quality-oriented procurement. The guidelines issued by the Department of Expenditure's Public Procurement Division now allowed the selection of bidders for works and non-consultancy services through alternative procurement methods like quality-cum-cost-based selection (QCBS). Earlier, under the General Financial Rules (GFR), 2017, which government agencies and ministries had to follow, QCBS was used only for procurement in cases where the quality of consultancy services was of prime concern. Two other additional methods—L1 and single-source selection—were also recommended in GFR 2017. According to the revised guidelines, L1 or 'least cost selection', would no longer be the only tendering format to select bidders for projects.

L1 was so far the preferred method used by ministries, public agencies and PSUs to select the lowest bidders to carry out standard or routine works/non-consultancy services like audit and engineering design of non-complex works. In times of early infrastructure development during UPA 1 and UPA 2, L1 had driven several private companies to make ridiculous bids, endangering their sustainability. In the L1 system, a bidder is selected only on the basis of the lowest cost with no 'technical score' qualification requirement while QCBS evaluates a bidder based on a combination of technical and quality scores. However, the maximum weightage for non-financial parameters could not exceed 30%. The revised guidelines allowed procurement agencies to use QCBS where the procurement had been declared to be 'a quality-oriented procedure by the competent authority' and where the estimated value of procurement did not exceed ₹10 crore. To declare a project fit for QCBS, a competent authority had been defined and the need for a technical committee comprising independent technical and financial members laid out. QCBS was also the preferred mode for international competitive bidding.

The arrest of former SBI chairman Pratip Chaudhuri in relation to a complaint by a loan defaulter caused a protest against undue vigilance action in bona fide commercial decisions. This was despite an assurance by FM Nirmala Sitharaman last year while announcing that banks should automatically extend loans to eligible MSME sector borrowers without the fear of the three Cs: CBI, CVC and CAG. In a similar vein, the review of decisions taken by the competent authority in procurement deserved proper guidelines to be followed.

The Centre instructed public authorities to refrain from 'routinely' appealing against arbitration/court awards relating to disputes involving publicly funded projects, unless there was a compelling case, including a realistic probability of success in court. As its instructions pointed out, there was a perception that such appeals were sometimes made to postpone the problem and defer personal accountability. Casual appealing in arbitration/court cases had resulted in payment of heavy damages/compensation/ additional interest cost, thereby causing more harm to the exchequer, in addition to tarnishing the image of the government. Indeed, with an ever-growing chasm between estimated and actual expenditure, procurement reform had the potential to be truly seismic.

2022

January

The past year, the economy struggled with inflation and sluggish demand, sometimes owing to logistical and supply chain nightmares. While the economy was hit by the second vicious COVID-19 wave in the first quarter, the second quarter showed a quick recovery in urban areas.

Despite a tepid Q1, as the pace of vaccination accelerated and cases declined from a high of 400,000 a day to 40,000 a day, the economy began to purr again. Resultantly, Q2 saw a turnaround with a pickup in capital goods imports, production of capital goods and cement production. Rural consumption, too, exhibited recovery in Q2, backed by a buoyant rabi harvest, good kharif prospects, government transfers and the MNREGA programme. Employment numbers improved in June–July and strengthened in September. While Q3 numbers for construction, too, would show some cheer, the sector had not regained its true momentum as during 2018–19 and 2019–20.

However, far-reaching policy measures were taken that could propel the sector in the future. These included a cut in corporate taxes, taxation reforms, introduction of the PLI scheme for thirteen major sectors, enhanced focus on infrastructure development and asset monetisation by the government, initiatives under the Atmanirbhar Bharat programme and proactive liquidity measures by the RBI. The mega schemes—the NIP amounting to ₹100 lakh crore and the National Monetisation Pipeline (NMP) involving

₹6 lakh crore—were also expected to provide a major thrust to infrastructure spending and uplift potential output.

Further, India's newfound success in inspiring innovation and entrepreneurship was validated as it added thirty-three unicorns (enterprises valued at over $1 billion each) in a single year and was the third highest hub for startups globally.

February

Infrastructure development was given a huge thrust in the Union Budget 2022–23 by the finance minister. The capital outlay was raised by 35% to ₹7.5 trillion and the fiscal deficit was contained at 6.9% of GDP. There were some noteworthy initiatives announced.

For instance, the allocation of ₹1 trillion to assist states in catalysing investments including those for PM Gati Shakti in the form of a fifty-year interest-free loan was over and above the normal borrowing allowed to states. The utilisation could include PMGSY, digitisation, optic fibre network, town planning schemes, etc. Data for the past five years (2016–17 to 2020–21) revealed that more than half the projects (52.3%) were taken up in five states: Gujarat, Maharashtra, Karnataka, Andhra Pradesh and Tamil Nadu. This would allow other states to follow suit.

After a gap of six years, urban planning a.k.a. the Smart Cities Mission was rejuvenated with the emphasis on nurturing megacities and reimagining Tier 2 and 3 cities. A committee was formed to resuscitate this vertical. Strategically, villages in border areas were covered under the Vibrant Villages Programme, which would include roads, housing, village infrastructure, renewable energy, etc. The contracts for laying optic fibre in all villages, including remote areas, would be awarded under BharatNet through a PPP in 2022–23 and was targeted to be completed in 2025.

The PM Awas Yojana had been delivering effectively and another 8 million houses were to be completed in both urban and rural areas with an allotment of ₹480 billion. Piped water for each household had been delivered to 55 million households, and another 38 million would be covered with an allotment of ₹600 billion.

The $5.9 billion Ken–Betwa Link Project, which transferred water from the river Ken to Betwa, aimed to provide irrigation benefits to 9.08 lakh ha of farmers' lands, drinking water supply to 6.2 million people, 103 MW of hydro and 27 MW of solar power. Five more draft DPRs of river links were finalised.

In the transportation and logistics sectors, the plans included highways for 25,000 km, 100 new cargo terminals to be built in the next three years, contracts for the implementation of multimodal logistics parks at four locations through the PPP mode and manufacturing 400 new-generation Vande Bharat trains with improved energy-efficiency. For the roads sector, which had slowed down after having executed 13,435 km in 2020–21 (an average of 37 km/day), the government had set a target of 12,000 km for the current financial year against which 5,118 km was constructed as on 30 November 2021 (barely 21 km/day). The government lowered the target for the year to 33 km/day from the 40 km/day set earlier. The original target was to build 14,600 km of highways in 2021–22.

The PM Gati Shakti Master Plan for Expressways was being formulated to facilitate faster movement of people and goods. The national highways network would be expanded by 25,000 km in 2022–23, and ₹20,000 crore would be mobilised through innovative ways of financing to complement public resources. Provision of surety bonds to fill in for bank guarantees was a welcome step to add to the capacity of existing EPC contractors and encourage new EPC contractors into the fold. Also, the Parvatmala scheme aimed at connecting the hilly regions was likely to see 60 km of eight ropeway projects take off. These would be environment-friendly, encourage the SME sector and boost tourism.

Further, several new-age businesses were recognised and provided for as an indication of the government's focus on the future and the youth. Encouragement to startups and sectors such as clean tech, drones, wearable devices, blended fuel, land record management, battery swapping, AVGC, 5G, etc., were laudable. And initiatives on skilling and education by using portals, television channels and digital universities, backed by the completion of the laying of the fibreoptic network by 2025, were steps in the right direction.

For the year 2022–23, the Fifteenth Finance Commission earmarked ₹229.08 billion for municipalities. Of this, ₹72.27 billion were earmarked for million-plus cities and ₹156.81 crore for non-million plus cities. The grant would be divided state-wise and devolved to the cities from the states based on their population. Accountability-based funding had got cities worried. Earlier, 80% was given as a basic grant and only 20% was linked to reforms. Now, with 100% of grants linked to performance, states had to work on a war footing. Grants were linked to safe water and energy resilience; this was crucial if India had to meet its aggressive SDG targets.

The projects planned under various corridors were substantial and could fill the vacuum in India's project pipelines. The industrial corridor programme was set to create greenfield, smart, industrial cities with sustainable 'plug-n-play' ICT-enabled utilities, which would facilitate manufacturing investments into the country by providing quality, reliable, sustainable and resilient infrastructure to industries. The government approved eleven such corridors consisting of thirty-two projects to be developed in four phases. Each would have multiple townships and industrial cities. The 701-km Samriddhi Expressway from Mumbai to Nagpur was creating nineteen new townships; one of them was already underway.

Other than roads and metro rail, the year 2022–23 was also expected to see irrigation, power, railways and mining with above-normal commercial expressions.

March

Russia invaded Ukraine and set in motion a series of actions that would have global repercussions. The oil price was set to boil, having breached $105 per barrel. The commodity cycle was also on a boil again. India's position to stay neutral was on trial, and the American favours that the country managed to secure were set to get tested. However, inflation was the real danger for India's economy as this war panned out.

Meanwhile, the results of the Uttar Pradesh elections were expected to indicate how much of the electorate favoured economic development and how much it favoured the caste issue. The state's report card on various parameters of development painted a sorry picture, unlike Bihar, which drove the state to development with its road networks during Nitish Kumar's tenure.

The PM's National Hydrogen Mission of producing 5 million tonnes of green hydrogen by 2030 and the related development of renewable energy capacity saw the green hydrogen and ammonia policy announced in February. Hydrogen and ammonia are considered future fuels and ideal substances to replace fossil fuels. As the production of these fuels is highly energy-consuming, using power from renewable energy to produce green hydrogen and green ammonia was one of the major steps towards COP26 commitments.

JCB invested ₹10 billion to scale up production of a new range of products at its latest factory in Vadodara, Gujarat—where the first phase would commence in April—boosting its strategy to export the new range of Make-in-India products. Exports for the company grew 300% the previous year, validating that India could be used as a sourcing hub for manufacturing products, even for markets such as the US and the UK.

Demand for housing in India continued to remain extremely robust, according to Deepak Parekh, Chairman, HDFC, who emphasised that the greatest mark of confidence was the strong pipeline of new launches, surpassing pre-pandemic levels.[75] The demand for housing continued to be from first-time homeowners as well as those moving into larger homes or houses in other locations. However, building material and construction costs were taking a toll. The rise in costs of raw materials was a concern—the price of pet coke increased by over 50%, while diesel price was up 14.4% year on year. Cement companies had already begun passing on the cost to retain profitability. The all-India average cement price increased by 5% year on year to ₹365 per 50 kg bag in January and seemed to be headed towards ₹400 per 50 kg bag. Labour and other construction costs also went up and, therefore, real estate prices were likely to firm up.

During 2021, the Brihanmumbai Municipal Corporation (BMC) approved 2,473 building projects, earning it a record ₹132 billion as premium fees from developers towards a built-up area of 150 million sq. ft, equal to roughly fifteen Nariman Point-sized real estate spaces on account of the 50% discount in development premium it offered to shore up its revenues. In comparison, about 1,995 projects were approved in the pre-pandemic year of 2019. These projects had a built-up area of around 90 million sq. ft. This was likely to see a spurt in real estate supply in Mumbai. We were likely to witness a sharp rise in real estate prices in lesser served areas versus more popular areas, which could face a glut.

April

Construction equipment sales suffered on account of multiple factors, the most noteworthy being the significant slowdown in road construction activity hitting a four-year low of 21.3 km/day over the period April to November 2021 compared to 25.8 km/day in the same period the previous year. Minister Nitin Gadkari acknowledged that the current pace of constructing 8,045 km until February 2022 worked out to 24.08 km/day, compared to the targeted 40 km/day, or 14,600 km for the full year.[76]

The Uttar Pradesh polls established that development was a key success factor. It was therefore expected that the states holding elections between now and 2024—Gujarat, Himachal Pradesh, Meghalaya, Nagaland, Tripura, Karnataka, Chhattisgarh, Madhya Pradesh, Mizoram, Rajasthan and Telangana—were likely to see an expeditious execution of road projects. NHAI has announced a ₹1 trillion plan with 100 aspirational districts that would build 5,795 km. In Karnataka, an MoU was expected that would give a big push to ring-road projects in different cities in the state. As per the MoU, the state government would have to share just 25% of the land acquisition cost and give exemption in GST/royalty for steel, cement and other construction materials. Other states were likely to follow.

Meanwhile, real estate demand was steadily rising. HDFC recently announced that it had disbursed a record ₹2 trillion home loans. The drivers were lower interest rates, stable property prices, the government's thrust on affordable housing, improved affordability, favourable demographics, increasing urbanisation and rising aspirations. The demand was from actual users and those wanting to upgrade to larger homes.

At the mega event Wings India, Civil Aviation Minister Jyotiraditya Scindia assured participants that while India had seventy-four airports in 2013–14, in the past seven years, sixty-six airports had been added, taking the total number to 140, including helipads and water aerodromes. He expected this number to reach 220 by 2024–25.

The railways had an estimated capital expenditure of ₹2.46 trillion for the upcoming fiscal year. Further, it would spend around ₹300 billion on the development of seventy-five stations across the country. While the railways procured 7,000 wagons the previous year, it was expected to procure 90,000 wagons over the next three years.

While all this was music to our ears, India's GDP forecast had been lowered to 4.6% by the UN, owing to the ongoing war between Russia and Ukraine, which was likely to cast a crippling effect on our costs. While Russia was expected to experience a deep recession this year, significant slowdowns in growth were predicted in parts of Western Europe and Central, South and Southeast Asia.

May

From FY2022–23, the top 1,000 listed companies in India (by market capitalisation) would need to prepare a 'business responsibility and sustainability report' (or BRSR), containing detailed environmental, social and governance (ESG) disclosures. The BRSR had to be a part of the annual report, which gets notified to the stock exchanges, published on official company websites and separately provided to shareholders. Before the BRSR became mandatory, the top 1,000 listed companies in India (by market capitalisation) had to publish a relatively shorter 'business responsibility report'.

In the current environment, the ESG agenda would remain a high priority for the engineering and construction industry. Governance would be a sensitive issue given the size and complexity of contracts, competitive bidding processes and the need to engage with both public and private stakeholders and prevent bribery, corruption and anticompetitive behaviour. The building and construction sector was responsible for 39% of carbon emissions globally, according to the World Green Building Council, and hence had to work hard to match the goals and commitments. Therefore, carbon reduction and environmental initiatives were a business imperative for contractors.

India ranked a lowly 120 among 165 countries in its progress towards achieving all seventeen SDGs (sustainable development goals), lower than Sri Lanka, Nepal and Bangladesh. Reliance Industries Ltd (RIL), Vedanta Ltd, JSW Energy and HDFC Bank all planned to go carbon neutral in the next few decades.

Good ESG scores were helping companies tap into newer pools of capital and build valuations to attract investors in these reorganised entities, while enhancing shareholder value.

Vedanta was restructuring its operations and could demerge and list its aluminium, iron and steel, and oil and gas businesses as standalone entities. Restructuring a mammoth like RIL meant transferring its gasification assets to a wholly owned unit, which would help it produce hydrogen to establish a hydrogen ecosystem, while JSW Energy was housing its green energy business in a new wholly owned unit, JSW Neo Energy Ltd, as it continued to keep the thermal business as part of the main company. The green business was expected to contribute more than 62% of JSW's earnings before interest, taxes, depreciation and amortisation.

Despite earlier assessments that the Russia–Ukraine war would be a short and swift strike-and-occupy exercise, it turned out to be a twister, disrupting supply chains and ballooning inflation to astronomical levels. All margins were under pressure. Companies were sitting with orders but their inability to supply products owing to critical part shortages was causing them to bleed. Fortunately, the building and construction industry was not facing these issues, although inflation caused by cement, steel and bitumen hit margins and time schedules.

Holcim, the owner of companies like ACC, Ambuja and Lafarge among cement brands, was India's second-largest producer of cement with a combined capacity of 45 million tonne, excluding Lafarge, which had a capacity of 8 million tonnes. Sweden, where Holcim is based, had the highest carbon tax rate worldwide at $137 per metric tonne of CO2 equivalent. Holcim decided to exit the Indian cement business and put it on the block. Adani and JSW groups were the frontrunners for this deal. Holcim's move may have been in line with its goals to reduce its carbon footprint to net zero. It even joined the Science-Based Targets initiative, detailing its net-zero pathway to 2050. Holcim would be a torchbearer in ESG within the building material industry.

June

Holcim's divestment of its preeminent position as the second largest cement manufacturer in India with brand Ambuja and brand ACC happened in a matter of days despite a price tag of over $10 billion. Not only did the deal close soon, the open offers it triggered were also rolled out in quick succession, making the total investment for the winning bidder, the Adani Group, $10.5 billion, plus another $3.5 billion towards the acquisition of shares through the open offer. The private sector, which had remained shy for the past eight years, was seen making a beeline for this acquisition, with JSW Group and Aditya Birla Group stitching solutions for finances and beating policy hurdles respectively.

This was one of the biggest deals in the history of building materials in India. The Adani Group was particularly proactive, snapping up airports, roads, ports, logistics, green energy and now cement too. In December, Adani Enterprises won contracts from the Uttar Pradesh government to build three stretches of the 594-km Ganga Expressway. The fourth section was awarded to IRB Infrastructure, where Adani's share of work was 80% of the total project. Now, Adani was in talks to raise ₹120 billion from SBI towards this massive project. Its capex plan for the next two years included $4.2 billion for airports and $2.2 billion for roads alone. The group's roads portfolio comprised fourteen projects with over 5,000 lane km, with an asset value exceeding ₹41,000 crore spread across India.

Meanwhile, it was heartening to see FM Nirmala Sitharaman proactively moving by imposing export taxes on steel, which had seen exports surge from 12 Mt to 18 Mt against a total annual production output of 120 Mt in FY2022. Excessive exports would have eventually led to high steel prices in the domestic markets and caused inflation. Tariffs on new iron ores and concentrates were raised to 50% from 30%, and duties on pellets hiked to 45% from zero. The government also removed import tariffs for coking coal and coke. These actions were expected to collectively help cool down the steel price steam.

The auction of mineral blocks stabilised as 186 mines had been put on sale so far. Of the 186 mineral blocks, twenty-eight were auctioned in the past two months and forty-six were successfully sold in FY2022, according to the Ministry of Mines.[77] In early May 2022, India faced a significant power crisis that severely impacted both industrial operations and daily life. Many industries came to a near standstill, while households endured unscheduled power outages lasting 8–12 hours, coinciding with an intense and early summer heatwave. The crisis even led to tragic outcomes, including patient deaths in hospitals due to power shortages. This situation brought to the fore the government's lack of preparedness in managing the coal and power sectors. The government's response was fragmented, with no clear strategy to address the ongoing crisis, which persisted until August. In response to the crisis, the government invoked Section 11 of the Electricity Act, compelling all imported coal-based thermal power plants to generate electricity under 'extraordinary circumstances'. The crisis was primarily attributed to a 'coal shortage', as many coal-fired power plants faced critical shortages in coal stocks. The looming power crisis and shortage of coal prompted Coal India to accelerate its plans. It was eyeing 12% growth in production during the current financial year and received environmental clearance for twenty proposals, which would add an incremental capacity of 22 Mt per year. Additionally, thirty-six mining projects were cleared by Coal India with a sanctioned capacity of 333 Mt and an incremental capacity of 220 Mt.

Through its implementing agencies, the government reportedly constructed 10,457 km of National Highways in 2021–22, a 24% decrease from the previous fiscal despite the downscaled target of 12,000 km (the earlier target was 40 km/day, which would have translated to 14,600 km). So, in effect, 4,143 km less than originally planned. However, according to Union Minister Nitin

Gadkari, it aimed to construct a record 18,000 km of highways in 2022–23 at a pace of 50 km/day! The FY2023 target was 72% higher than what was constructed in road length during the past fiscal year—a tall ask indeed. Further, the government planned to award construction contracts of 18,000 km in FY2023, according to the minister.

July

MoSPI monitors infrastructure projects worth ₹1.5 billion and above. Of 1,579 such projects, 425 reported cost overruns of over ₹4.8 trillion till March 2022; 664 projects reported time overrun. Expenditure incurred on the 1,579 projects till March 2022 was around ₹13.9 trillion, which was 51.9% of the anticipated cost of the projects.

Technologies in projects offer the benefits of precision, low wastage, higher productivity, integration and pre-emptive planning. The complexity of projects and their scale had propelled the need for adoption of BIM, 3D modelling, digital twins and AI. In parallel, the government enabled policies that favour the use of geospatial and drone technologies. Similarly, construction equipment with enhanced and advanced features was now appearing more within reach owing to the demands of projects and project developers.

August

L&T's consolidated orderbook was at a record of ₹363,448 trillion, with international orders having a share of 28%. CEO & MD S.N. Subrahmanyan had been at work chiselling away at restructuring the business with multiple verticals. He shaved off some businesses that were not profitable for the organisation any more. The company decidedly moved out of BOT (build-operate-transfer) and BOOT (build-own-operate-transfer) projects. It was also actively looking to exit the Hyderabad Metro. On the other hand, solar EPC, which was tiny earlier (with 25–50 MW projects), was now bagging gigawatt-scale orders, and the infrastructure and hydrocarbon businesses continued to grow.

L&T also intended to advance its green business portfolio, which constituted 38% of its standalone revenues in FY2022, including forays into new businesses of manufacturing storage batteries. The company's board approved entry into the green energy business through green hydrogen and derivatives and advanced chemistry cell batteries (such as lithium-ion batteries). These new businesses were proposed to be set up in FY2023 through joint ventures, with L&T having a dominant share. The company also identified green hydrogen, clean energy technology and offshore wind as new growth avenues.

Reliance announced plans to invest $80 billion and Adani Group announced plans to invest $70 billion in green energy projects. Reliance indicated its plans to make Gujarat net zero and carbon free. It proposed to invest ₹5 trillion in the state over a span of ten to fifteen years to set up a 100-GW renewable-energy power plant and green-hydrogen ecosystem development. It started the process of scouting land for the 100-GW project in Kutch, Banaskantha and Dholera, and requested 450,000 acres of land in Kutch.

Adani Group and France's TotalEnergies agreed to invest $50 billion over the next ten years in India to produce green hydrogen. These mega corps were targeting a scenario where green hydrogen would be available at a price of less than $1/kg. This, along with an economic scale of cycle hydrogen turbines and fuel cells, would enable India to reduce its dependence on energy imports and allow the transition to fossil-free fuels.

Renewable energy developers spent around ₹2.60 trillion on setting up 57.7 GW of solar power capacity in the country, with most projects coming from the private sector, and as per the normative cost of ₹4.5 crore per MW. Solar installations of 57.71

GW capacity were created, 48.7 GW were under installation and 16.7 GW were under bidding, totalling 123.1 GW.[78] The green energy opportunity was signalled by PM Modi when he announced the National Hydrogen Mission in August 2021. This ambitious plan built upon India's target of 450 GW of renewables by 2030.

Apart from green energy, the next big momentum was being driven by the roads sector, which was creating opportunities in logistics. The build-up of infrastructure investment in the country was resulting in improved mobility, which was set to bring about big savings for the economy, with logistics cost set to come down to 10% from the current 16–18% as per Union Minister Nitin Gadkari. Multiple ministries were making a coordinated effort under the Gati Shakti mission to transform mobility and build modern infrastructure.

Gadkari also emphasised that the use of renewable energy, including ethanol, electric mobility and liquefied natural gas (LNG)-fuelled trucks, would reduce the cost of transportation aided by an improved road network and interconnections between various modes of transport.

September

The regime change at the Centre in 2014 undoubtedly brought great focus on infrastructure and welfare service deliveries. From a spend of ₹5 trillion in the later years of the 2010 decade, infrastructure spending rose to over ₹10 trillion by 2018. Going forward, the national infrastructure agenda revived many schemes like Aadhar, BharatNet and the North–South–East–West Corridor, while new schemes like Bharatmala, Sagarmala, the Smart Cities Mission, AMRUT, the NIP and now Gati Shakti accelerated the initiatives.

That said, our fiscal deficit escalated, giving limited room for spending required for these initiatives. The country's fiscal deficit was projected at 6.4% of the GDP or ₹16.6 trillion for this fiscal year ending in March 2023, as against 6.71% for the previous year.

However, analysts were also predicting a rosier year ahead with an uptick in the private investment cycle. India was likely to be the fastest-growing Asian economy in the region in 2022–23, according to analysts at Morgan Stanley, who expected India's GDP growth to average 7% during this period—the strongest among the largest economies—and contribute 28% and 22% to Asian and global growth, respectively.[79]

Between April 2020 and March 2022, the construction sector drew in an FDI of $26.2 billion in townships, housing and other development projects, while construction in infrastructure activities attracted $27.92 billion during the same period. Policies conducive to infrastructure investments were paving the way for FDI—total FDI in FY2022 was $83.6 billion, up from $82 billion in FY2021, while in 2000, we attracted $3.58 billion. Despite higher deficits, FDI was expected to help accelerate infrastructure spending this year.

October

The road story in India had been trailing since the beginning of the financial year despite tall targets being expounded by the ministry. The pace of construction dropped to 19 km/day from last financial year's performance of 37 km/day. This fall was hurting contractors and construction equipment manufacturers.

The previous year, to boost the number of bidders, norms were diluted to include small packages of roads, which allowed the entry of small contractors. On the HAM front, aggressive bidding led to extremely low operations and maintenance (O&M) costs being quoted during HAM bids. In May, this norm was tweaked—only the Bid Project Cost (BPC) would henceforth be the criteria for HAM bid selection and the O&M would be a percentage factor of the BPC. This would thwart 'aggressive bidding'.

Yet, challenges remained in enhancing the pace of road construction. For the current average of 19 km/day to jump to 60 km/day, 21,900 km had to be constructed during the year. The ministry had constructed 10,237 km in 2019–20, 13,327 km in 2020–21 and 10,457 km in 2021–22. The current target required a jump of over 64% from the construction pace in 2020–21. Between September 2022 and March 2023, the ministry needed to construct 18,988 km, which meant a pace of over 90 km/day!

Even if one looked at the corelation of kilometres awarded and those constructed, the ministry would need to award 22,300 km or thereabouts. This was far beyond the capacity of the current framework given the past track record.

Meanwhile, the Maha Samruddhi Marg (the Mumbai–Nagpur Expressway) experienced delays despite a roaring start while the Coastal Road, Mumbai Trans Harbour Link and Navi Mumbai International Airport were all reported to be on schedule.

November

While efforts were converging at all levels to realise the dream of a powerful economy, we still needed several corrective measures. Our governments had not been empowered with majority support often enough, and when they did, there was little or no political will to liberate our economy from the clutches of corruption and cronyism, except during 1991. Now, though the current regime was well-intentioned and on the path of growth, it found it difficult to keep up the momentum.

Take the falling pace of road construction, for instance. The MoRTH secretary recently expressed that he was confident of building 12,000 km this financial year, which would give us a construction rate of 33 km/day. But having slowed construction to just 4,559 km in the first six months of this financial year, the pace of construction would have to accelerate to 47 km/day in the next six months—a mammoth ask. And while officials from

NHAI often contended that the spending on roads had been increasing over the past eight years, the fact was that we were spending too much of that money on land acquisition and less on project execution. Construction equipment companies were seeing orders dry up and contractors were bidding lower to keep the order book fat and impressive. Further, where was the application of the QCBS system over L1? It appeared this was only being applied to tenders of ₹10 crore and under to consultancy contracts, etc. This defeated a good idea completely. Appeals on arbitration orders had also been discouraged but this, too, was not being observed in its true spirit. So, while the ideas had reached the right ears and been translated into notifications, the executors were failing to implement them optimally.

All considered, with financial constraints at hand, did the government have the capability to accelerate its infusion as laid out in the NIP? Indications were that the government was now shying away from investment proposals and the private sector was driving the economy.

December

As the year drew to a close, the pandemic seemed like a distant nightmare with greater preparedness all around to handle a crisis of this nature. Meanwhile, there were newer disruptions such as inflation, supply-chain pangs, currency depreciation, war, sanctions, border disputes and pressure on the fiscal deficit. Still, India's economic growth was likely to outdo China's despite recent revisions, and we overtook the UK to become the fifth largest economy.

That said, the economic agenda was not getting the desired impetus. With government expenditure surging beyond budgeted levels on account of a rise in subsidies, the new recruitment drive for 1 million personnel and the stepping up in allocations for security and administrative preparations for the G20 summit to be held in India over the course of the next year, the fiscal deficit target of 6.4% of the GDP for FY2023 was seeming elusive. The government's allocation of ₹1.2 trillion owing to the extension of the Pradhan Mantri Garib Kalyan Anna Yojana (PMGKAY) of providing 5 kg of free foodgrain to 800 million households would need to be phased out if the deficit were to be contained.

Infrastructure spending was required to drive up GDP growth. In the current financial year, in the first five months, the ministries for railways and roads and highways spent nearly ₹3.24 trillion, nearly half the budgeted ₹7.50 trillion, mostly as capex. Along with these, other sectors that contributed cumulatively to 72% spending were telecommunications, housing and urban affairs. Affordable housing was another priority sector. Private-sector credit demand was now at an eight-year high. Sectors seeing strong loan demand ranged from infrastructure to real estate, iron and steel and new economy segments such as data centres and EV makers. In the past two weeks of October, lending was up nearly 17% to a year earlier. Lending to corporations, including small, medium and large businesses, was up 12.6% in September, the highest rate of annual growth since 2014. Further, about a quarter of current capital expenditure was linked to the PLI scheme.

Did the government have the appetite for another fight by launching labour reforms? Its agriculture reforms earned it a bloodied nose. Given that elections were due in mid-2024, would the government risk letting the opposition score on an issue like job security for labour? This was the rub. Without labour reform, the PLI scheme would remain a non-starter. All promises of creating employment would remain embedded in the effective rollout of the PLI scheme on the back of labour reforms.

The disinvestment target of ₹650 billion would not be met this year too. The proposed sale of BPCL did not materialise, the realisation from LIC was much lower than expected and proceeds of the IDBI Bank sale were expected only by June 2023.

So, there was fiscal deficit to contain that required the withdrawal of the foodgrain subsidy scheme, windfall taxes were not likely to generate as per targets, the disinvestment programme was at 38% achievement and the government was distracted by state elections. Amid all this, it was not likely to venture on launching labour reforms. All this would inevitably slow the pace of development that was desirable and possible.

2023

January

Highway construction this year was even slower than 2020, the first year of the pandemic. Data from MoRTH showed that only 4,766 km of the targeted 12,000 km of highways for FY2023 had been built from April to November, indicating a decline of nearly 7% from 5,118 km in the same period last year. NHAI awarded 5,382 km of highways from April till November, a decline of 4% against over 5,600 km of roads awarded a year earlier.

The government constructed 10,237 km of highways in the pre-pandemic period of FY2020 at 28.04 km/day. This increased in the first year of the pandemic when the country saw lockdowns, which indirectly helped accelerate construction. In FY2021, a record 13,327 km of highways were built at 36.51 km/day. However, in FY2022, the pace slackened to 10,457 km at 28.64 km/day .

MoSPI reported that the number of projects showing cost overruns as on 1 December 2022, was 22%, higher than 13% in March 2018, with a cost escalation of ₹4.5 trillion, 22% more than the original project cost, or roughly ₹1 trillion a year of escalation.

It now appeared to be a foregone conclusion that the roads target of 12,000 km would not be achieved. Even though the numbers during the April–November period were not too different from those of the previous year, the absence of any obstacles this year defied any confidence in the ability to muster up the numbers in the last four months.

The year 2022 was a mixed bag. While COVID-19 fears receded and order books began filling up, the infrastructure story did not accelerate after hitting a normal pace. Inflation hurt margins. Building material prices, particularly steel, took off vertically. Questions about the government's ability to spend money in infrastructure seemed validated with the tardiness in contracts awarded. Yet again, it diverted its core focus to elections. Exports were shaky, with Europe in economic doldrums. China had just about abandoned its COVID-19 policy of extreme caution but was hit with a pandemic wave. Inflation was currently being countered with monetary tightening, causing interest rates to be increased, which had begun to hurt demand. Cement was facing a demand slump and the rural areas, too, hit a pause button. However, the outcome of the rabi crop was likely to set it back on 'play' positively. The last quarter of this fiscal year was not likely to warm the industry's pockets even though costs had begun to rationalise. Credit disbursal was the lone bright star that continued to rise through the year.

According to CMIE, while the central government capex spending was up, state government capex spending, which was of comparable magnitude, was sluggish.[80] Also, new orders received by capital goods and construction companies dropped in July 2022 and remained low since then. The average monthly orders between July and October 2022 were to the tune of ₹142 billion, the lowest in many years.

February

At the Metro Rail Conference in Mumbai, Padma Vibhushan Dr E. Sreedharan expressed the need to enhance budgetary support as only ₹13,000 crore was allotted for the metro rail, while the roads and highways sector was accorded ₹2 lakh crore. Although we set up the first metro rail back in the 1970s with the Kolkata Metro, we have lagged behind in using it as a means of urban transport and have not recognised it as essential in urban planning, he rued. Now that cities are congested and travelling within the mega cities is becoming a nightmare, we have stepped up, the Metro Man added.[81]

Indeed, roads and metro-rail lines are the harbinger of development. The Union Budget was expected to provide funds to push the target for road construction above the 12,000 km that was set for 2022–23. The most optimistic target could be 18,000 km, which would mean a rate of 50 km/day. Given that construction is paused during the monsoon months, we would need a higher rate of up to 70 km/day after September 2023. Provisions for a metro rail were also likely to be stepped up. The railways would be another beneficiary of an enhanced allotment. Renewable and nuclear power were expected to be given priority too. Affordable housing would continue to accelerate. The real dilemma would be between welfare and infrastructure, given the fact that this budget would be the last before the general elections, as the next one would be a vote on account.

Exports were taking a dip as global demand was softening. Foreign investors were selling stocks and investing in China as it had begun opening and, after recording 3% GDP growth in the last quarter, was geared for a comeback.

As per the plans for the National Monetisation Pipeline (NMP) launched by the FM, ₹6 trillion was to be derived from FY2022 to FY2025. Against the set target of ₹1.62 trillion for asset monetisation for FY2022–23, the government was likely to fall short by ₹382 billion. The roads sector was to fetch ₹1.6 trillion up to FY2025 from among the assets the government was hoping to monetise. The FY2023 budget had earmarked ₹1.99 trillion towards the Transport Ministry, of which the capital expenditure was ₹1.877 trillion. The forthcoming budget was expected to enhance this by 10%. Among various sectors, coal, mines and ports and shipping were likely to surpass the asset monetisation target, while MoRTH was on track to achieve the target.

Talking of the roads sector, of late, with some high-profile deaths in road accidents, the focus shifted to road design. India, which ranked third in the number of road accidents (after the US and Japan), held the infamous record of the largest fatalities from these accidents. Moreover, the percentage of fatalities involving road users between eighteen and forty-five years of age stood at 69.80% for the year 2020. Notably, India's ranking in terms of fatalities was not a recent phenomenon. Poor design of roads was one of the key reasons, possibly because of bad engineering design, poor visibility because of obstructions or poor lighting and ignorance of soil and weather.

Against this backdrop, Union Minister Nitin Gadkari called for the rating of contractors on their financial and contract execution performance over the past five years. The dilution of stringent norms to attract more participation in some tenders led to the entry of some errant contractors who brought shame to the sector, he said.[82]

March

India's economic growth rate slowed to 4.4% in the December quarter. High input costs drove down profitability, especially for the manufacturing sector. However, construction grew by 8.4% against 5.8% in the previous quarter.

Would India remain immune to global volatility? Although the World Bank and other agencies seemed to think the country would be able to withstand these shocks with greater ease, past experience indicated that this elation of decoupling did not last very long as global headwinds caught up. The economic scenario was at inflexion point, when inflation was just about beginning to win the battle against growth. So far, none of the indicators were showing any worrying signs. But while commodity prices eased, they were still above pre-pandemic levels. Interest rates were increasing across the world, and rates in India were reaching a point where they would begin to hurt housing demand.

Irfan Razack, Chairman, Prestige Estates, expressed that he wanted to double the company's annual residential bookings in three years to ₹250 billion, mostly from his current markets like Bengaluru, Mumbai, Hyderabad and Chennai.[83] Given that the real estate market performed extremely well in 2022, his optimism, despite increasing interest rates, was due to the changing profile of the industry. India's millennials, who comprised 34% of the population, numbered close to 440 million. They were not waiting for eternity to buy their first house as was the trend two decades ago. In over twenty cities, the metro rail had begun to draw fresh contours to the existing cityscape, thus energising property markets. New properties with amenities were meeting the aspirations of the millennials. Incentives like lower stamp duty were good triggers for fence sitters. Easy availability of finance was allowing nuclear families to branch out from traditional joint family units. Job mobility had sown the seeds of independent nuclear units and availability of rental units eased the process to home ownership.

Union Minister Nitin Gadkari announced that his target was to complete 200,000 km of National Highways by 2025. This meant he planned to complete 60,000 km of road construction in three years which, at an average of 20,000 km per year, would mean a rate of construction of 55 km/day for three consecutive years! Notably, it was only in 2021–22 that we managed to construct at the rate of 37 km/day, the highest we have managed so far. This year appeared to be the best chance to meet the target of 20,000 km before the country slipped into election mode.

April

According to MoSPI, from among 835 delayed projects, more than 400 were delayed by twenty-five to sixty months and 130 projects had been under process for over sixty-one months. This meant that over 63% of projects were delayed for over two years and up to five years. The December 2022 report cited a cost overrun of ₹4.5 trillion or 22% of original cost. The various reasons cited included a delay in a tie-up for project financing, change in scope and finalisation of detailed engineering. These reasons indicated ill-preparedness or amounted to an excuse for non-fulfilment of project execution.

Virendra Mhaiskar, Managing Director, IRB Developers, expressed the view that tender conditions ought to be made more stringent.[84] He added that the government needed to tighten its qualification criteria in the award of tenders for road projects, as companies who put in bids often complained of cost overruns, which resulted in projects getting delayed. Issuing of a tender and its withdrawal or delay in awarding it were the first steps in tinkering with project costs. Bidding aggressively and then finding various reasons to change the scope of the project were the traditional ways by which several contractors managed to ward off competitive bidders. The Bandra–Worli Sealink project was originally set to be constructed at ₹4 billion in 2004 and went on to be constructed at ₹16 billion five years later. The contract was awarded to the lowest bidder, and when the awardee sought changes in the scope of the project, the developer, instead of putting the project up for a rebid, which would have kept the cost at reasonable levels of escalation, ended up taxing the state budget by 400%.

Project delays were costing ₹4.5 trillion, which was equal to 1.5% of the GDP—savings from this could potentially be used to triple the rural development budget from ₹1.6 trillion, double the railway budget from ₹2.4 trillion or increase the budget for roads by 50% from ₹2.7 trillion.

Completions by the private sector in 2022–23 slowed down too. In 2022–23, it was highly unlikely that it would manage to close the over ₹2.6 trillion worth of completions seen during

2021–22, as per a CMIE report.[85] Also, the 2.6 trillion was the deficit investment compared to last year; since last year, the private sector announcements were ₹3.8 trillion and this year, it was just ₹0.8 trillion, which was a 79.2% decline. Slow execution by the private sector was indeed cause for worry.

In other news, Indian Railways recently made headlines over its highest-ever wagon order of 84,000 wagons—it had typically purchased 12,000–15,000 wagons annually. The National Rail Plan projected that to handle planned freight levels over the next ten years, 28,000–32,000 wagons would be needed annually. The railways were indeed likely to be seeing huge investments as cited in the Union Budget of 2023–24, which provided for the highest ever budget of ₹2.4 trillion.

Further, with the opportunity that came our way owing to disruptions in the supply chain, India was being considered as an alternate manufacturing base. However, while the PLI scheme had been announced by the government and electronics had made some headway, no nation can achieve industrial prosperity without R&D. Our R&D budgets had been dismal. Although India's spending on R&D was consistently increasing across the past decade and nearly tripled from ₹394.38 billion in 2007–08 to ₹1.14 trillion in 2017–18, it figured at just 0.5%—for a $3 trillion economy, this was poor, standing even lower than Brazil (1.16%) and South Africa (0.83%).

May

MoRTH was reportedly investigating the reasons behind the failure in achieving road construction targets. While the yearly target was 12,200 km of roads, the cumulated distance of roads built was around 11,000 km. This was a marginal improvement upon FY2023, when 10,457 km of highways were constructed against a target of 12,000 km. The ministry ordered a scrutiny, as part of which NHAI had been asked to provide all the data on highway construction and awards, including on construction that was nearing completion. Data from the National Highways and Infrastructure Development Corp Ltd, Indian Roads Construction Corp and Border Roads Organisation (BRO) would also be studied as part of the investigation.

In other news, Monetary Policy Committee member Jayanth Varma commented that more interest rate hikes had been undertaken than necessary to tackle inflation. According to him, inflation could fall below 5.5%, provided crude oil prices did not rise and the monsoon progressed normally.

The Nasscom Strategic Review 2023 reported the creation of 290,000 new jobs in FY2023. But India's top software companies were making up to 30% fewer campus offers this year for the 2023 batch compared to the previous year, as a slowdown in their Western markets was causing uncertainties. This led analysts to forecast that net hiring of engineers by Indian IT companies would crash by close to half in the next fiscal year starting April, compared to FY2023. This could upset the demand balance unless other sectors make up for the shortfall.[86]

Certain businesses, such as Bharti Airtel, MakeMyTrip, Flipkart, Uber, PepsiCo, EY and Deloitte were hiring STEM talent in large numbers, paving the way for an alternate source. Then, there was growing demand for tech talent by auto companies, EPC companies and over 300 startups; 80% of early-stage start-ups were looking to increase their workforce in 2023. Overall, it was certain that FY2023 would see a moderation of tech talent hiring in the Indian IT/technology industry; it remained to be seen whether other industries would be able to make up for this decline.

Meanwhile, there was worry about private-sector projects that were shying away from reaching commercial production. The reason could lie in unutilised capacities and tardy demand. According to CMIE, crude steel capacity rose from 91 million tonne in 2011–12 to 154 million tonnes by 2021–22. But again, capacity utilisation was down from 81.8% to 77.8%. Cement capacity increased from 228 million tonnes in 2010–11 to 593 million tonnes in 2020–21. Capacities in the industry remained underutilised. Capacity utilisation stood at 69.5% in 2021–22. There was no compelling reason for private-sector entrepreneurs to go through with their announcements in capex.

CMIE reported that, in steel, there are 347 projects that aimed to set up 239 Mt of additional capacity. This was more than 1.5 times the current outstanding capacity. Of these, thirty-nine projects involving nearly 71.3 Mt of capacity were overdue for completion, but the promoters seemed to be in no hurry to commission the projects. Upon completion, these alone could raise steel capacity by almost 50%.

Similarly, there were 182 cement projects on hand, envisaging the establishment of 425 Mt of additional capacity over the current 600 Mt or so. Projects to set up 79 Mt of cement capacity were overdue for completion.

June

Under the Parvatmala Pariyojana, the National Ropeways Development Programme, Union Minister Nitin Gadkari announced plans to develop 250+ projects with a ropeway length exceeding 1,200 km over a span of five years. He emphasised upon PPP under HAM, with 60% contribution from the government. Additionally, the promotion of ropeway component manufacturing under the Make in India initiative was said to be a priority. In fact, during a visit to Austria, the minister invited Austrian manufacturers to invest in ropeway systems.[87]

NHAI began to accept bid security and performance security in the form of electronic bank guarantees (e-BG) issued by various banks through the National E-Governance Services Ltd (NeSL) platform. It was also considering the use of insurance surety bonds as an additional method for submitting bid security and/or performance security deposit.

While the roads sector readjusted its targets, the railways achieved an all-time high of 5,243 km of track laying in 2022–23 compared to 2,909 km in 2021–22. The average track laying rate reached 14.4 km/day. The railways were also rapidly progressing towards accomplishing the mission of 100% electrification and becoming the world's largest green railway network. However, the question arose whether the pace, for both railways and roads, would be maintained as we approached the upcoming general elections or whether the commitment would waver.

Delays in projects were not unfamiliar, as evidenced by an official report indicating that out of 1,566 infrastructure projects, 384 experienced cost overruns exceeding ₹4.66 trillion in the January–March 2023 quarter. Even the new parliament building, inaugurated by the prime minister, faced a challenge regarding the grant of environmental clearance. The Supreme Court had given the green signal to the ₹13,500-crore Central Vista revamp project finally only on 5 January 2021. The previous month, the Telangana CM K. Chandrashekar Rao inaugurated the Secretariat building in Hyderabad, standing 265 ft tall and covering 10.5 lakh sq. ft in a sprawling 28-acre area. Although the foundation stone was laid on 27 June 2019, work only commenced in January 2021 owing to delays caused by the COVID-19 pandemic, court cases and other issues. Hence, both projects obtained clearance through the courts in January 2021 and were completed in just over twenty-five months. These projects benefited from the support of influential offices. When there is political will, there is a way.

July

'India will be the third largest economy soon. We are not only growing bigger but we are also growing faster. When India grows, the whole world grows.'[88] These were PM Modi's words to a Joint Session of the US Congress during his visit to the US. In the year of its G20 Presidency, India was clearly able to secure the attention of the world.

Minister Gadkari announced the expansion of the road highway network in the Northeast, with projects worth over ₹2 trillion underway in the region. He highlighted that the total length of national highways had increased from 91,287 km in 2013–14 to 145,240 km in 2022–23, a remarkable rise of over 59% in a nine-year period. During the challenging year of 2020–21, highway construction reached its peak, with a daily construction pace of 37 km and a total of 13,327 km of highways built. However, the pace declined in FY2022 and FY2023. Recent reports indicated efforts to set a target of up to 2,000 km for NHIDCL to achieve an overall construction of approximately 14,000 km this year.

While road construction targets proved elusive, construction stocks became part of mid-cap portfolios for investors. This development allowed company promoters to leverage their shareholding as collateral for easier borrowing and potentially pursue follow-on offers to raise additional equity and reduce debt.

The real estate sector witnessed significant growth and diversification over the past five years. Factors such as the rise of e-commerce companies and start-ups, the demand for logistics and data centres, luxury residential high-rises and hotels propelled the sector to new heights. Consolidation led to a portfolio of high-quality developers and India's favourable investment policies attracted interest despite foreign currency fluctuations. Knight Frank's report earlier in the year highlighted simultaneous growth in major real estate segments, including office, residential, warehousing and retail, driven by changing attitudes towards home ownership, return to work, increased hiring and the proliferation of e-commerce. In 2022, annual sales increased by 34% year-on-year, reaching a nine-year high with 312,666 units sold.[89]

In Bengaluru, India's first post office building constructed using 3D printing technology was nearing completion on Cambridge

Road. The Halasuru Bazaar Post Office would be housed in a 1,100 sq ft facility, with a cost of approximately ₹2,090 per sq ft. L&T was overseeing the construction and the technology had been approved by the Building Materials and Technology Promotion Council (BMTPC), with the structural design validated by IIT Madras. A fully automated 3D printer was being utilised in an open-to-sky environment, marking Karnataka's first public structure built using 3D technology. The cost and time advantages of this technology were expected to encourage further adoption and scale in the construction industry.

August

The increased adoption of construction technology was heartening. The Indian edition of the KPMG Global Construction Survey 2023 reaffirmed the industry's enhanced engagement with technologies being used in construction.[90] One example is the digital twin.

Using real-time data and artificial intelligence (AI), digital twins become virtual, living mirrors of their physical counterparts, providing opportunities to simulate everything from infrastructure and construction to traffic patterns and energy consumption. The digital replica is created with digital drawings, plans and IoT sensors. The plans and drawings are the foundation of the physical item in a virtual space. Sensors then collect data from it and sync it with the digital model to create a real-time replica.

The National Urban Innovation Stack in India was exploring policy initiatives to enable the creation of layers of digital data and allowing out-of-the-box solutions to urban challenges. Singapore and Shanghai both have complete digital twins that work to improve energy consumption and traffic flow, and even help plan developments.

While digital construction had relevance, particularly in metro rail and high-speed rail projects, the need for skilling and training had never been so acute. The crane accident in Thane on 1 August 2023, when twenty workers and engineers were killed during the third phase of the construction of a viaduct on the Samruddhi Expressway in Maharashtra, highlighted the need for safety in execution. The 2.28 km-long viaduct was being constructed by Navayuga Engineering and Singapore-based VSL India. Of the viaduct's 114 segments, 98 had been successfully constructed using the same launcher.

Crane collapses are common globally, with over forty to sixty people dying every year. Over 25% of these accidents occurred owing to errors during crane assembly or disassembly; another 25% occurred during operation or lifting. Of the deaths, over 50% were the result of workers being struck by objects or equipment and over 20% involved the crane operator.

September

India became only the fourth country to land a spacecraft on the moon—and we had our share of reasons to feel like we were 'over the moon'! Over the past twenty-five years, the country had built up gross domestic savings of $12 trillion and over the coming twenty-five years, this number was expected to surge to over $100 trillion. What took twenty-five years to happen would take five years to reach the same quantum in most aspects. The value of real estate under construction, which was ₹4.6 trillion in 2009, was ₹22.8 trillion in 2022. Residential real estate sales clocked 3.6 lakh units in 2022, creating a new peak surpassing 2014 levels.

India had also become an increasingly attractive location for multinationals across a wide range of industries, with FDI inflows having reached a new record high of $85 billion in FY2021–22. The gross inward FDI was $71 billion in 2022–23.

Further, India, not China, had the second-largest road network in the world after the US, spanning about 6.332 million km, comprising national highways, expressways, state highways, major district roads, district roads and village roads. NHAI awarded total projects of 6,003 km with a value of ₹1.26 trillion during FY2023. A provisional target of constructing about 13,800 km had been set for 2023–24.

Now, all infrastructure projects over ₹500 crore required approval from the Network Planning Group (NPG). The group comprised representatives of all infrastructure ministries to ensure that their planning conformed to the objectives of the Gati Shakti Master Plan. The approval of the NPG was required before the project was cleared by the Public Investment Board (PIB) or the Department of Expenditure. The NPG recently approved 100 projects worth ₹5.89 trillion (out of a total ₹12 trillion worth projects under Gati Shakti). Of this, forty road projects totalled an investment of ₹3.65 trillion. In addition, forty railway projects worth ₹95,704 crore and eight urban development projects with an investment of ₹79,016 crore were also given the go-ahead.

Nevertheless, challenges persisted. Delays, for one, continued to plague the infrastructure sector. According to the July 2023 report by the Project Monitoring Division, 809 projects were delayed, and 213 projects were behind schedule even after being granted extensions. The road sector had the greatest number of delayed projects at 262, followed by railways at 115 and the petroleum sector at 89.[91]

October

Did you know that L&T's quarterly revenue was double that of its nearest competitor's annual revenue? S.N. Subrahmanyan, Chairman and Managing Director, formerly took the baton from retiring chairman A.M. Naik recently and had already embarked on changing the dynamic quotient of the company. He diversified the revenue through an acquisition in the IT space (Mindtree) and shed businesses (the electrical and automation business to Schneider Electric) the company did not want to hold on to. In its FY2022–23 results, it notched annual order inflows of over ₹2 trillion, taking its total order book to over ₹4 trillion, nearly equal to its market capitalisation. In fact, over the past nine years, under the Modi Government, its turnover doubled from ₹570 billion to ₹1.10 trillion.

Indeed, the administration's keenness to drive the infrastructure story rapidly heralded a black swan opportunity for construction companies. In this case, the coming together of multiple positive factors simultaneously had the potential to multiply the impact ten times. The Gati Shakti initiative reduced the time taken for DPRs, which would accelerate the time taken for launching projects. Roads and metro rail have always been the drivers of infrastructure development but Indian Railways also gathered speed, especially with high-speed rail projects. The sector received the highest-ever capex allocation of ₹2.6 trillion, with many projects aimed at capacity augmentation and traffic decongestion.

The railways further announced plans to develop seven new high-speed rail (HSR) corridors in the medium to long term, the feasibility studies of which were initiated. In recent years, there has been a thrust on the development of semi-HSR corridor projects, of which track and systems packages worth ₹250 billion were expected to be finalised in the next five years. ICRA estimated that metro rail projects would provide business opportunities of about ₹800 billion in the next five years and, consequently, the metro-rail network was expected to expand by 2.7 times over the same period. Further, the previous month, the prime minister launched the Amrit Bharat Station Scheme. The ₹250 billion project would cover the development of 508 stations spread across sixteen states and union territories.

Also, real estate and building projects were ushering in a new range of opportunities, including airports, hospitals, stadia, retail spaces, educational institutions, IT parks, office buildings, data centres, high-rise structures, mass housing complexes, cement plants and industrial warehouses. Opportunities in water were being driven by the Jal Jeevan Mission, aimed at providing piped drinking water to 192 million rural households by 2024. Since its inception, over 128 million households had been provided tap water. With the general elections scheduled for 2024 and several state elections around the corner, the government was working on a war footing to complete its mission.

With the announcement of 'Amrit Kaal' as a period where the government envisioned a prosperous and inclusive India, in which the fruits of development reached all regions and citizens and included a technology-driven and knowledge-based economy with strong public finances and a robust financial sector, this was expected to be a defining decade for India.

November

Here are some observations after over twenty years of monitoring and researching the Indian construction sector.

Our spending on infrastructure, which was around ₹10 trillion per annum between 2008 and 2018 now needed to grow by double to meet the needs of the NIP. The capacity of contractors and construction companies expanded from an operating revenue of ₹160 billion in 2003 to over ₹3 trillion—up nearly eighteen times over twenty years. On 30 April 2003, the market capitalisation of L&T was $1.09 billion; now, it was $510 billion. The construction equipment market was around 7,000 units or ₹45 billion; now, it was 107,776 units. JCB had a turnover of ₹5.5 billion then; now, it had crossed ₹120 billion. L&T was planning to target international revenues of ₹10 billion in fiscal 2002; in FY2023, it had reached ₹686.87 billion—roughly sixty times in twenty years!

New York-based *Engineering News Record* (ENR) magazine, which is over 106 years old, annually publishes a list of top international contractors and design engineering firms. In the latest list of design engineering firms, three Indian companies were featured, while five companies featured in the 250 international contractors' list. However, China had over eighty companies and Turkey over forty companies on that list. Why were Indian companies not of that scale? How could Indian companies scale up?

Unfortunately, there were no easy answers nor any easy solutions. With margins of 5% at net levels, the contracting company had a sword hanging over its head, and any delay in the project could push it towards arbitration or a long process of recovery of money. The risk undertaken by the enterprise did not provide any premium to it.

Firms that are well-capitalised can absorb risks. Further, they have expensive experts on board and do not bid for projects with a bidding war among multiple competitors as they like to enter projects with better margins. During the 2009–12 period, though, several contracting companies defied the sustainability norms and bid aggressively. Finally, they were not even getting any white knights to rescue them from insolvency.

December

Wrapping up the year, there was a fair share of heartening news. The NIP, which was launched with 6,835 projects, had expanded to capture over 9,288 projects with a total outlay of ₹108.88 trillion between 2020 and 2025. It was followed by the NMP, giving the fillip to the possibility of asset churning by bringing back more capital. Financing had been an Achilles' heel in the infrastructure story; as projects have a long gestation period, financing was very critical. Hence, in the FY2022 budget, the government announced the NMP plan to raise ₹6.6 trillion by FY2025.

Considering the huge size of the infrastructure financing market, it needs to attract both debt and equity capital. The size of infrastructure lending market for PPP/private-sector projects in FY2024 was estimated at $32 billion, with banks/NBFCs expected to finance $20 billion. The balance $12 billion would need to be raised from other sources, including pension/provident/insurance/sovereign funds, private credit, etc.

With the government laying emphasis on capital recycling through capex outlay and parallel monetisation plans for infrastructure development, InvITs (infrastructure investment trusts) were gaining traction as yields showed continued uptick and resilience during volatile market conditions. For example, in the roads sector, assets under management (AUMs) crossed over ₹1 trillion, with InvITs emerging as the preferred holding structure. InvITs, conceptually like mutual funds, raise capital to invest in income-generating assets like highways, power transmission, etc. While developers have set up their own InvITs, of late, financial institute-driven InvITs were raising a lot of capital. MoRTH was trying to reduce the debt burden of NHAI, which had run into ₹3.4 trillion. Its asset monetisation efforts had brought in ₹100 billion, but much more was yet to come. Could NHAI InvITs pave the way for retail investment too?

As outlined in the recently adopted Vision India 2047 document, between FY2024 and FY2030, India was set to channel ₹143 trillion into infrastructure projects, more than double the ₹67 trillion expended in the preceding seven financial years. This surge in investment is anticipated to predominantly target sectors such as roads and power, with nascent areas like EVs, solar, wind, and hydrogen also gaining momentum.

Gati Shakti was enabling quicker DPRs and higher contract awards, and faster execution possibilities with technologies were enabling better business opportunities. However, our skill development and capacity building were trailing, impeding the adoption of technology. Further, while we increased the pace, we needed to look at sustainable financing. NHAI's debt had reached ₹3.48 trillion, tripling over the past five years from ₹1.22 trillion in 2018. A huge amount of money was being poured into land acquisition. The Land Acquisition Policy was the first step in shooting ourselves in the foot. Paying the cost of land at four times the market price did not only escalate project costs but allowed cash circulation and caused social upheavals. Land pooling concepts that proved successful in several projects, with added provisions of annuities to farmers, could have been explored.

What's more, while the race to build infrastructure lays emphasis on speed, we needed to look deeper. Transportation, for one, ought to be designed well and built with materials that can last a lifetime. Our buildings and commercial complexes, too, should not be crumbling and leaking; otherwise, while we struggle to pay high maintenance costs, we also lose productivity. Given the ₹100 trillion bet on infrastructure, we ought to get the best returns on our investments.

Safety was an issue seemingly off the grid. The recent tunnel collapse at Uttarkashi showed there was no provision for an escape route in the plans in the eventuality of the soil caving in. Given the fragility of the soil in that region, this should have been a mandatory provision. Now, all twenty-nine under-construction tunnels were being audited for safety.

Any proposed highway running longer than 100 km needs environmental clearance. The Silkyara tunnel, part of the 900 km Char Dham project, needed environmental clearance too. The race to complete the project before the forthcoming elections led to splitting the project into fifty-three separate sections, with none of them over 100 km in length, thereby skirting the environmental impact assessment. In June 2018, the NHIDCL awarded the tender for tunnel construction to Navayuga Engineering (NEC), which contracted Bernard Gruppe, a German-Austrian engineering consultancy, to design and build the tunnel. On its website, Bernard Gruppe stated that since the start of tunnel driving, the geological conditions proved to be more challenging than predicted in the tender documents. NEC needed to build an escape route for workers in the case of an emergency during construction, which it failed to do. Apart from providing an escape route, the channels were also supposed to help relieve workers from the contamination caused by gases generated underground.

It was indeed unfortunate that despite all the technologies we were embracing, including AI, we were unable to extricate our workers from the Silkyara tunnel in Uttarakhand and had to resort to 'rat mining' operations. While the rescue was heart-warming, the uncertainty of our abilities was unnerving.

CHAPTER THREE

WHY AREN'T WE THERE YET?

Despite glorious global reviews of the Indian economy, our capitalists remain wary of investing. The China Plus One policy seemed to have been a super opportunity but, contrary to popular perception, Vietnam and Cambodia seem to have benefitted the most out of it, rather than India. The PLI scheme has been a non-starter except for the mobile phone manufacturing sector. Now, the jury seems to be out on whether the scheme will build our competitive advantage or break it. On infrastructure, the desired pace is elusive. We continue to lose over ₹4 trillion on account of project overruns annually, and this figure keeps growing despite the PM Gati Shakti initiative to enhance the speed of DPRs and GST implementation to facilitate the free movement of goods after disbanding octroi and excise.

Why is the bureaucracy dragging its feet? Why is private capital still shy? And why is a majority government unable to instil a sense of confidence in private industry to embark on an aggressive adventure or unleash the animal spirits? Finance Minister Nirmala Sitharaman has likened Indian corporates to the legendary Lord Hanuman who, as per mythology, did not have an idea of his own strength! In her view, private capital needs to be made aware of its strength and prodded to action.[1]

It appears the government has not yet cracked the code to business and entrepreneurship. For instance, there are more SMEs that have shut down than ever before—reportedly, the number of MSMEs closed since the government's Udyam registration portal launch on 1 July 2020 post-COVID has jumped to 35,680 as of 5 February 2024, as per government data.[2] Out of total closures, 13,290 units were shut in FY2022–23 while FY2022 saw the closure of 6,222 MSMEs and 175 units in FY2021. In the current financial year, as of 5 February, 15,993 MSMEs have closed their businesses. FDI is still not commensurate with the prospects for such a fast-growing nation—net FDI in India, i.e. the difference between inflows and outflows, fell to $10.6 billion in the financial year ending 31 March 2024 (FY2024) from $28 billion the previous year, which is a drop of 62.14%, according to the RBI.[3] And, as mentioned earlier, the private sector is still reticent: its share in infrastructure investment in FY2022–23 reverted to the level seen during the pandemic in 2020, according to the latest National Accounts Statistics data released.[4]

The share of private non-financial corporations in gross fixed capital formation (GFCF, a proxy for infrastructure investments) dipped to 36.2% in FY2023 compared to 36.3% in FY2022. Let us delve deeper into various aspects of the infrastructure story and examine the hits and misses over the past ten transformative years.

The Hits

Undeniably, the past ten years have seen a huge change in the lives of Indian citizens.

Eliminating pilferage and limiting corruption was made possible with schemes like Aadhar and Direct Benefit Transfer. In fact, using technology for administration has limited corruption and enhanced accountability.

Delivery of welfare, which includes electrification of villages, water on tap, rural roads and insurance schemes, made its mark. According to a NITI Aayog discussion paper, multidimensional poverty in India declined from 29.17% in 2013–14 to 11.28%

in 2022–23, with about 248.2 million people moving out of this bracket during this period.[5] National multidimensional poverty measures simultaneous deprivations across three equally weighted dimensions of health, education and standard of living that are represented by twelve sustainable development goals-aligned indicators. These include nutrition, child and adolescent mortality, maternal health, years of schooling, school attendance, cooking fuel, sanitation, drinking water, electricity, housing, assets and bank accounts. At the state level, Uttar Pradesh topped the list, with 59.4 million people escaping poverty, followed by Bihar at 37.7 million and Madhya Pradesh at 23million. These gains were credited to many government initiatives and schemes targeted at improving specific deprivation aspects.[6]

The country had some success in *setting goalposts for bureaucracy*: India's ease of doing business reforms have centred around streamlining and digitising regulatory compliance processes throughout the entire business lifecycle, from incorporation to the cessation of operations. For example, in the Union Budget 2023–24, the government declared a reduction in over 39,000 compliances and the decriminalisation of more than 3,400 legal provisions. Also, companies and LLPs can now be incorporated using the Centre's National Single Window System (NSWS), which offers various central and state government approvals in one place, as well as the MCA21 portal of the Ministry of Corporate Affairs.

What's more, the introduction of NCLT for bankruptcy and dispute resolution mechanisms have proved to be extremely beneficial in *eliminating legal hurdles*, and the introduction of GST and faceless assessments have streamlined processes and increased the number of tax payers, thus *enabling tax reform*.

The greatest success, however, of the past ten years has been the *digital transformation* of the country. Today, almost every Indian (among 1.4 billion) has a digital ID that provides online authentication using a fingerprint, iris, OTP (one-time password) and face. And 80 million transactions a day are undertaken with this system. This online verification, which was also called 'Know Your Customer' (KYC), was later made a requirement to open a bank account or get a mobile connection. On these building blocks, more services were offered, such as DigiLocker (a digital wallet), digital signature, and Unified Payment Interface (UPI) for instant payments from the mobile. During COVID-19, this helped transfer $4.5 billion into the bank accounts of 160 million beneficiaries, facilitated distribution of 2.5 million vaccinations in two years and helped Indians obtain vaccine certificates on their mobiles in real time.[7]

According to the World Bank, between 2014 and 2017, one of every two new bank accounts opened in the world was in India.[8] In December 2022 alone, 8 billion digital payment transactions were processed in India. The total volume of digital payment transactions increased from 20.71 billion in FY2017–18 to 134.62 billion in FY2022–23 at a CAGR of 45%. In FY2023–24, digital payment transactions reached 116.6 billion till 11 December 2023. Retail digital payments in India have grown from 1.62 billion transactions in FY2012–13 to over 147.26 billion transactions in 2023–24 (till February 2024), i.e., an approximate ninety-fold increase over twelve years.

Today, India accounts for nearly 46% of the world's digital transactions (as per 2022 data). UPI has become the most talked about fast payment system not only in India but across the world. It has been the biggest contributor to the growth of digital payments in the country. The share of UPI in digital payments reached close to 80% in 2023. At a macro level, the volume of UPI transactions increased from 430 million in calendar year (CY) 2017 to 117.61 billion in CY2023. Apart from being a user-friendly interface and facilitating QR code-based payments, UPI has evolved to include advanced functionalities, such as offline payments through near field communication (NFC) technology (UPI Lite X), payments through feature phones (UPI 123Pay), and AI-based conversational payments (hello! UPI).[9]

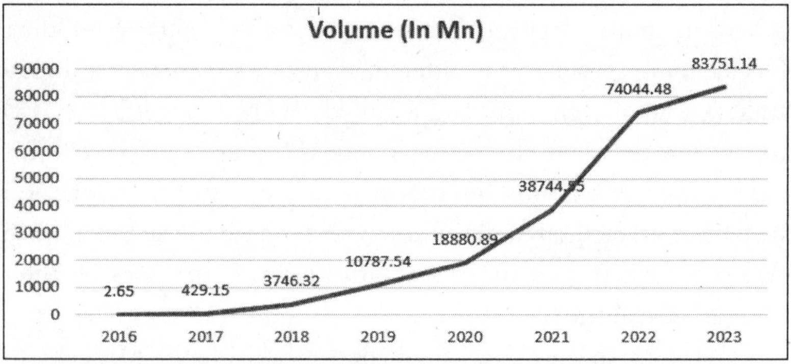

Source: Inder Pal Singh Sethi, 'Digital Payments driving the growth of Digital Economy', *National Informatics Centre*, https://www.nic.in/blogs/digital-payments-driving-the-growth-of-digital-economy/.

The Centre is eyeing the export of a full range of indigenously-designed 4G and 5G stacks in 2024 as part of its policy to attract investments and use the technological outreach as a key foreign policy bet. Several countries such as Kenya, Mauritius, Papua New Guinea and Egypt, among others, have shown interest in Indian telecom technology. India has received inquiries from at least fifteen global telecom operators, as well as bilateral inquiries from nine nations. All these requests will be systematically met and Indian telecom technology will make its way abroad in the second half of 2024.

As the leader of the G20 in 2023, India has been able to raise an extraordinary level of awareness about digital public infrastructure (DPI) among countries of the Global North and South through the interventions of the G20 Digital Economy Working Group, the new high-level Task Force on DPI for Economic Transformation, Financial Inclusion and Development, and several G20 Engagement Groups. Today, the

DPI model has emerged as a key Indian offering to the world, and is being considered, adopted or adapted by nations at very different stages of development. As foundational population-scale tech systems, DPIs enable the flow of individuals (through digital identity systems), money (through real-time SWIFT payment systems) and information (through consent-based, privacy-protecting, data-sharing systems). India Stack's pioneering, integrated architecture helped us become the first nation to develop all three foundational DPIs: the Aadhaar unique identity, UPI and the Data Empowerment and Protection Architecture (DEPA). Broadly, in 2024, India is likely to seek to understand more closely what different countries would like to do—and in some cases are already doing—in the DPI space, and to provide them the necessary assistance. The country is well placed to do this, given its legacy of cooperation and knowledge-sharing through the Modular Open Source Identity Platform (MOSIP) and, more recently, through its MoUs with partner nations.

Finally, 2024 ought to be marked by a rise in global awareness about the link between DPIs and AI development efforts. Large volumes of data are a critical component of DPIs, and they could be an asset for training AI models, provided that the principles of data privacy and security are firmly upheld. As part of DEPA 2.0, for example, India is already experimenting with a solution called Confidential Clean Rooms, which are hardware-protected secure computing environments where sensitive data can be accessed in an algorithmically controlled manner for model training. As more countries begin to understand and implement these approaches, DPIs could help unleash a new wave of AI-based solutions.[10]

The Misses

However, there are many issues that continue to plague the government and aspects it has failed to deliver on, or is yet to.

On the economics front …

Private investment is one of the pillars of economic growth. According to World Bank estimates, it fell from 31% of the GDP in 2011 to 22% in 2020.[11]

Indeed, private investment increased from under 15% of the GDP in 1980–81 to almost 30% in 2011–12 but has since fallen to around 25%. The rise came in phases. In the first phase, from the mid-1980s to 1990, the private investment rate rose from 10% of the GDP to around 15%. The next jump came in the mid-1990s from 15% to 20%. The third jump came in 2004–05, when private investment increased sharply again to cross 25% of the GDP and helped propel the economy to a period of rapid economic growth, averaging over 8% from 2003–04 to 2011–12, peaking at 30% of GDP.

The components of private investment—corporate and non-corporate—present some interesting differences. Corporate investment rose sharply from 5% of the GDP to almost 10% after the economic reforms of 1991 but slumped again after 1996–97. From 2004–05, we again see a very sharp increase in corporate investment to 16% of the GDP in 2007–08 and falling sharply after the global economic crisis to around 12%. Non-corporate investment, which is a mixed bag of small and medium enterprises, household and real estate investment, hovered around 10% of the GDP from 1980–81 to 1999–2000 and then started rising to around 17% by 2012–13. But since then, it has dropped to around 14% of the GDP.[12]

India must see a revival of private investment to around 30% of the GDP, which together with public investment of at least 6%, will allow GDP growth of over 8% on a sustained basis. But with slower growth and a banking system saddled with considerable non-performing loans, reviving private investment will not be easy. India also suffers from other factors that have reduced competitiveness. India has a huge public infrastructure deficit and declining public investment. Public investment typically crowds in private investment.

However, despite a surge in public investment in FY2023, the private sector is still sitting on the fence. As per analysis by the National Institute of Public Finance and Policy, to achieve more than 8% growth, India must increase public investment to around 14–15% of the GDP, depreciate the real exchange rate by at least 10% and increase the growth of credit to over 10% of the GDP. This is the policy package that many fast-growing countries such as China followed over a twenty- to thirty-year period to sustain double-digit growth.

According to data from CEIC and Bank of Baroda Research, the number of industrial investment proposals fell from 612 in July 2021 to 118 in July 2022. Even gross fixed capital formation (GFCF) numbers for FY2023–24 indicate a sequential slide quarter on quarter. As these reflect fixed assets, including construction, machinery and equipment, it was a concern. However, the share of GFCF in the GDP, which was falling in 2022–23, has been arrested.[13]

That said, in the Union Budget 2023, the Centre amped up capital investment with an outlay of ₹10 lakh crore, a 33% jump from the budgeted capital spending in the previous year. Yet, it was not able to entice private capital.

In an article published in February 2024, Mahesh Vyas, MD & CEO of the Centre for Monitoring Indian Economy (CMIE), iterates that although the capital spending of the central government trebled in four years, the private sector continued to remain tepid. He comments that though the Centre has been increasing its capital spending, it has reduced spending by central public-sector enterprises. He makes his point by giving an example of the government's revised estimate of capital spending in 2022–23, which was slated to increase by nearly 21%. However, he points out that the internal and extra-budgetary (IEBR) support to central government enterprises declined by 20.2% during the same period. The budgeted IEBR for 2023–24 was only 4% higher than the Budget Estimate (BE) of 2022–23. He warns that as central government enterprises are mostly in capital-intensive industries, starving them of capital would have an impact on the overall capex cycle in India.[14]

Indeed, the Centre's commitment is relatively inadequate in India's overall investments or the GFCF. The total central government spending on the capital account in 2022–23 is estimated at ₹7.3 lakh crore, less than 10% of India's total fixed capital formation in the year. In 2020–21, its share was less than 8%. This is one of the reasons holding back enhancement of private investment.

The geopolitical uncertainty resulting from the war in Ukraine is also making corporate India more cautious with its investments. Already, exports have been slowing, dropping 12% year on year in December 2022 to $34.5 billion (₹2.8 lakh crore) and putting additional pressure on the manufacturing sector.[15]

The National Accounts Statistics from MoSPI shows that private GFCF during the five fiscal years of FY2018–22 averaged 10.3% of the GDP. This is a significant fall from 11.5% in FY2013–17. Private GFCF slipped below 11% in FY2018 and continued at 10% in both FY2021 and FY2022. Examining the back series of 2011–12 GDP, private GFCF collapsed from 16.8% in FY2008. The *Monthly Economic Review* (MER) of August 2023 shows a falling graph of private GFCF (as a percentage of the GDP) in Q1 of FY2024. The RBI's September 2023 bulletin indicates that growth in overall GFCF (government plus private) was 8% in Q1 FY2024, lower than the previous nine quarters. MoSPI data shows growth in overall GFCF falling from 25.6% in FY2022 to 17% in FY2023, averaging 9.5% during FY2013–23 (current prices).

Thus, not just private GFCF, even overall capex (government and private) is losing steam. The Centre's capex in Q1 FY2024 grew at 59%, much lower than the states' capex growth of 74.3%.[16]

Of the six use-based Index of Industrial Production (IIP) indices, growth in four fell sharply during April–July 2023 compared to FY2023—primary goods fell from 11% to 4.5 cent, capital goods from 22.4% to 4.8%, intermediate goods from 9.5% to 2.8%, and consumer durables from 19.7% to –2.7%. Only two indices registered higher growth: infrastructure/construction goods rising from 8.8% to 12.2% and consumer non-durables from 0.1% to 6.8%.

Among three sectoral IIP indices, growth in two slipped sharply: manufacturing fell from 10.2% to 4.8%, and electricity from 13.2% to 2.9%. The third, mining IIP, saw moderate growth from 6.1% to 7.3%. Overall IIP (general IIP) growth slipped from 10% to 4.8%. The capacity utilisation and IIP numbers do not point to a revival of private investment. Credit growth has shifted from being driven by 'large industry' to 'personal loans' for consumption expenditure. Personal loans overtook large industry in FY2020 and industry and services in FY2022. This trend continued in FY2023 and Q1 FY2024. Credit flow to infrastructure improved marginally by about 1.5% between June 2022 and June 2023.

On the demand side, GFCF is likely to be the key driver of growth, while consumption demand is expected to be weak. GFCF is projected to grow by 10.3% in real terms, primarily due to government capital expenditure. As a percentage of the GDP, GFCF is expected to rise to 29.8% in nominal terms, the highest since 2014–15, and 34.9% in real terms. Consider the following facts: growth in manufacturing GVA is falling, growth in consumption demand (PFCE) is declining, growth in government expenditure (GFCE) is decreasing, and RBI estimates that GDP will sequentially slow from 7.8% in Q1 to 5.7% in Q4 of FY2024. Additionally, FDI inflows saw a sharp decline of 43% in 2023, dropping to $28 billion from $49 billion in 2022, according to UNCTAD. This significant fall contributed to India's drop to the fifteenth spot in global FDI inflows in 2023, down from the eighth position in 2022.[17]

Consider the following facts, which indicate that the trend is not moving up. This is because the economy, which has been supported by government expenditure, has not been able to stimulate private investment. Now even the capacity of the government to undertake public expenditure is likely to get capped by fiscal deficit targeting, as stated by FM Nirmala Sitharaman in her Union Budget announcements for FY2024–25:

- Growth in manufacturing GVA is falling.
- Growth in consumption demand (PFCE) is going down.
- Growth in government expenditure (GFCE) is going down.
- As per RBI estimates, the real GDP growth for 2024–25 is projected at 7.2% with Q1 at 7.3%; Q2 at 7.2%; Q3 at 7.3%; and Q4 at 7.2%. Growth in FDI inflows has shown a significant decline.[18]

Year	FDI Inflows (Billion USD)	Change (%)
2012	28	-
2013	26	–8
2014	32	24
2015	40	27
2016	44	10
2017	40	–9
2018	39	–2.5
2019	44	14
2020	57	30
2021	44	–23
2022	49	10
2023	28	–43

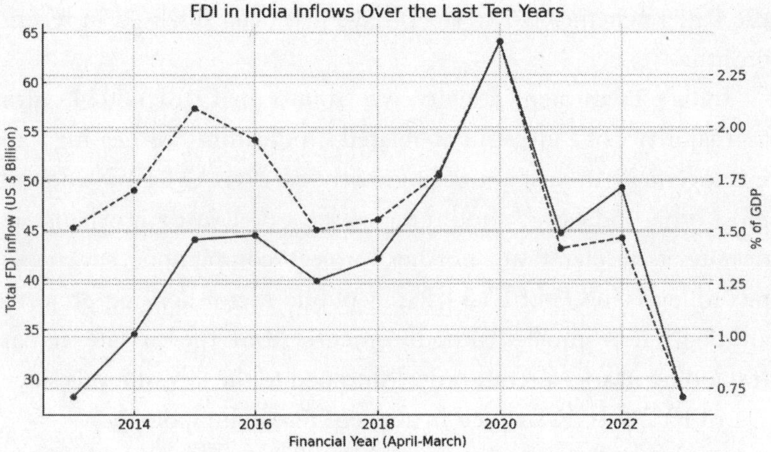

Source: 'India Foreign Direct Investment 1960-2024', *Macrotrends*, https://www.macrotrends.net/global-metrics/countries/IND/india/foreign-direct-investment; Ruchika Chitravanshi, 'India sees 43% decline in FDI inflows in 2023, drops to 15th spot', *Business Standard*, 20 June 2024, https://www.business-standard.com/economy/news/india-sees-43-fall-in-fdi-inflows-in-2023-drops-to-15th-spot-unctad-124062000868_1.html.

The *Production-Linked Incentive (PLI) scheme* has been the bedrock of the government's plan to promote domestic manufacturing after COVID-19. The scheme is currently operational across fourteen sectors, targeting manufacturing capacity addition of ₹5 lakh crore and employment generation of 3.6 million. The government is reportedly willing to spend ₹2.8 lakh crore spread over the next seven years in the form of financial capital support.

Three years since the commencement of the PLI scheme, the government has received investment commitments for ₹3 lakh crore by 733 applicants. About ₹62,500 crore of capex has been spent till FY2023 (i.e. 21% of committed capex and 12% of planned capex). Most of the capex activity under the PLI scheme is bunched during FY2024–26 as the final contours of some of the larger schemes (solar, steel) have just been finalised in recent months.

India's investment activity was robust in Q1 FY2024, with a majority of investment-related indicators witnessing an improvement in year-on-year growth vis-à-vis Q4 FY2023, and most other indicators continuing to see a double-digit expansion, despite a deceleration. 'Further, project completions surged to record levels in Q1 of FY24, led by public-sector housing projects, although new project announcements from the private sector (excluding a large aircraft order) slumped to the lowest levels since Q1 of FY21,' ICRA added in a recent research report.[19]

Metric	Value
Investments received	₹1.03 lakh crore
Production/sales due to PLI	₹8.61 lakh crore
Employment generation	6.78 lakh people
PLI exports	₹3.20 lakh crore
Number of applications received	746
Number of MSMEs benefitting	176

Note: Information up to November 2023

Four years after its launch, only the large-scale electronics manufacturing sector, including mobile phones, has significantly benefited from the PLI scheme, attracting considerable investments and boosting production and exports. Other sectors like pharmaceuticals, food processing, IT hardware and drones show some promise, but on a much smaller scale.

Sectors such as automobiles, auto components, drug intermediaries and APIs, medical devices, specialty steel, white goods, textile products, solar PV modules and ACC battery need to catch up. Overall, the PLI scheme's disbursals have been disappointing. Despite an announced outlay of ₹1.97 lakh crore over five years starting from 2021–22, only ₹9,700 crore have been disbursed, less than 5% of the total outlay.[20]

The government has consistently failed to achieve its *divestment* targets over the last ten years. Yet, it keeps assigning targets that, on the face of it, seem unrealistic. Divesting government equity in public-sector enterprises (PSEs) has proven to be quite volatile even for the BJP-led NDA government over the last nine years, despite a handful of mega transactions like the privatisation of debt-ridden erstwhile national carrier Air India and public listing of LIC. As many as 159 disinvestment transactions have taken place in the past nine years, government data reveals.[21] In terms of strategic sales, the Union Cabinet gave in-principle approval to thirty-six cases of PSEs, subsidiaries and JVs since 2016. But of the thirty-three cases being handled by the Department of Investment and Public Asset Management (DIPAM), strategic disinvestment transactions have been completed in only ten, including the privatisation of Air India. Interest from investors has also proven to be a stumbling block and getting the right price is a prime consideration.

Take, for instance, the disinvestment of Air India, which took three attempts over a period of twenty years before it could be sold off to the Tata Group. In the case of LIC, the IPO size was cut to 3.5% from the planned 5% because of choppy capital market conditions. Meanwhile, the operationalisation of the National Land Monetisation Corporation (NLMC) is underway but could take some time. The NLMC, which was approved by the Union Cabinet in March 2022, aims to monetise land and other non-core assets of central PSEs that are being taken up for strategic sale and closure. The Department of Public Enterprises, which is the nodal ministry in charge of this initiative, has recently selected international property consultants, including SBI Capital Markets and CBRE South Asia, to provide transaction advisory services for monetisation of such assets.[22]

Just when we thought multiple *taxes* had been merged administratively into GST and technology had paved the way for faceless assessments, we realised we had been presented with another authority with special powers that would haul up businesspersons.

Indeed, GST officials (not below the rank of joint commissioner) have the authority to search and seize any commodities, documents, or anything that would aid in legal actions, and empower the appropriate police to search and seize such objects and information at any time and in any location. If the GST commissioner has reasonable grounds to think a taxpayer has committed a violation, he has the authority to order their arrest by any appropriate officer. Further, if the officer determines that the person is subject to a penalty that is not covered under the act, the officer may issue an order levying the penalty.

This is arbitrary and allows room for corruption. Besides, the department is given targets that it fulfils by laying astronomical claims of penalties and evasion. Such is the level of overreach in terms of the claims made that if one were to collate the claims versus amount settled, one would observe that the amounts were fictitiously overstated to impress seniors or overwhelm the assessee into confessing, obliging or caving in.

In June 2023, chartered accountant and Manipal Group chairperson Mohandas Pai in a tweet reacted to a report that said 6,500 high-net-worth individuals (HNIs) would leave India in 2023, calling the trend 'very worrisome' and attributing it to 'tax terrorism'.[23] The former chief financial officer (CFO) of Infosys added that the Ministry of Finance was making life more difficult for HNIs and that too much tax terrorism and too much complex compliance needed to ease. (Pai was referring to the announcement by the finance minister in Parliament, before the passage of Budget 2023–24, that there would be tax collected at source (TCS) of 20% on credit card payments for overseas travel.)

On 11 November 2020, the prime minister had stated that the country was moving from tax terrorism to tax transparency. He added that this change had come because of the 'Reform, Perform and Transform' approach. Stating that rules and procedures were being reformed with the help of technology, he said, 'We are performing with clear intentions and, at the same time, transforming the mindset of the tax administration.' He expressed the view that when the difficulties of the country's wealth creators are reduced, they get protection, then their trust grows in the country's systems. He added that the result of this growing trust is that more and more partners were coming forward to join the tax system for the development of the country. He also remarked that along with the reduction of tax and simplicity in the process, the biggest reforms were related to the dignity of honest taxpayers, to protect them from trouble.[24]

The GST system was introduced in July 2017. Monthly GST collections have steadily increased over the years, with this year's average at ₹1.66 lakh crore, up from ₹1.51 lakh crore in 2022–23. However, GST is far from complete and needs substantial work—from reducing the number of tax slabs to widening its scope to include key items such as fuel products, among others.

Recently, cables and wires company Polycab was raided by GST authorities and the media carried reports that over ₹1,000 crore of unaccounted cash sales were found. This report brought the stock price of the company crashing by 20% on the same day. The true picture will only emerge after due diligence by the department, but releasing this kind of a statement even before the figures had been verified leaves the company and its shareholders in a very vulnerable position. In such cases where there has been an observation by authorities, they ought to maintain utmost secrecy or else the chance of clarification or even a containment of the crisis will be lost.[25]

The CAG under Vinod Rai had also issued claims of astronomical figures associated with the 2G telecom scam and the coal scam that were baseless and sensationalist at best. Although there was no doubt that a scam occurred, the claims made were audacious and enough to scare any foreign or domestic investor looking at investing in those sectors.[26]

In January 2024, we still had over 50 million pending cases in court. In 2021, in a speech at NALSAR University, the Chief Justice of India N.V. Ramana, said the total number of pending cases was 32.45 million. That implies a growth rate of nearly 18% every year. The economy is growing at 6%, the population is growing at 0.8%, but the backlog of the case load is growing at 18%. The aggregate case load data can be broken down into how many cases are pending for less than one year, between one and three years, and so on. Nearly 25% of all cases have been pending for more than five years. According to a 2018 report from PRS Legislative Research, one-fourth of all cases with high courts were pending for over ten years, with an aggregate number of over 1 million. Allahabad High Court had the highest pendency, with over 7 lakh cases.

The reasons are not far to seek. The first is the inadequate number of judicial officers. Across the board, there are an average of 20% unfilled vacancies; these numbers are even greater in the higher judiciary. In a speech in December 2022, the chief justice said 6.3 million cases were considered delayed because of the non-availability of counsel. And another 1.4 million cases were delayed as they awaited some kind of document or record. Why should this be the case when the whole system is being digitised? Another significant reason for the piling up of cases is due to appeals made by government officers when judgments are delivered against the department concerned. For instance, if a lower tribunal gives an order against the income tax claims of the government, the officer involved would almost surely appeal, even if it were an open-and-shut case. This is for fear of being accused of corruption or collusion.[27]

One of India's biggest challenges is—and has always been—*corruption*. According to 'The Impact of Corruption on Growth and Inequality', a report published by Transparency International (TI),[28] at the macro level, research generally shows that corruption has a detrimental, direct effect on economic development and growth. As per the Corruption Perceptions Index by TI, India is ranked 85th among 180 countries. Although the situation is much better than 2013 when the country was ranked 94th, India has a long way to go to tackle this perverse phenomenon.

According to the TI survey, in the wider Asian region, India has one of the highest incidences of bribery and use of personal connections to access key public services such as health and education. It cited state services, particularly courts, police, the revenue department and hospitals, as the most corrupt bodies. The report claims that government servants are involved in 90% of corruption cases. Similarly, in 51% of cases, a bribe is paid for the timely delivery of service.

Historically, the infamous License Permit Raj, which curbed foreign investment and severely stifled competition in the name of a 'socialist economy', created a black market for everything and the smuggling of imported goods became a norm. The real turning point for India's culture of graft began with the commencement of economic reforms and liberalisation in 1991. While economic reforms led to the end of licensing for industrial activities and the abolition of import quotas, thereby removing many corrupt practices, this did not reduce graft. The same phenomenon continued in some form or the other in several key sectors, particularly minerals, natural resources and services. For example, the opaque and arbitrary allocation of coal blocks and the telecom spectrum (2G) set the stage for the UPA 2 government losing power in the 2014 elections.

In response to the 2011 anti-corruption stir by Anna Hazare, who demanded to have a Lokpal or Ombudsman, the UPA 2 government passed the Lokpal Bill in 2013 to tackle big-ticket graft. The NDA government took more than four years to appoint the members of the Lokpal. Ironically, this much-promised institution has remained largely invisible in the fight against big-ticket corruption. Yet, what has done more for the anti-corruption crusade is the enactment of the Right to Information (RTI) legislation in 2005. The RTI Act helped unearth scams related to the Adarsh Housing Society in Mumbai and the Commonwealth Games in Delhi. However, not only has the current regime curtailed the powers of the chief information commissioner (CIC) via administrative changes and constitutional amendments, it has restricted the scope of the RTI application too in recent years.

The appointment of heads of public-sector companies, senior police officers, tax officers and such other powerful government officials needs scrutiny, as somewhere there lies the root of the evil. Creating a system of appointment as per merit for such appointments and then a review system for performance can cleanse the system.

~

Foreign and private investors worry about the impact on their projects due to regime changes. Successive governments, at the state or Centre, have given them cause for concern.

In recent times, even before Y.S. Jagan Mohan Reddy took oath as Andhra Pradesh chief minister in May 2019, he had announced his intent to probe some of his predecessor N. Chandrababu

Naidu's projects, including the ₹1.1 trillion development of the new capital, Amaravati, and the ₹55,550 crore Polavaram irrigation project. Similarly, a day after Shiv Sena chief Uddhav Thackeray assumed the top job in Maharashtra in November 2019, he put on hold the construction of a contentious metro car shed and, soon after, ordered a review of other major infrastructure projects, including a high-speed train between Mumbai and Ahmedabad, costing over ₹1 trillion.

Even if an infrastructure project is fully or partially funded by the government, a state, if ruled by a different party or coalition, may refuse to play ball. And the state's cooperation is essential to acquiring the requisite land and executing the project. In July 2019, Andhra Pradesh decided to review the power purchase agreements (PPAs) it had signed with wind and solar power developers, saying the tariffs were kept high to benefit some players. This put 5,200 MW of projects—and their ₹21,000 crore debt—at risk, according to CRISIL. Reddy also terminated a ₹3,217 crore hydel power contract and withdrew hundreds of acres allotted for infrastructure, industrial and real estate projects. A project awarded to a Singapore consortium to create a startup district in Amravati was also scrapped.

Another landmark case of policy flipflops or getting into the crosshairs of political adversaries was Lavasa, India's first planned hill city, which was being built on 25,000 acres in Pune district. The (central) Ministry of Environment and Forests raised objections to the environmental clearances given by the Maharashtra government to the project in 2002 and 2004. Lavasa's main shareholder was Hindustan Construction Company (HCC), which owned 64.99%, while the remaining stakes were held by the Avantha Group, Venkateshwara Hatcheries and Pune-based Vinay Maniar. The project's initial promoters included Sharad Pawar's daughter Supriya Sule and her husband Sadanand Sule, who withdrew from the project in 2004. In 2012, observing that the project nods were given without environmental and cabinet approvals, the CAG rapped the Maharashtra government for 'total lack of transparency' in the selection of the project. The government order halted all construction work for a year.

Though the government later allowed it to go ahead by paying penalties and ensuring full compliance to regulations, the debt started weighing heavily on Lavasa as it struggled to pay interest on it. After Lavasa failed to meet its payment obligations, Raj Infrastructure Development India, one of its creditors, filed a bankruptcy petition against the company, which was admitted in 2018. Nearly five years later, the NCLT cleared the sale of Lavasa to Darwin Platform Infrastructure. The NCLT order envisaged a payout of ₹1,814 crore over eight years, including ₹929 crore to lenders and a spend of ₹438 crore on delivering fully constructed houses to homebuyers. There are 837 homebuyers whose claims have been admitted. Their admitted claims total ₹409 crore. The total claim amount admitted by the company, including from lenders and operational creditors, is ₹6,642 crore. The resolution plan envisages the delivery of fully constructed properties to homebuyers within a period of five years of receiving environmental clearance on an actual cost basis. Homebuyers will have to pay actual future construction costs to Darwin towards obtaining constructed properties in the project. In April 2024, Lavasa's creditors invoked a ₹25-crore performance guarantee provided by Darwin Platform Infrastructure Ltd (DPIL). DPIL was to make a down payment of ₹92.50 crore for working capital to keep Lavasa running. It has not paid the money yet.[29]

There are many ways in which the problem of policy flipflops can be resolved. Contracts between government and companies are one-sided. Adoption of the FIDIC contract system—a globally recognised template—would put contractors on an equal footing with the government. Other measures include empowering state infrastructure regulators like electricity regulatory commissions so that they are free of the influence of state governments; establishing a national body, along the lines of the NCLT, dedicated to infrastructure, with separate benches for subsectors like roads and ports; and creating a national project board by an act of Parliament. All projects above a certain threshold must be registered with the board and all MoUs and agreements should be submitted to government bodies. A dedicated dispute resolution commercial court with a permanent full bench should be attached to the board. Any breach of promise should be dealt with swiftly by the court.

India's small informal sector firms, employing over 75% of the manufacturing workforce, struggle to compete globally owing to their scale and productivity limitations. In contrast, China's manufacturing sector, dominated by firms with over 1,000 workers, enjoys much higher productivity. For India's small-scale units to thrive, they need to evolve into medium and large-scale industries, achieving higher productivity and wages. Key obstacles include restrictive *labour laws*. The Union Government's consolidation of twenty-four labour laws into four codes aims to introduce flexibility, especially the Industrial Relations Code, which permits firms with up to 300 workers to hire and fire without government approval. However, effective implementation by states, given labour laws are in the Concurrent List, is crucial.

India's Factories Act has been considered a barrier to the growth of the manufacturing sector because of its complex compliance requirements. The act mandates stringent regulations regarding safety, health and welfare conditions in factories, which can lead to significant operational costs and bureaucratic hurdles, particularly for smaller firms. These compliance demands can hinder the ability of SMEs to scale up and achieve higher productivity levels.

The Factories Act 1948, read with fifty-eight rules, contains over 8,682 imprisonment clauses; the Legal Metrology Act 2009, to establish and enforce standards of weights and measures, read with twenty-nine rules, has 391 imprisonment clauses; the Electricity

Act 2003, read with thirty-five rules, has 558 imprisonment clauses; and the Motor Vehicles Act 1988, read with nine rules, has 134 imprisonment clauses.[30]

Labour participation is key to the growth matrix. Goldman Sachs projects India will beat the US by 2075 to emerge as the second largest economy, while also surpassing Japan and Germany.[31] These projections imply that global growth will average a little under 3% per year over the next ten years and will be on a gradually declining path, primarily reflecting slower labour force growth. Global population growth has halved over the past fifty years, from 2% per year to less than 1%, and is expected to fall to close to zero by 2075. That is where India's chance lies.

India's large population is clearly an opportunity. However, the challenge is productively using the labour force, by increasing the participation rate. That will mean creating the opportunities for labour to get absorbed and simultaneously training and upskilling them. The labour force participation rate (LFPR) is defined as the section of the working population in the age group of 16–64 in the economy currently employed or seeking employment. People who are still undergoing studies, housewives and persons above the age of sixty-four are not counted in the labour force.

India's current population is estimated to be a little over 1.4 billion and roughly 64% of that—or about 900 million—falls in the working age cohort. Every year, however, a little over 10 million youth join the workforce. This is a matter of concern, as the LFPR in India has been around 50% for a long time and the employment statistics have not improved much. In comparison, LFPR is 73% in the US, 76% in China and 78% in the UK. Even if India were to increase its LFPR by one percentage point every year until it reaches a LFPR of 70%, around 95 million non-agricultural jobs will have to be created over the next twenty-five years considering the rate at which the total population is estimated to increase, according to experts from Dun & Bradstreet International.[32]

Let us look at female labour participation in particular. India is home to about 663 million women, of which approximately 450 million fall in the working age of 15–64 years. India's female labour force participation rate (FLFPR) had been showing a sharp declining trend over the past three decades, from 30.2% in 1990 to an all-time low of 17.5% in 2018, as per reports by the World Bank, Centre for Monitoring Indian Economy (CMIE) and the Periodic Labour Force Survey (PLFS). Unlike the downward trend India has seen in the FLFPR since the 1990s, the 2020–21 PLFS for all ages shows a significant improvement in the past three years, going up from 17.5% to 24.8% (for women aged 15 and above, the rate increased from 23.3% in 2017–18 to 32.8 in 2020–21). A recent press release from the Ministry of Finance highlights that this improvement can be attributed to a range of factors, including progressive labour reform measures, better employment trends in the manufacturing sector, increasing share of self-employed people, and a rise in formal employment levels.[33]

The global FLFPR is 52.4% (age 15+) and has been at a similar level for the past three decades. However, in developing countries and emerging economies, there is a significant variation. In the Middle East, North Africa and South Asia, this rate is approximately 25%, whereas it reaches up to about 66% in East Asia and sub-Saharan Africa. According to the PLFS, we have approximately 166 million women either working, seeking work, or available for work. Of the population of working women, more than 90% work in the informal sector. They are either self-employed or casual workers, predominantly in the agricultural and construction sectors. This means they face increased exploitation, poor working conditions, lack of mobility and higher risk of violence. This discourages women from entering the workforce. A recent NITI Aayog report states that women in India spend 9.8 times more time than men on unpaid domestic chores (against a global average of 2.6 as reported by UN Women). Globally, unpaid care work is the key reason that women are outside the labour force.[34]

India's ability to attract and retain talent is another issue to consider. Developed by the prestigious INSEAD, the Global Talent Competitiveness Index (GTCI) index measures how countries and cities grow, attract and retain talent. It claims to provide 'a unique resource for decisionmakers to understand the global talent competitiveness picture and develop strategies to boost their economies'. The index uses two sub-indices: input and output. Input measures regulatory and business environments, as well as steps being taken to foster talent and retain it, while output evaluates the quality of talent.

With a ranking of 103, India's performance in the GTCI is the worst among the BRICS group of countries. China remains at the top of the group at 40, while Russia is at 52, South Africa at 68 and Brazil at 69. 'In the years to 2020, India saw its talent competitiveness increase but it has regressed in each of the three years since,' notes the report. 'A major reason for this fall is a slump in business sentiment, which has had a detrimental effect on the ability to "attract talent" (now 132 of 134) – whether that is talent from overseas (127 in "external openness" sub-pillar) or from within the country (129 in "internal openness").' It also refers to 'an increased skills mismatch and a greater difficulty in finding skilled employees, pushing India to 121 in both the "employability" sub-pillar and the "vocational and technical skills" pillar'. The report records 'global knowledge skills', the second of the output-related pillars, as India's best-performing area, where innovation and software development are driving its 69th position in the talent impact sub-pillar.

According to the report, other emerging countries have shown improvements on this index, with China, Indonesia and Mexico being cited for special mention. 'Several of the largest emerging economies are among the best improvers over the past decade. Notable examples: China has moved from being a talent mover to a talent champion; Indonesia is one of the countries with the greatest strides in talent competitiveness over the past decade;

Mexico has moved from being a talent laggard to a talent mover; and Brazil has progressed and may well soon be categorised as a talent mover.'

Singapore, Switzerland and the US are among the top three countries on the scale.[35]

On the infrastructure front …

A major issue plaguing the infra sector is *project delay*. The MoSPI reports every quarter on the status of delayed projects above ₹150 crore. In a report issued in November 2023, of a total of 1,788 monitored projects valued at ₹150 crore and above, 411 reported cost overruns, while 837 experienced delays. The original implementation cost was ₹2,478,446.60 crore, with an anticipated completion cost of ₹2,909,526.63 crore, indicating an overall cost overrun of ₹431,080.03 crore.

Reasons for time overruns reported by implementing agencies included delays in land acquisition, obtaining clearances, lack of infrastructure support and state-wise lockdowns owing to COVID-19 in 2020 and 2021. Other factors include delays in project financing, detailed engineering and scope changes, tendering, ordering, equipment supply and law-and-order issues. Despite the Gati Shakti initiative, the benefit of accelerated pace and higher accuracy of DPRs has not accrued. In fact, the cost overrun is higher than the entire railways and roads budget put together! A prime reason for project delays has consistently been problems with land acquisition—this factor is the costliest element in shaping the cost matrix of infrastructure can throw all calculations into a tailspin.[36]

Land continues to be the biggest cause of project delay and project cost inflation. It continues to cause litigation and is a contributor to India losing out on FDI. A study conducted by Prosperiti.org, called 'The State of Regulation Report', has compared ten states on factory land lost to building standards and the opportunity cost of land lost. Based on land lost to four building standards (ground coverage, setbacks, parking and floor area ratio), it has ranked states on building restrictiveness. According to the survey, a factory in India is likely to lose 50% of land, or more, to building standards. Overall, Haryana is the least restrictive state for constructing a factory, followed closely by Tamil Nadu and Telangana, while Odisha, Bihar and Delhi are the most restrictive for factories of all sizes.

Here are the other key findings:

- Our entrepreneurs are paying full price for half use.
- A large factory can generate 130–255 more jobs by halving the land lost.
- Standards penalise small factories more than large factories. Still, large and mega factories end up losing 55% of their plot on average across states.
- Of the four standards, factories lose the most amount of buildable footprint to setbacks and parking. In Bihar, a small factory can lose up to 77% of land to setbacks alone. A 500-employee factory in Maharashtra needs estimated space for sixty-seven cars, 304 two-wheelers and six trucks.
- Only five out of ten states recognise that ground coverage is a redundant standard. In other states, this redundant standard can lead to a deadweight loss of land owing to overlaps with parking and setbacks.
- On average, factories across states are only allowed to create floor space up to 1.3 times the plot size.
- Our standards often surpass standards set by countries that are ten times India's per capita GDP.

Land use is largely regulated by state-level building and construction laws. Over the past few years, states have begun to recognise the importance of releasing unbuilt land through revising building bylaws. But these efforts are unsystematic and reactive. For example, the Haryana Building Code 2017 has been amended ten times since its promulgation (Housing Board 2018). At least five of these amendments institute more liberal standards. Some states have introduced sector-specific relaxations. For example, Gujarat and Uttar Pradesh have promised relaxation of building standards for IT office spaces, warehouses and logistics parks. Creating exemptions sector by sector gives only selective relief. There is value in a more comprehensive review based on costs and benefits. Land is the biggest cause of litigation, according to a recent study—over two-thirds of complainants are being affected by land dispute issues.

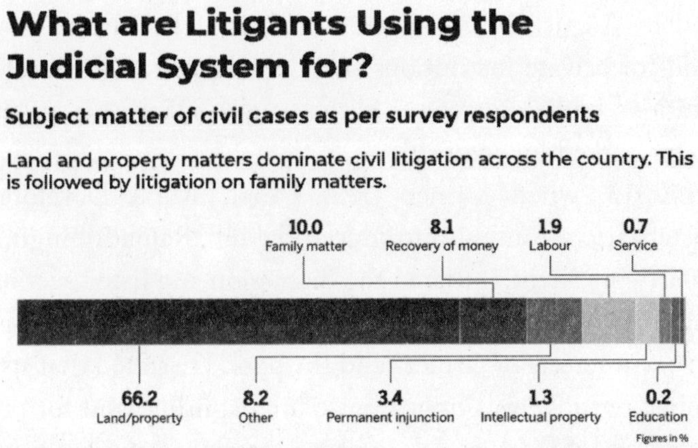

Source: 'Access to Justice Survey 2015-16', *Daksh*, https://dakshindia.org/wp-content/uploads/2016/05/Daksh-access-to-justice-survey.pdf.

Digitisation of land records is a key concern. In 1999, the Ministry of Rural Development (MoRD) published a Vision Document for the Computerisation of Land Records to standardise the management of land. For the first time, this document discussed the standardisation of a Land Information System. Now is the time to develop and implement a national policy on land records. The decade-old National Land Record Modernisation Programme (NLRMP) aimed at improving land records was rechristened the Digital India Land Record Modernisation Programme (DILRMP) but, fundamentally, the scheme has remained the same despite low-to-middling success across states. Although land is a state subject, it is for the Centre to incentivise states to undertake reforms and provide knowledge and capacity-building platforms.

Land acquisition in India is currently governed by The Right to Fair Compensation and Transparency in Land Acquisition, Rehabilitation and Resettlement Act 2013 (RFCTLARR Act, 2013), which came into force from 1 January 2014 after the Land Acquisition Act of 1894 was replaced. In December 2014, the NDA government promulgated an ordinance amending the Land Acquisition and Rehabilitation Bill, which had originally been passed in August 2013. Its provisions included the acquisition of land for private institutions such as hospitals and educational institutions and doing away with social impact assessments in areas earmarked for acquisition.

In 2013, when former UPA Union Rural Development Minister Jairam Ramesh introduced the bill, Rajnath Singh, then BJP party president, initiated the discussion and listed sections of the bill that, in the party's view, did not display enough seriousness about the interests of farmers and the poor. He stated that its idea of 'public purpose' was only a guise for acquiring land for private industry and SEZs; social impact assessment must always be carried out and the urgency clause that bypassed this provision must be done away with; a retrospective clause for farmers who had not yet received compensation when the process of acquisition was not yet complete must be included; and compensation under the bill must be enhanced.

As for farmer reforms, the NDA government's own initiatives were poorly presented, leading to a stand-off with the farmers. Ultimately, the resolution, which would have been a landmark agricultural reform, was withdrawn.

India has traditionally followed the L1 principle of procurement where the lowest cost *tender* is selected. In the L1 system, a bidder is selected only based on the lowest cost committed to complete the work. There is no weightage for technical score in the final evaluation and the responsive technically qualified proposal with the lowest evaluated cost is selected.

How do you select a contractor without issuing a tender? A private company does not have any such issue doing so, but a state or central body has to follow mandated procedures. Then, how does the government manage to allot and award contracts to companies that would surely deliver without having to issue tenders? The Motera stadium was awarded to L&T by the Gujarat Cricket Association, whose president was Amit Shah, and they wanted it to be ready with a seating capacity of 132,000, which would make it bigger than the Melbourne Cricket Ground (capacity of 100,024), making it the world's biggest. Built at a cost of ₹800 crore within five years, it was first opened to the public in 2020 for the Namaste Trump event, organised for US President Donald Trump. Similarly, the Ram Mandir contract was awarded to L&T and Tata Consulting Engineers by the Ram Janmabhoomi Teertha Kshetra, a trust set up in 2020. Probably, the criticality of completing the land acquisition and construction so it met the deadline of January 2024 was a key consideration over the cost. The construction of the Ram Mandir will be completed by December 2024. Right now, only the ground floor has been built. Work on the other two floors was resumed after the Praan Pratishtha ceremony. So, when quality and criticality are of utmost importance, an autonomous body is a great vehicle to grant contracts and move a project at great speed.

According to MoSPI, India is losing over ₹4 trillion owing to project delays. Thus, time is precious and should be made the essence of any contract. Several contracts, once won, seek amendments in design and feign 'doctored' environmental reasons. The changes allow them to raise cost estimates and retain the contract award despite changes in the terms. On 29 October 2021, quality-cum-cost based selection (QCBS) was introduced, paving the way for a revised system that incorporated merit and not simply the cost. This system was recommended where the procurement has been declared to be a quality-oriented procurement (QOP) by the competent authority and for procurement of non-consulting services, where the estimated value of procurement (including all taxes and option clause) does not exceed ₹10 crore. Now, in a notification dated 1 November 2023, a clarification has emerged where the limits for applicability of the QCBS system have been withdrawn and it can now be applied for all non-consultancy contracts for quality-oriented projects too. This is not yet mandatory but its application will be allowed in procurement processes.

The L1 selection method made it impossible for quality infrastructure, as everyone was competing to deliver the cheapest alternative. Companies that wanted to raise money or their stature at the stock market would bid low and grab contracts to inflate their order books. However, when it came to execution, such firms realised too late that they were unable to execute the projects in the required timeline or at the cost they had won the tender at. They then either pleaded to surrender the project or went bust. Now that we have indicated the ambitious target of becoming a $30 trillion economy by 2047, we cannot allow our scarce resources to be utilised for low-hanging fruits.

The current dispensation in procurement follows the traditional method that stems from the transitionary nature of public accountability, which is that action and execution on display should be evident in a short time and the lifecycle of a project is incidental. Other than mega projects like the metro rail, the Atal Setu and Statue of Unity, projects like a bridge, highway and other infrastructure that does not command national attention, the specifications do not necessarily mandate that the project last a specific number of years. Thus, corresponding material, technologies and design are sourced to meet current execution deadlines and available budgets rather than engineered with the objective of making them available for use for the desirable life of such projects. If we are budgeting ₹11.11 trillion in 2024–25, why should it not last us for a hundred years?

The government has failed to create capacity among companies that could potentially help build the infrastructure for the $5 trillion economy.

L&T remains the bellwether construction company with a topline revenue of ₹2.10 trillion for FY2023–24, of which international revenues contributed ₹95,086 crore, constituting 43% of total revenues. Even at ₹3 trillion of domestic orders, L&T commands a 25% share in total infrastructure project announcements. But if India has added more than 50,000 km of national highways since 2014, why have we been unable to create several L&Ts? In December 2023, the Union Minister of Road, Transport & Highways Nitin Gadkari cited that in the preceding nine years, his ministry has allocated projects exceeding ₹50 lakh crore and streamlined the contract approval process by refining existing policies. Then how come the next ten companies make up only half of L&T's turnover and the balance companies make up only one-fourth of it?

If India aims to India aims to elevate its road infrastructure to match that of the US within the next five years, as stated by Gadkari, where is our capacity to undertake these projects? If, as per CRISIL, investment in infrastructure is projected to double by 2030, reaching an estimated ₹142.9 lakh crore from ₹66.7 lakh crore during 2017–23, which are the companies that will shoulder this? If we are hoping that foreign construction companies like Bechtel will join in this massive infrastructure ramp-up, we will need to address the reasons they have stayed away so far.[37]

Company Name	Revenue (₹ in cr)	Profit (₹ in cr)
		(Financials for 2023–24)
Larsen & Toubro	126,235.85	9,304.33
Megha Engineering & Infrastructure	33,000.00*	2517.00*
NCC	18,314.41	631.48
Tata Projects	17,596.00	139.09
Kalpataru Projects International	16,759.66	533
Afcons Infrastructure	13,646.88	449.76
Dilip Buildcon	10,537.30	422.03
Navayuga Engineering	8200.00*	330.00*
NBCC	8,251.81	344.36
GR Infraprojects	8,013.25	1,977.43
Dineshchandra R Agarwal Infracon Pvt. Ltd	7,987.00	292
Ashoka Buildcon	7,841.28	442.76
PNC Infratech	7,726.96	849.79
ITD Cementation India	7,588.49	376.62
APCO Infratech Pvt. Ltd	6,041.67	520.36
Hindustan Construction Co	5,167.70	178.57
HG Infra & Engineering Ltd	5,134.34	545.49
J Kumar Infraprojects	4,907.61	328.59
Jaiprakash Associates Limited	4,907.61	328.59

Company Name	Revenue (₹ in cr)	Profit (₹ in cr)
Patel Engineering	4,521.03	285.6
KNR Constructions	4,233.15	493.83
Ahluwalia Contracts (India)	3,891.94	375.55
Welspun Enterprises	2,552.75	285.15
PSP Projects	2,486.76	123.9
Ramky Infrastructure	2,137.12	360.22
Capacite Infraprojects Ltd	1,899.68	114.03
RPP Infra Projects	1,378.82	65.51
SPML Infra	1,268.20	4.82
BL Kashyap & Sons	1,224.37	34.9
Madhuccon Projects	1,205.67	–10.27
Sadbhav Engineering	1,077.46	–264.67
Simplex Infrastructures	1,028.73	–71.89
GPT Infraprojects Ltd	1,009.84	60.74
Man Infraconstruction	804.80	195.46
Vascon Engineers	775.17	61.42
SEPC Ltd	606.56	22.67
IL&FS Engineering & Construction Company Ltd	332.62	–77.19
AGI Infra Ltd	301.39	52.1
Brahmaputra Infrastructure Ltd	221.11	17.19
Adwait Infratech Ltd	209.92	21.33
MBL Infrastructures	184.15	6.63
Consolidated Construction Consortium	146.04	665.67

Company Name	Revenue (₹ in cr)	Profit (₹ in cr)
Artson Engineering	128.78	6.05
Shristi Infrastructure Development Corporation Ltd	109.49	–18.4
Coromandel Engineering Co	96.68	–4.4
Sanmit Infra Ltd	96.65	4.47
Atlanta Ltd	96.17	49.07
Tarmat Ltd	89.79	–1.13
Reliance Industrial Infrastructure Ltd	82.70	10.21
IVRCL Infrastructures & Projects	80.70	–2696.08
PBA Infrastructure	79.80	2.45
Conart Engineers Ltd	49.49	3.08
Sadbhav Infrastructure Projects Ltd	43.20	–562.11
Total	**352,308.55**	**20,127.16**

Note: 1) Consolidated Construction Consortium Ltd's profit is higher than their revenue because it has received a write-off from lenders due to its resolution under the Insolvency & Bankruptcy Code, which increased its profit.

2) IVRCL is indebted to various financial creditors and operational creditors to the tune of approximately ₹12,908 crore and is undergoing a settlement process under the Insolvency & Bankruptcy Code.

3) Megha Engineering & Infrastructure and Navayuga Engineering's turnover and PAT figures are estimated based upon their provisional figures reported for six-monthly and nine-monthly performances for the same financial year.

A key variable affecting India's manufacturing potential is *cost-competitiveness in logistics.* Costs are about 14–18% of GDP, according to the *Economic Survey* 2022–23. The government aims to lower these costs to below 10% to be more in line with major Asian exporters. The PM Gati Shakti initiative is a promising measure where multiple plans are integrated by geospatial tagging to integrate most efficient infrastructure solutions.

Improving road and rail connectivity will help cut logistics costs. There is already a noticeable acceleration in national highway building, with the government expecting construction to reach 33 km/day in FY2024, almost double the 17 km/day achieved in FY2016. The share of containers being shipped by rail is also rising—it is forecast to hit 23.5% in FY2024 and 33% in FY2030, according to the government. India lags behind Japan, South Korea and mainland China in export infrastructure and efficiency, particularly in terms of port capacity.

To narrow this infrastructure gap and become the global manufacturing destination of choice, India will need massive upgrades covering areas such as rail, ports and freight corridors. The country needs to reduce its reliance on transshipments via hubs such as Singapore and Hong Kong to help manufacturers avoid potentially lengthy transit times. This means adding efficient high-capacity ports that can handle the largest container ships or incentivising operators to introduce direct services to major markets. It will also entail strengthening links with global container carriers and freight forwarders. India has an opportunity to increase its share of global container shipments and bulk commodities, even if North Asia will likely continue to be the driver of global container volumes, according to S&P Global's Trade Analytics suite.[38] Accelerating port infrastructure development will be key to achieving this. Port capacity and container throughput have experienced robust growth in India over the past five years. Looking forward, capacity will have a CAGR of 2.7% from 2023–30, with container traffic achieving

6.5%, based on estimates from CRISIL, an S&P Global company.

On 19 June 2024, the Cabinet approved the construction of a major port at Vadhavan near Dahanu in Maharashtra's Palghar district at a cost of ₹76,200 crore. As reported by ANI, Minister Ashwini Vaishnaw said, 'It will be an integral part of the IMEC (India-Middle East-Europe Corridor). It will be constructed by a JV of the Jawaharlal Nehru Port Authority and Maharashtra Maritime Board. It will be one of the top 10 ports in the world.' The Cabinet also okayed the road connectivity between the port and national highways by MoRTH and rail linkage to the existing rail network and the upcoming Dedicated Rail Freight Corridor by the Ministry of Railways.[39]

India has the fourth-largest *railway system* in the world, following the US, Russia and China. As of FY2023 (January 2023), Indian Railways had 13,523 passenger trains and 9,146 freight trains. As of FY2022, it had a total route network of 68,103 km. Indian Railways has logged the highest-ever electrification of sections covering 6,015 route kilometre (rkm) in a single year in 2020–21. More than five times electrification was achieved from 2014–21 compared to 2007–14. Indeed, the railways are close to completely running on electricity.

However, though the railways carry over 20 million passengers daily, they haven't got the attention they deserve. An audit by the CAG of India last year revealed that the ₹2.5 lakh crore spent on building rail infrastructure over the last decade has not been adequate to improve its 'mobility outcomes'. The challenge for the government has been to yank this vast network spanning a running track length of over 128,305 km into the modern era, leaving behind the colonial legacy of overcrowded trains, poor facilities and dirty washrooms.

India's worst train disaster in two decades—a collision in Balasore, Odisha, in mid-2023 that killed at least 275 people and injured hundreds more—has renewed concerns over the safety of the railways. Indian trains run on mixed tracks, with both passenger and goods trains running on the same track. Thus, the lines are mostly over-utilised and clogged and the time available to carry out routine maintenance activity is compromised.

Year	Number of Train Accidents
2010	165
2011	131
2012	121
2013	115
2014	105
2015	107
2016	104
2017	73
2018	59
2019	52
2020	44
2021	35
2022	34
2023	38

As in March 2023, the Indian railway network spanned 104,647 km of running track length and 68,426 km of route length. Indian Railways is rolling out tenders for 10,000 km of Kavach, an automatic train protection system, to prevent accidents due to human error resulting in signal passing in danger and speeding. It has so far tendered 6,000 km of Kavach system deployed on 1,465 route km and 139 locomotives (including electric multiple unit rakes) on the South Central Railway. It has received the patent for Kavach and tenders are in proof for another 10,000 km. The system involves complexities and has to be customised for every train. The plan is to deploy Kavach on the entire 70,000 rkm to ensure the safety of passengers.

The railways have constantly lost out to roads in freight and airlines in passenger comfort and travel, continuing to cede its revenues and turning into a loss-making proposition. Only in recent years has the sector begun to make moves to restore its original glory. But it is a work in progress. The government has invested nearly $30 billion in the sector by manufacturing semi-high-speed trains, modern coaches and locomotives and redeveloping stations—part of a broader upgrade to transport infrastructure. What is close to becoming a reality after eighteen long years is a project of connecting the Eastern and Western Corridors. The Dedicated Freight Corridors are likely to change this as they accelerate the movement of cargo and relieve the passenger routes free of cargo and good movement. The 1,337-km Eastern Dedicated Freight Corridor (EDFC) from Ludhiana in Punjab to Sonnagar in Bihar is fully operational, and the 1,506-km Western Dedicated Freight Corridor (WDFC) from Jawaharlal Nehru Port Terminal in Navi Mumbai, Maharashtra, to Dadri in Uttar Pradesh, is 88% (around 1,300 km) operational. Over 90% of the 2,843 km of railway corridors dedicated to freight transport—built at a cost of ₹1.24 lakh crore—is operational. Reportedly, against the dedicated freight corridor's optimum capacity of 480 trains per day on both arms together, there are 300–320 running currently (200 on EDFC and 100 on WDFC); the average speed is 55–60 kmph (maximum is 100 kmph), compared to 20 kmph on the Indian Railways freight service.[40]

Cities occupy only 3% of the land mass, but are the engines to our country's growth and contribute over two-thirds to its GDP although they host only 30% of the country's population. The number of inhabitants in Indian cities is estimated to have increased almost fourfold between 1970 and 2018, from 109 million to 460 million. Already the second-largest urban community in the world, the country is expected to add another 416 million people to its cities by 2050 and have an urban share of population of 50%.[41]

The Ministry of Housing & Urban Affairs has taken up initiatives such as Pradhan Mantri Awas Yojana, urban and rural, smart cities and metro rail.

Mission	Up till 31 Dec 2022	Up till 31 Dec 2023	Growth
PMAY			
Houses grounded	107.30 lakhs	113.53 lakhs	6.23 lakhs
Houses completed	67.10 lakhs	79.02 lakhs	11.92 lakhs
Person days generated for gainful employment	727 crores	864 crores	137 crores
Consumption of steel	100 lakh metric tonne	120 lakh metric tonne	20 lakh metric tonne
Consumption of cement	443 lakh metric tonne	526 lakh metric tonne	83 lakh metric tonne
AMRUT			
Completed projects	₹33,478 crores	₹43,573 crores	₹10,095 crores
Of the grounded projects, works physically completed	₹67,437 crores	₹75,256 crores	₹7,819 crores

Mission	Up till 31 Dec 2022	Up till 31 Dec 2023	Growth
Water tap connections	136.62 lakhs	187.40 lakhs	51 lakhs
Sewer connections	103.40 lakhs	147 lakhs	43.6 lakhs
LED street lights	97 lakhs	99 lakhs	2 lakhs
AMRUT 2.0			
Approved projects	₹94,955.12 crores	₹153,573.75 crores	₹58,618 crores
Water tap connections to be added/serviced	2.36 crores	3.66 crores	1.30 crores
Sewerage connections to be added/serviced	60 lakhs	1.01 crores	41 lakhs
Contracts awarded	0	₹32,703 crores	₹32,703 crores
Water distribution network to be laid/ replaced	58,707 km	1.02 lakh km	43,550 km
Sewer network to be laid/ replaced	15,498 km	28,458 km	12,960 km
WTP capacity to be added/ augmented	7,071 MLD	9,701 MLD	2,630 MLD
STP capacity to be added/ augmented	2,158 MLD	3,939 MLD	1,781 MLD
Water bodies to be rejuvenated	1,518	2,135	617
Mission	Up till 31 Dec 2022	Up till 31 Dec 2023	Growth

Mission	Up till 31 Dec 2022	Up till 31 Dec 2023	Growth
PMAY			
Houses grounded	107.30 lakhs	113.53 lakhs	6.23 lakhs
Houses completed	67.10 lakhs	79.02 lakhs	11.92 lakhs
Person days generated for gainful employment	727 crores	864 crores	137 crores
Consumption of steel	100 lakh metric tonne	120 lakh metric tonne	20 lakh metric tonne
Consumption of cement	443 lakh metric tonne	526 lakh metric tonne	83 lakh metric tonne
AMRUT			
Completed projects	₹33,478 crores	₹43,573 crores	₹10,095 crores
Of the grounded projects, works physically completed	₹67,437 crores	₹75,256 crores	₹7,819 crores
Water tap connections	136.62 lakhs	187.40 lakhs	51 lakhs
Sewer connections	103.40 lakhs	147 lakhs	43.6 lakhs
LED street lights	97 lakhs	99 lakhs	2 lakhs
AMRUT 2.0			
Approved projects	₹94,955.12 crores	₹153,573.75 crores	₹58,618 crores

Mission	Up till 31 Dec 2022	Up till 31 Dec 2023	Growth
Water tap connections to be added/serviced	2.36 crores	3.66 crores	1.30 crores
Sewerage connections to be added/serviced	60 lakhs	1.01 crores	41 lakhs
Contracts awarded	0	₹32,703 crores	₹32,703 crores
Water distribution network to be laid/ replaced	58,707 km	1.02 lakh km	43,550 km
Sewer network to be laid/ replaced	15,498 km	28,458 km	12,960 km
WTP capacity to be added/ augmented	7,071 MLD	9,701 MLD	2,630 MLD
STP capacity to be added/ augmented	2,158 MLD	3,939 MLD	1,781 MLD
Water bodies to be rejuvenated	1,518	2,135	617
Smart Cities Mission			
Total projects	7,744	8,010	266
Completed	5,040 projects worth ₹93,529 crores	6,627 projects worth ₹1.32 lakh crores	1,587 projects worth ₹38,471 crores
SBM			
Waste processing	74% of total 1.52 lakh TPD	77.19% of total 1.57 lakh TPD	

Mission	Up till 31 Dec 2022	Up till 31 Dec 2023	Growth
PM SVANidhi			
No. of loans sanctioned	45.03 lakhs	81.14 lakhs	36.11 lakhs
No. of loans disbursed	38.75 lakhs	76.62 lakhs	37.87 lakhs
Total loan amount disbursed	₹4,548.99 crores	₹10,114 crores	₹5,565 crores
SVANidhi Se Samriddhi	33.52 lakhs	58.85 lakhs	25.33 lakhs
Metro rail			
Total operational	830.8 km	905.42 km	74.62 km
Smart Cities Mission			
Total projects	7,744	8,010	266
Completed	5,040 projects worth ₹93,529 crores	6,627 projects worth ₹1.32 lakh crores	1,587 projects worth ₹38,471 crores
SBM			
Waste processing	74% of total 1.52 lakh TPD	77.19% of total 1.57 lakh TPD	
PM SVANidhi			
No. of loans sanctioned	45.03 lakhs	81.14 lakhs	36.11 lakhs
No. of loans disbursed	38.75 lakhs	76.62 lakhs	37.87 lakhs
Total loan amount disbursed	₹4,548.99 crores	₹10,114 crores	₹5,565 crores

Mission	Up till 31 Dec 2022	Up till 31 Dec 2023	Growth
SVANidhi Se Samriddhi	33.52 lakhs	58.85 lakhs	25.33 lakhs
Metro rail			
Total operational	830.8 km	905.42 km	74.62 km

Source: 'Transformational interventions undertaken to develop urban infrastructure and strengthen urban governance, since 2014: Hardeep S Puri', *Press Information Bureau*, 12 January 2024, https ://pib.gov.in/PressReleasePage.aspx?PRID=1995507.

The Smart Cities Mission has failed to meet its objective and been reduced to a project management corporation. Launched in 2015, it covers 100 cities that were selected through various rounds of competitions held from January 2016 to June 2018. The selected cities had five years from their selection to complete the proposed projects, meaning the original deadlines were from 2021 to 2023. After the COVID-19 pandemic broke out, the deadline for all 100 cities was fixed to June 2023 in 2021. In May last year, the ministry again extended the deadline, this time to 30 June 2024. The failure of the mission lies in its inability to convince the citizens that meaningful interventions have been made in the city that have uplifted the lives of its citizens although the Mission had mandated that the plan had to have the 'buy-in' of citizens. There are no City Development Plans (nearly 65% of Indian cities are devoid of local area plans, zonal plans and master plans), which are an integrated set bringing together local, state and central plans to provide a meaningful perspective to the citizens, who can in turn indicate their 'buy-in' or seek better urban solutions for their local development. As a result, there is chaotic, unbridled growth.

India's rapid urbanisation requires more urban planners. Estimates indicate that the country will need 300,000 urban planners by 2023. Every year, 1,800 urban planning graduates pass out from forty-nine institutes, including the School of Planning and Architecture Bhopal, New Delhi and Vijayawada, but most jobs are in the public sector, mainly municipalities. These positions are often filled by general cadre officials rather than specialists, leading to generalists supervising specialists. Short tenures of one to three years for IAS officers hinder project completion. Municipalities also lack sufficient funds and autonomy, causing masterplans to remain unimplemented. For urban planning to become a viable career, a shift from just creating plans to focusing on implementation strategies is needed.

India's employment in the construction sector is estimated to grow to 100 million to attain economic growth targets, according to a report by Knight Frank India. The construction sector, which is the second-largest employment generator in the country, is estimated to employ 71 million of the workforce by 2023. More than 80% of this workforce is unskilled and only 19%, that is 1.3 million of the workforce in the real estate sector, are skilled employees, the report says—4.4 million are core skilled employees, which includes engineers, technicians, clericals workers, etc., and 6.9 million are vocationally trained. According to the National Skill Development Council (NSDC), 87% of employees (both skilled and unskilled) are absorbed by the real estate sector, while 13% are absorbed by the infrastructure sector.[42]

Indian manufacturing is dominated by low-skilled labour, in contrast to the upskilled workforce found in services. This difference reflects the central government's focus on services-driven economic growth in recent decades, which has naturally driven higher skill development in this sector. Increasing skill levels in manufacturing would aid India's efforts to become a global manufacturing hub. The lower skill level in Indian manufacturing means that each employee added just $8,076 of value on average in 2021, according to S&P Global Market Intelligence. That is far behind the $18,308 achieved in Thailand and the $34,402 seen in Malaysia. This skills shortage is a key risk for manufacturers wanting to move up the value chain, jeopardising India's bid to be a manufacturing hub.

Further, only a meagre 9.8 million construction workers of the total 32 million in the country are registered. Tripura, Manipur and Lakshadweep are the states/UTs that employ the highest number of registered workers in the construction sector. Interestingly, a significant number of women forms a part of the unorganised construction workforce. The education and training capacity offered through various schemes currently is inadequate to meet the demands of the large percentage of unskilled workers in the Indian labour market. The education system often does not deliver the required number of specialists across project management, engineering, surveying, contract management and skilled/semi-skilled labour. Findings from the National Sample Survey Office (NSSO) also reconfirm that over 97% of individuals between 15 and 65 have no exposure to any training. Thus, the immediate need is to expand the reach of training providers and set up models and institutes with the capability to scale.

Indeed, there is a lack of adequate skilled contractors for the existing number of projects. Organisations, especially PSEs, have recommended the establishment of a few contractors' training institutions. There is a near absence of formal training and skill certification systems and institutions and overreliance on conventional sourcing of manpower for workers. Worryingly, there is a perceptible reduction in the share of new trainees in construction engineering streams (civil, electrical and mechanical engineering) with a lack of interest of institutions to raise intake levels.

Segment	Employment Base in million		
	2013	2017	2022
Building, Construction & Real Estate	40.14	51.95	66.62
Construction of Buildings	35.52	45.97	58.96
Demolition and site preparation	0.34	0.45	0.57
Electrical plumbing and other construction installation activities	1.00	1.29	1.66
Building completion and finishing	3.27	4.24	5.44
Infrastructure	5.28	7.45	9.93
Construction of roads and railways	4.28	6.04	8.05
Construction of utility projects	0.79	1.12	1.49
Construction of other civil engineering projects	0.18	0.26	0.35
Other specialized construction activities	0.02	0.03	0.04
Overall Sector	45.42	59.40	76.55

Source: 'Human Resource and Skill Requirements in the Building Construction and Real Estate Sector', Volume 5, *KPMG*, https://skillsip.nsdcindia.org/sites/default/files/kps-document/Building-Construction-Real-Estate%20%281%29.pdf.

All that said, the future looks bright with the NDA government assuming office for the third time and reiterating its commitment to infrastructure development.

A key part of achieving this will be the NIP. Launched with 6,835 projects, it has expanded to capture over 9,288 projects with a total outlay of ₹108.88 trillion between 2020 and 2025, according to a statement by the Ministry of Finance.[43] The NIP comprises brownfield and greenfield infrastructure projects of above ₹100 crore across both economic and social infrastructure and includes projects implemented by all the states and UTs of India and twenty-two infrastructure ministries, iterated the ministry. It is expected to improve project preparation, attract investments (both domestic and foreign) into infrastructure, and prove crucial for the country to become a $5 trillion economy by FY2025.

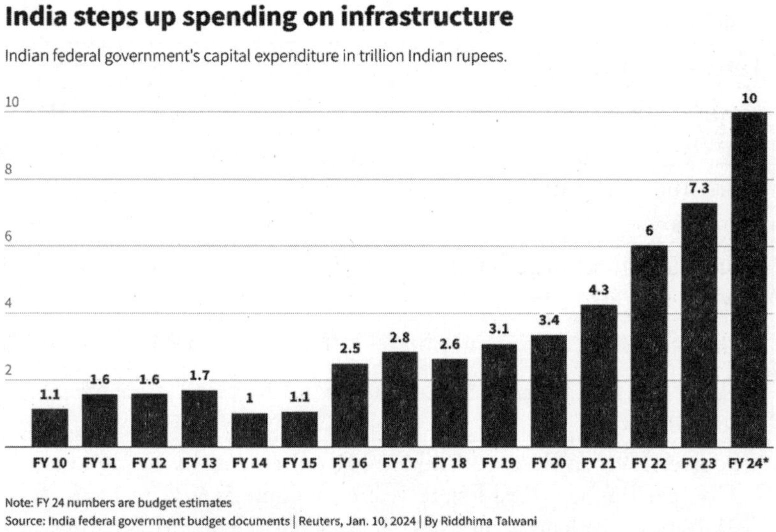

Source: Shilpa Jamkhandikar and Ira Dugal, 'Mumbai gets a makeover as India binges on bridges, roads and rail', *Reuters*, 11 January 2024, https://www.reuters.com/world/india/mumbai-gets-makeover-india-binges-bridges-roads-rail-2024-01-11/.

As per data released by the National Statistical Office (NSO) in early 2024, India's GDP is estimated to reach ₹296.58 lakh crore in FY2023–24 at current prices.[44] Taking ₹83 for a dollar as exchange rate, the size of the economy would be around $3.57

trillion in 2023–24. India is currently the fifth largest economy in the world after the US, China, Japan and Germany. By 2027–28, India is projected to surpass Germany and Japan to become the third largest economy. Referring to the Viksit Bharat ('developed India') goal, FM Nirmala Sitharaman has indicated, 'The estimate that India will be at least a $30 trillion economy by 2047 is a conservative estimate.'[45]

To make this vision a reality will require zeal and commitment to forge ahead along with willingness to course-correct where required based on the lessons of the past.

Where We Stand

Category	Number (in crore)
Population*	144
Aadhar card holders	136
Internet users	120
Mobile subscribers	114
Total enrolled voters	95
E-commerce users	80
Smartphone users	65
OTT subscribers	50
Social media users	40
UPI users	30
Food delivery platform users	28
BHIM payment users	20
Digital learning users	9.3
E-Sanjeevani healthcare users	9.2
Health insurance users	51.4
Stock market users	8
Mutual fund investors	3.5

*Of this, 37% is urban and 63% rural.[46]

CHAPTER FOUR

FAST FORWARD TO VIKSIT BHARAT

Centuries ago, Persia (modern-day Iran) and Mesopotamia (modern-day Iraq) were regions renowned for their prosperity. Around 330 BCE, Alexander the Great, as he transitioned into adulthood, set his sights on Persia, aiming to make it the crown jewel of his conquests during his expansive campaigns. The Roman Empire, established in 27 BCE and lasting until 476 CE in the West and 1453 CE in the East, was another symbol of enduring prosperity. The Ottoman Empire, which reigned from 1299 to 1922, extended its reach into Europe and beyond, dominating as a land of immense wealth and influence. During these periods, India, often referred to as the 'Golden Bird', was also known for its immense riches and thriving culture.

Fast forward to 2024, and India has surged to become the fastest-growing economy in the world, ranking among the largest global economies. In contrast, the empires that once reigned supreme for centuries have faded into history, their former glory now a distant memory. In the language of stock-market investing, India is a breakout stock. In the stock market, a breakout stock refers to a stock whose price moves beyond a defined resistance level (upper limit) or support level (lower limit) with increased volume. This movement signifies a significant change in investor sentiment and can indicate the beginning of a new trend, either upward or downward. Breakouts can be crucial for traders and investors as they often signal a substantial price move and can present lucrative trading opportunities. Here, I am indicating an upward trend. Multiple facets of India's potential are showing the promise of reaching optimal efficiency at the same time, and this is being recognised by stakeholders, both domestic and global, creating a tectonic shift.

In his book *The Third Wave*, published in 1980, Alvin Toffler described a transformative period in human history characterised by the transition from the industrial society (the Second Wave) to the information age or the post-industrial society (the Third Wave). This tectonic shift, as Toffler outlined, encompasses several key changes in society, economy and technology. India is benefitting—after missing the second wave that was the result of the Industrial Revolution that introduced mass production, centralised industries and urbanisation—it is now riding the third wave. The third wave is the 'Information Age' marked by transition to a knowledge-based economy, decentralised production and advanced technologies.

India has emerged as the world's 'services factory', driven by robust growth in its services exports, particularly in the IT and business process outsourcing (BPO) sectors. According to a report by Goldman Sachs, India's services exports reached nearly $340 billion in 2023, with a compound annual growth rate (CAGR) of around 11 per cent since 2005. This growth rate is nearly double the global average and significantly outpaces the growth in goods exports.[1]

The country's emergence as a global hub for services is further bolstered by its immense pool of skilled professionals, particularly in the technology sector. This 'brainpower talent pool' has been a significant factor in India's ability to attract and retain global business. India produces over 1.5 million engineering graduates annually, making it one of the largest talent pools in the world. Indian engineers and IT professionals are highly sought after for their expertise and innovation, contributing to the country's reputation as a preferred destination for global companies seeking high-quality and cost-effective services.

Additionally, Global Capability Centres (GCCs) have played a crucial role in this transformation. India hosts more than 1,300 GCCs, which are offshore units that handle critical business functions such as R&D, IT support, customer service and financial management for multinational corporations. These centres have not only generated employment for millions of Indians but also enhanced India's stature as a global services hub by providing sophisticated and high-value services.

Moreover, India's strategic focus on digital services and remote working capabilities has positioned it to capitalise on the increasing global demand for these services. This transformation into a global services hub underscores India's growing influence in the global economy and highlights its potential to drive future economic growth through its skilled workforce and competitive services sector.

Here are some key figures:

- Services exports in 2023: Nearly $340 billion
- CAGR since 2005: About 11%
- Number of GCCs in India: Over 1,300
- Engineering graduates produced annually: Over 1.5 million

This growth in services exports, the proliferation of GCCs and the large number of engineering graduates illustrate India's dynamic shift towards becoming a powerhouse in the global services industry, leveraging its talented workforce and technological advancements to cater to global demands.[2]

In 1980, both India and China were of the same economic size, but then China embraced reforms and grew rapidly, while India fumbled over its various political upheavals. In 1990, India's per person income was $367 and China's was $317. That was the last time we were ahead of that country. In 2000, we were at $1,357 and China was at $4,450. In 2022, India was at $2,388 and China at $12,720. India's liberalisation opened our doors to faster growth. But this growth could not keep pace with theirs. China grew at 11.7% in the 1990s (versus our 5.6%), then 16.5% in the 2000s (against our 6.5%) and then 8.8% in the 2010s (versus our 5.1%). (In 1995, China was ranked sixth largest in terms of GDP, and fifteen years later, by 2010, it had attained its place as the second highest. Currently, India is the fifth highest in GDP terms and it is vying to be the third largest economy in terms of GDP before 2030.)

However, now, India is at a point of inflexion where it can propel itself to high growth for a continuous period of a couple of decades to somewhat emulate what China managed in the three decades from 1980 to 2014, where it grew by nearly 10% per annum. But then, walking five steps and retreating three is not going to cut it. India needs a transformative approach. Ideas that would make a transformative change in outcomes. If the country were to grow at a rate of 6% per annum for the next twenty-three years, it would achieve a GDP of $13 trillion. At 7%, the GDP would touch $15 trillion, and with an annual growth rate of 8%, it could touch $23.31 trillion. But to achieve a GDP of $30 trillion by 2047, the desirable GDP annual growth rate would have to be 9.19%.

The real question: Are we fine with GDP as the metric of measurement? Attaining a high GDP and its consequent per capita income does not guarantee that we would have provided equal opportunity to our citizens in education, health and infrastructure, i.e., social and physical infrastructure. Inequalities in society may continue and may even turn for the worse. Communal disturbances, civil disobediences, public outrage … all may be at flash point during this period and may cause an implosion.

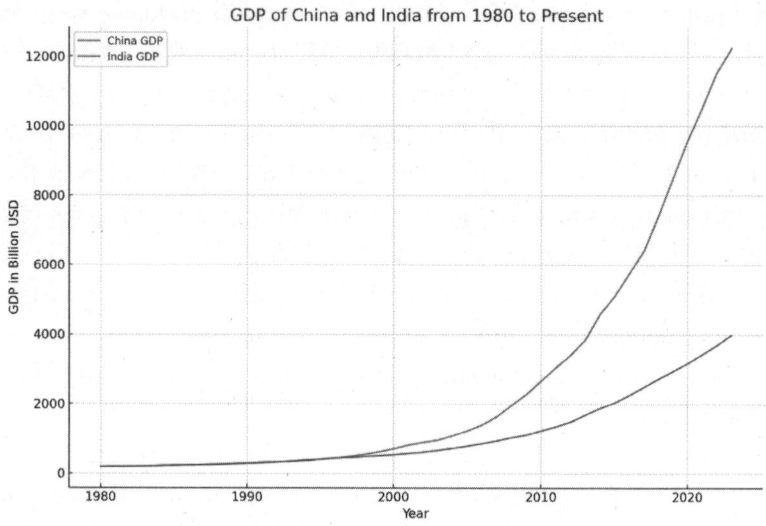

This chart shows how growth diverged from 2006, making China into a behemoth (GDP in billion USD). Between 1980 and 1990, there was no difference between the economies. We, too, had a chance to grow after liberalisation in 1991. This chart tells you that given India's current position, it is set to achieve high growth if stays true to its course.

Source: 'China vs India - GDP Comparison', *MGM Research*, 26 November 2019, https://mgmresearch.com/china-vs-india-gdp-comparison/.

Transformative Change 1: Outcome-Based Policy Approach

Why not look at another metric, the metric of outcomes? In this approach, we should get an organisation like NITI Aayog to provide the benchmark metrics of various countries and set our own targets. For example, according to the *Annual Status of Education Report* (ASER) *2023* by the NGO Pratham, approximately 26% of children aged 14–18 in rural India cannot read a Class 2 level textbook in their regional language.[3] Can we set a metric in education of a desirable outcome of 100%

for an ability to read and write in Class 2? Similarly, in India, compulsory education ends at age 14. To work full time in the organised sector, you must be 18. Only about 5.6% of all youth in this age group are doing vocational courses. Can we set a desirable outcome of 50% of all youth in this age group? Such outcomes can be set for infant mortality, maternal mortality rate, and so on. See the table below:

Metric	Current status	Global comparison
Infant mortality rate (IMR)	25.5 deaths per 1,000 live births (2024)	Higher than Sri Lanka (6), Bangladesh (24), Nepal (24), Bhutan (23)
Maternal mortality rate (MMR)	103 per 100,000 live births (2017–19)	Higher than China (18) and Russia (17)
Child malnutrition	35.5% stunted, 19.3% wasted, 32.1% underweight (NFHS-5 2019–21)	Higher than global averages and worse than many developing countries
Access to clean water and sanitation	6% lack access to clean drinking water, 15% lack basic sanitation	Falls short of UN SDG targets and is higher than many developing countries
Literacy rate	77.7% (2021); gender gap: 84.7% (men), 70.3% (women)	Lower than global average, lagging behind countries like Sri Lanka and China
Gender inequality	Ranks 140th out of 156 countries in the Global Gender Gap Report 2021	Significant gender disparities in various sectors

Metric	Current status	Global comparison
Healthcare infrastructure	3.5% of GDP spent on healthcare	Among the lowest in BRICS nations and lower than many developing countries
Environmental quality	Severe air pollution in cities like Delhi	Ranks poorly in global air quality indices
Income inequality	Top 10% holds 77% of total national wealth	Comparable to Latin American countries like Brazil and worse than many developed nations

While I was heading the Smart Cities Council India, which I founded along with the Smart Cities Council Global based in Washington DC, I had repeatedly pointed out, through my articles and papers presented to the Ministry of Housing and Urban Affairs (MoHUA), that as the very idea of a 'Smart City' was being misunderstood by people at large, it ought to be renamed 'Smart Area Development'. The whole intention of the Smart Cities Mission was to create a model smart area that imbibes the principles of urban planning and marries them to technology such that outcomes in the form of citizen satisfaction and city sustainability are attained so that, in turn, the rest of the city gets inspired to replicate the ideas. I had further proposed that, after the term of the mission was coming to an end, an outcome report ought to be published outlining the benefits obtained because of the initiatives conceptualised and executed using the funds provided. The outcomes I had in mind were such as a reduction in crime due to provision of good lighting and Swachh Bharat mission initiatives where dark corners in downtown areas of cities are illuminated and kept clean resulting in a drop in crimes;

improvement in health or a drop in diseases owing to cleanliness and regular disposal of garbage; or better attendance in schools by young girls because proper sanitation facilities were provided in schools. These instances could be cited as case studies of success. If an outcome-based approach is used, NITI Aayog can compute the budgets required for us to achieve targeted outcomes, and that is how our definition of Viksit Bharat should be defined. So, while we can pursue the objectives of a $30 trillion GDP by 2047 that would put India second only to China in the global pecking order, we ought to also have parallel targeted outcomes for a holistic development plan.

Transformative Change 2: Vocational Training

Construction, spanning real estate and infrastructure, is India's second-largest employer with a workforce of 71 million, according to Knight Frank India (KFI) and the Royal Institution of Chartered Surveyors' (RICS) 2023 report, 'Skilled Employment in Construction Sector in India'.[4]

The National Skill Development Council (NSDC) estimates that 87% of the construction industry's employees are absorbed by the real-estate sector, while 13% work in infrastructure. However, only 19% of the 71-million workforce is skilled, and that is a matter of concern, especially as employment in the construction sector is estimated to grow to 100 million by 2030 to meet growth targets. To align the curriculum with industry needs, a collaboration is needed between academia and industry. Academic institutions must incorporate more practical experience, internships and industry-relevant projects. Interventions like site visits, guest lectures from industry experts and live projects are essential.

The dual education system combines apprenticeships in a company and vocational education at a vocational school in one course. This system ensures that students receive both theoretical and practical training, which makes them job-ready immediately after graduation. This system is being followed in Germany. Akin to Germany, Switzerland's vocational education and training (VET) system integrates academic and practical learning, with students spending part of their time in school and part in a real work environment. Something, surely, to think about.

Meanwhile, the government has introduced the National Apprenticeship Promotion Scheme (NAPS), which mandates that companies with over thirty employees have at least 2.5% of their workforce as apprentices, with the percentage going up to 15%. To encourage more employers to take up apprentices, it announced a direct benefit transfer last year wherein the government directly transfers 25% of the stipend or ₹1,500 per month, whichever is lower, directly to the bank accounts of apprentices. The number of apprentices engaged under NAPS has increased from 570,000 in FY2022 to 920,000 in FY2024. But as per the India Employment Report 2024 jointly published by the International Labour Organisation (ILO) and the Institute of Human Development (IHD), the proportion of educated young people possessing at least secondary education, among the total unemployed youth has nearly doubled from 35.2% in 2000 to 65.7% in 2022.[5] Therefore, while initiatives and schemes are instituted for the educated unemployed youth, the youth at school need to be trained in specific skills that can give them alternate employment opportunities.

Transformative Change 3: Women Workforce

For India to harness its demographic dividend, it makes sense for the country to ensure both genders work towards the common objective of making it a developed nation. A paper published by the World Economic Forum in 2018 had estimated that India's GDP would go up by 27% if the female labour force participation rate (LFPR) was the same as the male one. A survey in 2019 showed appalling statistics with regard to the female LFPR in

India—according to World Bank indicators, it was lower than that of Saudi Arabia, Afghanistan and Pakistan, some of the most conservative Islamic nations. According to the survey, only one out of five women in India work.[6]

According to the definition of the International Labour Organisation (ILO), LFPR is a measure of the proportion of a country's working-age population that engages actively in the labour market, either by working or looking for work; it provides an indication of the size of the supply of labour available to engage in the production of goods and services, relative to the population at working age. The accompanying table gives the female LFPR of selected countries, expressed as a percentage of the female population over 15 years of age.

Country	**1990**	**2019**
Nepal	55.3	82.9
Vietnam	73.5	72.5
Ghana	57.2	61.7
China	73.2	61
United Kingdom	51	56.8
United States	57.3	56.1
Germany	52.2	54.3
Indonesia	55.7	50.7
Japan	49.2	51.6
United Arab Emirates	41.5	53
Malaysia	47.9	55.2
South Africa	47.8	47.1
Bangladesh	60.5	36.4
Turkey	49.2	38.5
Sri Lanka	37.3	34.2
Saudi Arabia	14.2	15.6
Afghanistan	9.1	21

Country	1990	2019
Pakistan	14.7	20.8
India	29.4	21.5
Egypt	19.2	19.6
Iran	13.4	14.8

The table shows that India's female LFPR is now lower than what it was back in 1990. Indeed, in 1990, our female LFPR was well above that of Saudi Arabia, the UAE, Pakistan, Afghanistan and Bangladesh. And this has happened despite India's higher GDP growth rate.

Source: 'Labor force participation rate, female (% of female population ages 15-64) (modeled ILO estimate)', *World Bank Group*, https://data.worldbank.org/indicator/SL.TLF.ACTI.FE.ZS.

However, five years later in 2023, the Periodic Labour Force Survey (PLFS) Report 2022-23, released by India's MoSPI on 9 October 2023, indicated a sharp improvement and that the female LFPR in the country had greatly improved by 4.2 percentage points to 37.0% in 2023. The government ascribes the improvement to its initiatives for girls' education, skill development, entrepreneurship facilitation and safety in the workplace.

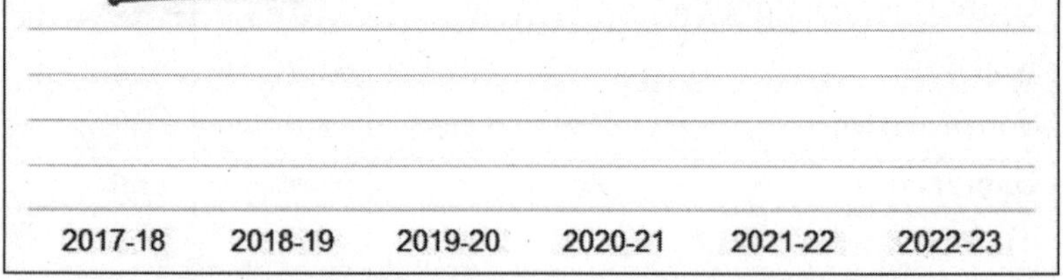

Source: 'Nari Shakti Surges Ahead!: Female Labour Force Participation Rate Jumps to 37.0%', *Press Information Bureau*, https://pib.gov.in/PressReleasePage.aspx?PRID=1967291.

According to the findings of the Observer Research Foundation (ORF), the overall increase in women's participation in the labour force is driven by more rural women joining the workforce. PLFS data shows that the LFPR increased by 5 percentage points for urban women and 14 percentage points for rural women. This could partly be linked to a more accurate measurement of women's work, according to several analyses. Women in India, and many developing countries, are widely engaged in unpaid economic work—different from care work or domestic work, like working on farms or family enterprises for instance—for which they are neither paid nor recognised as workers. The data being collected now is more cognisant of the historical mismeasurement of women's work and might be the reason for the increase in FLFPR. Women unpaid workers rose from 31.7% of total women workers to 37% from 2017–18 to 2022–23. An investigation into and resolution of the causes that hold back women from joining the paid workforce, such as provision of security, creches, sanitation facilities, etc., could accelerate their willingness and consequently alter the results favourably.[7]

In any case, it is a good sign and will have a transformative impact. Another reason could be the rise in women's participation as enterprise owners or under the self-employed category. The proportion of self-employed women rose to its highest at 70.1%, up from 60% in 2021–22. The category of self-employed has two sub-categories in PLFS: own account worker and employer and unpaid helper in household enterprises. More than half the women worked as unpaid helpers in family enterprises. Obviously, then, the capture of numbers under unpaid helpers has ensured that women doing domestic chores are being counted as LFPR, but what is significant is the rise in enterprise owners. This is probably owing to the efforts of the Pradhan Mantri MUDRA Yojana, which extends microcredit for entrepreneurship, where nearly 70% of beneficiaries are female. And 84% of loans sanctioned under Start-Up India have also gone to female beneficiaries. The government seems to have caught on to this weakness and is working towards improving the inclusion of women in the LFPR. A continuous improvement on this ratio can have a transformative impact in attaining India's objectives.

Transformative Change 4: Research and Development

Indian corporates have historically underinvested in research and development (R&D) compared to their global counterparts. India's gross expenditure on R&D as a percentage of GDP or the gross expenditure on research and development (GERD) has remained around 0.7%, which is significantly lower than that of countries like South Korea (4.5%), Japan (3.2%), Germany (3.0%), the USA (2.8%), France (2.2%), the UK (1.7%) and Canada (1.6%). India's spending is even lower than that of BRIC nations. China spends 2.1% and Brazil 1.3% while Russia spends a bit over 1%.[8]

The Big 5 big-tech companies—Amazon, Alphabet, Apple, Meta and Microsoft—collectively spend about $200 billion every year on R&D. In 2021–22, Amazon's expenditure on R&D was over $73 billion. Globally, the big pharmaceutical companies spend 20% of their revenue on R&D. The innovation spend is currently dominated by the US.[9]

The business sector in India contributes significantly less to the gross expenditure on R&D (about 37%) compared to businesses in the top ten economies, which average 68%. This discrepancy exists despite India offering more liberal tax incentives for R&D than those economies. The Indian government disproportionately shoulders the burden of R&D funding, contributing 56% of the gross expenditure, which is three times the average contribution by governments in the top ten economies. Despite these efforts, India's gross expenditure on R&D stands at 0.65% of the GDP, much lower than that of the top ten economies.

Academic institutions already have invested in research facilities, but these are not being utilised as well as they ought to be. Collaborations between academia and industry are essential, creating a mutually beneficial relationship where institutions equip students with vital skills and businesses gain a ready talent pool.

The Indian IT industry has gained a reputation as a provider of outsourced services rather than a producer of innovative products. Here are some reasons for this trend:

- *Service-oriented business model*: The industry's success has largely been built on providing cost-effective services to global clients, which has led to a focus on labour-intensive projects rather than product innovation.
- *Risk aversion*: Developing new products involves significant risk and investment, which many Indian IT firms have traditionally been reluctant to undertake. This is compounded by the industry's emphasis on maintaining stable profit margins.
- *Talent and skill gaps*: While India has a large pool of IT professionals, there is often a gap in the high-end skills required for product development, such as advanced research capabilities and innovation management.
- *Limited access to venture capital*: Compared to the US, there is less venture capital available for high-risk, high-reward technology ventures in India, making it harder for startups to develop and launch new products.

Given the facts, there is need for a transformative approach to enhancing our R&D quotient by deploying policy initiatives for industries that deserve such allocation because of the nature of the business. Take South Korea, for example.

South Korea's investment in R&D has seen significant growth over the decades. In the early 1990s, the country's R&D expenditure was about 2% of the GDP. By 2019, this figure had risen to over 4.5%, making the country one of the highest R&D spenders in the world relative to its GDP. For instance, Samsung's

R&D expenditure grew from about $6.2 billion in 2007 to nearly $19 billion in 2021. South Korea's focus on R&D has propelled its semiconductor industry to the forefront. Samsung Electronics and SK Hynix are two of the world's leading semiconductor manufacturers. In 2020, Samsung held a significant market share in the global memory chip market, accounting for approximately 43.5% of DRAM and 34.1% of NAND flash memory markets. The revenue from semiconductor exports grew from $10 billion in 1998 to over $90 billion in 2020.

R&D investment has also been crucial in the consumer electronics segment. Companies like Samsung and LG have become global leaders in various product categories, including smartphones, televisions and home appliances. The country's emphasis on R&D is evident in its high number of patent filings. Samsung and LG are among the top companies globally in terms of patent applications, highlighting their commitment to innovation. In 2020, Samsung Electronics filed over 6,000 patent applications, indicating a robust pipeline of new technologies and products.

In India, the next wave of artificial intelligence (AI) and machine learning (ML) needs to be incubated internally with the infusion of R&D capital so that Indian companies do not remain cogs in the wheel of another country's product development.

Transformative Change 5: Technology Upgrade for MSMEs

The government is running multiple schemes to make finance available for the upgradation of technology for micro, small and medium enterprises (MSMEs). These include schemes like the credit-linked capital subsidy and technology upgradation scheme (CLCS-TUS) and the zero-defect zero-effect (ZED) certification. An amount of ₹2,900 crore has been allocated for the same and, in 2018–19 alone, ₹980 crore was disbursed. But this idea needs a massive drive. The Industrial Training Institutes (ITIs), which were offered to the private sector for public–private partnership, have not achieved success. The latest Union Budget 2024–25 has introduced a new centrally sponsored scheme, as the fourth scheme under the prime minister's package, for skilling in collaboration with state governments and industry. As per the finance minister, 2 million youth will be skilled over a five-year period and 1,000 ITIs will be upgraded in hub-and-spoke arrangements with outcome orientation. Course content and design will be aligned to industry skill needs, and new courses will be introduced for emerging needs. While I chaired a public–private partnership ITI in Navi Mumbai for ten years, I realised that the guidelines are not clear for the private organisations—while large corporations can execute the scheme as they have CSR obligations too, medium-sized companies may not find it worth their while, as bureaucrats handling the schemes have their own relationships and arrangements that they wish to continue to nurture and find the introduction of private organisations a new equation to handle. These officers should be shuffled so that they too start the upgradation process on an even keel with the private organisations.

With 63.4 million MSMEs employing a workforce of 111 million contributing 30% to the GDP and 48% to exports, this sector deserves a lot more attention. The RBI estimated an overall credit gap in the MSME sector to be between ₹20 trillion and ₹25 trillion. This highlights the significant unmet financial requirements for the growth and technological advancement of MSMEs. As exports have been struggling to grow, PLI schemes are yet to take off and private capital has been shy for several years. The onslaught of demonetisation, coupled with compliance burden of GST and debt legacy, has added to the woes of MSMEs. They need a transformational infusion of relief. With 19.6 million MSMEs in manufacturing with a workforce of 36 million, a targeted approach to uplift this sector can have immense benefits.

Transformative Change 6: Using Private-sector Experience

While framing rules, incentives and some schemes, the government often consults trade bodies and experts for advice. However, for various reasons, it has not provided a platform for such expertise to be infused into making a significant contribution.

The Department of Personnel and Training (DoPT) invited applications for positions at the joint-secretary level and above to facilitate fresh perspectives and expertise, enhancing the policymaking process and implementation. In 2023, only twenty vacancies were announced (four joint secretaries and sixteen directors/deputy secretaries). In 2021, over 2,000 applications were received. Given new initiatives and new-age businesses like Startup India, AI, cybersecurity, Open Network for Digital Commerce (ONDC) and Government e Marketplace (GeM), intake from the private sector can prove to be a transformative infusion of expertise and experience that can propel these ideas to higher orbits. Countries like the UK, US, Australia, Canada and Singapore have been using such programmes and benefitting from the expertise of the private sector.

Even when the government invites suggestions from chambers of commerce and other associations during pre-budget exercises or when at times they seek a dialogue before introducing a new scheme, the system they adopt is not conducive to getting honest opinions. We see that industry leaders are invited by the finance minister for pre-budget discussions. I am told that while they exude confidence in articulating what deficits need fixing when they meet in a waiting room, they clamp shut as soon as they walk into the minister's chamber, and the finance minister just about manages an exercise in confirmation bias.

Transformative Change 7: Image Upgrade for Infrastructure

The construction industry faces challenges in attracting workers, particularly among rural youth who seek better work environments. L&T, India's largest construction company and largest employer of construction workers, employs over 250,000 workers—however, it is also constantly at its wit's end trying to source more, considering its burgeoning orderbook. It is clearly a challenge. During COVID-19, despite the lockdown, construction was an essential activity, but workers walked to their homes in Uttar Pradesh, Bihar and so on during the great migration of that time. Then, as the fear of the pandemic eased, L&T had to offer to fly its workers to Mumbai in a chartered plane for them to collectively kick off project work.

Construction jobs are physically demanding and often involve working in harsh conditions. Social media and widespread broadcast of people living better lives, higher risks of injury and inadequate safety measures deter potential workers. Many rural youths are now better educated and aspire for white-collar jobs that offer more comfort and security. There is also a preference for urban areas with better living standards and job opportunities in sectors like IT and services.

Given this challenge, a nationwide media campaign needs to be run whereby national icons (perhaps from the field of cinema) address the public at large, donning hard hats or doling out advice on safety at sites, thus enhancing the esteem associated with this work. In our movies, the construction worker has generally been shown in distress or undergoing adverse circumstances. The stereotypical portrayal of this protagonist needs to be replaced by someone who is adept at using hand tools and equipment, who is braced on tall structures well equipped with harnesses and undertakes daring feats. Besides, the rising popularity of modular construction and prefab will also necessitate footage of the manufacture of the elements and walls at a factory followed by onsite assembly. Today's construction worker is essentially going to work at the factory or operate cranes assembling prefabricated portions of the structures onsite.

Transformative Change 8: Pan India eShram Card for Unorganised Labour

The Ministry of Labour & Employment launched the eShram portal on 26 August 2021 to create a comprehensive National Database of Unorganised Workers, which is seeded with Aadhaar. As on 21 April 2023, over 288.7 million unorganised workers have registered on the portal. A unique identity for construction workers, which enables their Jan Dhan account and carries their provident fund details would be a great smart card! It would allow money to be credited to their account even as they work on casual basis in different states and cities and could also be linked to accident and life insurance, thus providing full security!

Instead of increasing budgets in MGNREGA, companies should be asked to fund training of workers under CSR in order to get an equivalent amount of tax break. The MGNREGA fund should be only extended if the worker manages to get training credits.

In March 2020, the Union government had issued an advisory to all states and UTs to use funds with their Building and Other Construction Workers (BOCW) Welfare Boards to help people engaged in the unorganised sector. The states had around ₹52,000 crore in funds at the time with about 35 million registered construction workers, as per the advisory. In a press release issued in June 2020, the Union Labour Ministry said that the states disbursed ₹4,957 crore in cash assistance to around 20 million registered construction workers. Around 17.5 million transactions were done directly into their bank accounts.

The BOCW Act 1996 governs construction activities and mandates a BOCW Welfare Board in every state. These boards run on a cess that is 1% of a construction project's total cost. Experts and activists have long called for a pan-India labour card that does away with the requirement of working for at least ninety days in a state to get any benefit. This model of charging 1% of the project cost as a means of funding the support system for workers is a step in the right direction.[10]

The Andhra Pradesh government under then Chief Minister Chandrababu Naidu had introduced such a scheme where the cess on project cost was used to fund the training of construction workers. Experts have also called for simplification of registration, renewal and other processes, along with streamlining of norms across states. Provision of such a fund that could then leverage some insurance, too, could be a source of much relief, given that the workers have safety concerns and are worried about looking after a large family if they were to become incapacitated. Enhancing the welfare of workers and providing them an identity that allows them to access their provident fund, medical and other social security benefits, already being provided by the government or through the largesse of the BOCW Welfare Board, could not only streamline the availability of workers but also encourage other unemployed youth to explore employment opportunities in construction.

Transformative Change 9: Cooperative and Competitive Federalism

Typically, states governed by the ruling party at the Centre are quick to take up initiatives launched by the Union government, while states ruled by other parties procrastinate.

India's federal structure is characterised by the synergistic and cooperative interaction between the Centre and state governments. Although there are exceptional situations such as national security and defence, where the Centre holds more power, the overall framework remains federal.

Effective coordination mechanisms between the Union and the states are essential. Institutions like the National Development Council, Finance Commission and zonal councils have played pivotal roles in promoting cooperative federalism. The central government has undertaken several initiatives to enhance this cooperation:

- States have been granted more autonomous powers in various matters.
- The Planning Commission has been replaced by NITI Aayog, symbolising a shift towards cooperative federalism.
- The Indian constitution's Schedule VII delineates powers through three lists: the Union List, State List and Concurrent List, the latter embodying the spirit of cooperative federalism.
- The introduction of GST serves as a common platform for both the Centre and the states, replacing numerous indirect taxes with a comprehensive and uniform tax system.

That said, competitive federalism encourages competition between the states and the Union, as well as among the states themselves. This approach fosters an environment where states and the Union government strive to outdo each other in various domains. The selection of smart cities through competitive bidding exemplifies this philosophy. The Fifteenth Finance Commission has also prepared an index to evaluate the individual performance of states, with financial allocations based on their performance.

In the current era, states are proactively enhancing the ease of doing business and improving living standards. They are initiating reforms in sectors such as administration and health. Examples include the state-sponsored Rythu Bandhu scheme in Telangana and the KALIA scheme in Odisha, which complement the central government's PM Kisan Yojana.

The Centre encourages states to be smart, simple, accountable and responsive to their populations. There is a mutual understanding that innovation is crucial for socioeconomic progress in the country. This mutual pursuit of excellence underscores the role of competitive federalism in shaping and developing the nation.

Cooperative federalism emphasises decentralisation, empowering state governments to take decisions closer to the ground. This is fundamental to a vibrant democracy, ensuring that governance is more responsive and accountable to the people. Competitive federalism fosters a healthy competition among states to improve their performance in various sectors. This leads to innovative policies, better governance and improved service delivery. States strive to outperform each other in areas such as ease of doing business, thus attracting investments and social welfare schemes. As states are evaluated based on their performance, this benchmarking promotes accountability and encourages them to achieve higher standards of governance and public service delivery. The 15th Finance Commission's performance-based devolution of funds exemplifies this approach.

However, in India, this has been a mixed bag. In West Bengal, which is ruled by the Trinamool Congress (TMC), resistance was encountered for the Centre's Pradhan Mantri Awas Yojana (PMAY). The state government accused the Centre of not consulting it adequately and politicising the scheme. Funds for the housing scheme were suspended following political conflicts, impacting implementation in the state. Similarly, the Aam Aadmi Party (AAP)-ruled Punjab showed resistance to the PM-KISAN scheme. There were delays in the state government submitting beneficiary data to the Centre, resulting in delayed transfers of funds to farmers.

Similarly, the Communist Party of India (Marxist)-ruled Kerala initially resisted the Ayushman Bharat scheme. The state had concerns over integrating its own health scheme with the central initiative, fearing loss of control over its health policies and a potential duplication of benefits. On the other hand, Uttar Pradesh, ruled by the BJP, quickly adopted the Swachh Bharat Mission. The state government actively promoted the construction of toilets and sanitation facilities, aligning with the Centre's objectives. This led to significant improvements in sanitation coverage across the state. Madhya Pradesh, also under BJP rule, swiftly implemented PMAY. The state government collaborated closely with the Centre to expedite the construction of affordable housing for the poor, making it one of the top-performing states under this scheme.

For a vibrant democracy, there must be decentralisation of power and the states must simultaneously work in a competitive spirit to provide the best possible outcomes to their people. There is already lopsided growth in our country and this attitude of non-cooperation will only enhance the inequality.

Transformative Change 10: Tourism, the Next Software

In the updated list of international tourist arrivals for the top twenty countries, India ranks twentieth with 17.9 million international tourists.

Here is the updated table:

Rank	Country	International tourist arrivals (millions)
1	France	89.4
2	Spain	82.7
3	United States	79.4
4	China	65.7
5	Italy	64.5
6	Turkey	51.2
7	Mexico	45.0
8	Thailand	39.8
9	Germany	38.8
10	United Kingdom	37.7

Rank	Country	International tourist arrivals (millions)
11	Japan	32.1
12	Austria	30.8
13	Greece	27.8
14	Malaysia	26.1
15	Hong Kong	23.8
16	Russia	23.6
17	Canada	22.2
18	Poland	21.1
19	Netherlands	20.9
20	India	17.9

The table below indicates the scope of tourism revenue that can be transformative. Look at the data on India's earnings from international tourists over the past ten years:

Year	Revenue ($ billion)
2013	18.4
2014	20.3
2015	21.1
2016	22.9
2017	27.3
2018	28.6
2019	30.1
2020	6.0
2021	8.8
2022	16.4
2023	20.0

As one can observe, we have not been able to greatly increase our earnings in the last ten years. A country like Turkey, which has had runaway inflation, earns over 2X our earnings; Thailand earns double our earnings; even Malaysia earns 30% more than India. With the history, coastline, biodiversity, mountain ranges, rivers and jungles we are blessed with, it is a pity that we are at the bottom of a list of countries that have much less to offer. Considering our infrastructure of new airports, improved rail connections, flight connections and hotels operated by major brands, this sector can be a big revenue earner and employment generator. We need to market our jungle safaris, coastlines, festivals, monuments, religious places, mountains, yoga retreats and Ayurveda health resorts, markets, food, even marriage celebrations, which are on every Westerner's bucket list, all on the back of our newly developed infrastructure.

Transformative Change 11: Stop Buying Land for Road Construction

If the financials of NHAI are logjammed owing to expansion of the roads programme, stop buying land for road projects. Just the Bharatmala Pariyojana's budgeted cost ballooned to nearly double at ₹10.64 lakh crore due to input costs and land acquisition costs across the project length of 34,800 km. This is ₹31.6 crore per km! Assuming that 20% of a project cost is sunk in land acquisition, over ₹2 lakh crore would have been paid for land acquisition alone. That too at four times the market price! Instead, it should roll out the land-pooling scheme that has been experimented with in Andhra Pradesh and the NAINA region in Navi Mumbai. In Amaravati in Andhra Pradesh, for instance, for each acre surrendered by farmers towards contribution to the land for the capital, the farmers were provided:

- 1,000 sq. yards of residential land;
- 250 sq. yards of land for commercial purposes;

- 450 sq. yards for commercial purposes if the land was fertile and located near the river;
- An annuity of ₹30,000 per acre for non-fertile land and an annuity of ₹50,000 for fertile land. The annuity was subject to a 10% annual increase for ten years.

The scheme has multiple advantages. Landowners become stakeholders and can be guaranteed annuity or rent. They do not get a windfall that throws their life off balance. They can be provided a marginal land piece as part of the compensation package so that they can continue tilling. (This scheme has also been introduced in China.) The budget for roads is then deployed only towards their construction. Meanwhile, NHAI must continue to monetise toll-yielding assets by attracting long-term funds from foreign investors and use the money to construct roads.

Transformative Change 12: FIDIC Contracts

While India's ranking in ease of doing business improved to the 63rd position from 180th position among 190 countries, the country was still ranked 115th in paying taxes, 163rd in enforcing contracts. Fear of tax reprisals due to the ghosts of the retrospective Vodafone case constantly discourage international firms when it comes to investment in India.

The construction sector here does not subscribe to any standard form of contract. However, contracts published by FIDIC (the Swiss-based Fédération Internationale des Ingénieurs-Conseils, or the International Federation of Consulting Engineers), the Institute of Civil Engineers and the Indian Institute of Architects are often used. Apart from these, many government organisations have their own standard contracts, suiting their department's needs. There is a lack of uniformity in contract terms and formats. India's track record in arbitration is abysmal and is an invitation to bankruptcy for mid-sized contractors due to the exorbitant fees charged during the process. FIDIC contracts clearly define the roles, responsibilities and obligations of all parties involved (employer, contractor and engineer), reducing the scope for disagreements and delays. They are designed to allocate risks fairly between the parties. This balanced approach helps in reducing the burden on any single party and encourages a more collaborative working environment. Even the UK laws have undergone changes, but the Indian Contract Act 1872 continues to be the foundation of our contractual legal system. Laws that leave room for multiple interpretations contribute to two injustices:

1. They delay justice, as arguments and counterarguments cause the case to go on and on.
2. For an investor, they cause anxiety due to the unpredictability.

The FIDIC contracts could help enhance confidence of international investors in the Indian construction market, leading to increased investment and participation in large-scale projects.

Transformative Change 13: Renewable Energy

In 2023–24, India imported approximately 232.5 mt of crude oil. This translates to about 4.6 million barrels per day (bpd), making India one of the largest importers of crude oil globally. India imports oil to the value of $220 billion or ₹16 trillion. If all vehicles would turn electric, the saving in import would be to the tune of $114 billion per year, considering 70% consumption on road transport alone, so we could actually cut the import of oil by half and save approximately ₹8 trillion at the crude oil rate of $80 per barrel.

The auto component industry is a significant employer in India, and the transition to EVs is expected to change the nature of jobs. While there may be fewer jobs in traditional component manufacturing, new opportunities will arise in the production of

EV-specific parts. However, these new jobs will require different skill sets, necessitating substantial reskilling and upskilling of the workforce. The transition presents opportunities for Indian manufacturers to innovate and capture new markets. Companies are already investing in R&D and forming partnerships to build capabilities in EV technology. This can potentially position India as a significant player in the global EV market.

The rooftop solar scheme in India, particularly under the PM-Surya Ghar: Muft Bijli Yojana, is expected to install rooftop solar systems in 10 million households, which could add up to 30 GW of solar capacity. This rooftop solar capacity is expected to generate approximately 1,000 billion units (BUs) of electricity and reduce CO2 emissions by 720 mt over the twenty-five-year lifespan of the systems, helping India's net-zero commitment by 2070.

Transformative Change 14: Decentralisation

The share of municipal revenue in India's national GDP is relatively small, accounting for about 0.6% to 0.7% in recent years. According to the RBI and other reports, municipal revenue receipts in India have ranged from 0.61% of GDP in 2017–18 to 0.72% in 2019-20. This is significantly lower compared to other countries, with municipal revenues/expenditures accounting for 7.4% of GDP in Brazil and 6% in South Africa.

The Fifteenth Finance Commission has recommended that urban local bodies publish audited annual accounts as a prerequisite for accessing grants, and the government has accepted it. Effective decentralisation relies on local bodies having adequate resources and the autonomy to prioritise expenditure decisions. Reform programmes in various developing countries and transition economies, such as Poland, Chile, Argentina, South Africa and China, have shown that granting autonomy to local units for decisions on investment incentives and capital market access provides a strong foundation for reforms. In China, for instance, town and village enterprises were given extensive powers over resource mobilisation, user fees and recruitment of experts, in addition to their existing implementation responsibilities. That said, among the countries mentioned, only South Africa has implemented comprehensive devolution of powers to the third tier. In China, the reforms did not pertain to political freedom. Political decentralisation offers a more durable 'rational-legal' framework, integrating decentralisation into political and civic discourse. India has the potential to lead in creating space for political decentralisation.

Transformative Change 15: Global Education Hub

The Indian civilisation, with all its faults and inequalities, was a knowledge-based one, like any other great civilisation. The revival of the modern Nalanda University, with a 455-acre campus in Bihar inaugurated by the prime minister in June 2024, rekindled the idea of India when it held a position of eminence in education during the Gupta Empire period in 5th century CE.

While this revival through the Nalanda University Act has seventeen participating countries supporting it as an international institution for pursuit of intellectual, philosophical, historical and spiritual studies, the current education global landscape has evolved to a different level. India is one among the three largest higher education systems in the world. According to the All-India Survey on Higher Education (AISHE) 2021–22, India had 1,168 universities, 45,473 colleges, 12,002 standalone institutions, 15.98 lakh (~1.6 million) faculty members and 43.3 million students enrolled in our higher education system. Despite such a large student base, our gross enrolment ratio (GER) in higher education is just 28.4%. Further, none of our higher education institutions are in the global ranking of the Top 100 Institutions, a list dominated by universities from the US, UK, Canada and Australia.

Although graduates from India's IITs, IIMs and other institutes of repute are highly sought after across the world, these institutes do not feature among the top institutions of global repute. Till, a couple of decades ago, most students going overseas went for postgraduate education. Today, they also do so for undergraduate and sometimes even high-school education. What is also striking is that even as more Indian students go overseas, fewer foreign students are coming to India. According to data collected by the Ministry of External Affairs, the number of Indian students studying overseas was estimated to be 1,324,954 in 2022.[11] By comparison, the number of foreign students studying in India was estimated to be 46,878 in 2022, according to the All-India Survey on Higher Education conducted by the Union Ministry for Human Resources Development.[12] While most Indian students going overseas are concentrated in the US, Canada, Australia and the UAE, most foreign students in India are nationals of Nepal and Afghanistan. There was a time when Indian universities attracted many students from Africa. These numbers have dwindled, with many Africans headed to China.

Globally, around 254 million students are currently enrolled in universities around the world with an overall GER of 42%. According to the UNESCO Institute of Statistics, in 2021, there were over 6.4 million international students globally, up from 4.1 million in 2012. With an average annual spend of $50,000 per student on tuition fees, accommodation and other living expenses, the size of the international education market can be pegged at $325 billion, assuming 6.5 million students. It is estimated that Indians comprise 20%, or 1.3 million of this market, in terms of number of students.

By applying the same financial metrics, the current annual spend by Indian students studying abroad can be estimated at around $65 billion. By 2030, this figure could well surpass the $100 billion mark. Given the excitement we display at the savings in foreign exchange outgo owing to domestic manufacture of the iPhone in India, which has saved $14 billion in FY2024, the figure of $65 billion racing towards $100 billion deserves equal attention, if not more. NITI Aayog CEO B.V.R. Subrahmanyam announced that India is targeting to enrol half a million foreign students in higher education by 2047.[13] But given how foreign students are choosing other countries, NITI Aayog needs to explore all such areas of discontent, which may range from infrastructure to job opportunities.

India's rise as a global education hub can be beneficial in more ways than one:

- Saves foreign exchange of $100 billion;
- Creates opportunities for student housing and allied social infrastructure like restaurants, medical centres, shopping and entertainment centres;
- Allows Indian companies to have the benefit of top global talent for recruitment;
- Can improve the research quotient in academic institutions;
- Enhances tourism in the long run;
- Helps heighten the innovation quotient in the country.

In Conclusion

As I complete this book, I hear the deafening roar of the resounding expectations of a 400-plus victory for the NDA at the general elections. The expectations fanned by senior politicians see the stock market rise to a crescendo only to come crashing the following day as the results are declared—although victorious, the victors stand disappointed. Our democracy resurges as the electorate serves the report card by casting its ballot.

At the beginning of this chapter, I wrote about the empires that were the toast of the world 2,000 years ago and now lie bathed in grime, dust and blood. But today, India is poised for greatness. Its potential has been recognised, its deficiencies have been exposed and are being worked upon. It is strong enough to ward off the threats and has the wisdom to pursue the opportunities that will take it to the orbit of the most powerful nations of the world.

It is time for Viksit Bharat. The pieces are in place. With political will, they will come together to realise our dreams—for infrastructure, progress and sustained development. Jai Hind. Jai Bharat.

Notes

Introduction

1 Margaret Thatcher, 'Speech to Conservative Women's Conference: 22 May 1985', *Margaret Thatcher Foundation*, https://www.margaretthatcher.org/document/106056.
2 'The World in 2050: The long view: how will the global economic order change by 2050?', *PWC*, https://www.pwc.com/gx/en/research-insights/economy/the-world-in-2050.html.

Chapter 2: The Road to 2014

1 'Summary of Economic Survey 2010-11', *Press Information Bureau*, 26 February 2011, https://pib.gov.in/newsite/PrintRelease.aspx?relid=70169#:~:text=The%20growth%20rate%20has%20been,grow%20around%205.4%20per%20cent.
2 Shishir Asthana, 'Private bidders see profits in govt rejected road projects', *Firstpost*, 20 December 2014, https://www.firstpost.com/business/private-bidders-see-goldmine-in-govt-losses-in-road-projects-51724.html.
3 PTI, 'NHAI to utilise Rs 1,352 cr negative grant in road devt', *Business Standard*, 20 January 2013, https://www.business-standard.com/article/economy-policy/nhai-to-utilise-rs-1-352-cr-negative-grant-in-road-devt-109050400207_1.html.
4 Yaruqhullah Khan, 'India's total toll collections rise 35% on-year to Rs 64,810 cr in FY24, target for FY25 at Rs 70,000 cr', *Moneycontrol*, 12 April 2024, https://www.moneycontrol.com/news/business/indias-total-toll-collections-rise-35-on-year-to-rs-64810-cr-in-fy24-target-for-fy25-at-rs-70000-cr-12626331.html.

5 'Federation Of Noida Residents Welfare ... vs Noida Toll Bridge Company Ltd. And ... on 26 October, 2016', *Indian Kanoon*, https://indiankanoon.org/doc/42525153/.

6 'Agreement between Maharashtra State Road Development Corporation Ltd and Mhaiskar Infrastructure Pvt. Ltd and Ideal Road Builders', https://msrdc.in/Site/Upload/GR/Conession%20Agreement%20of%20Mumbai%20Pune%20Expressway.pdf.

7 'Infrastructure Today India Opportunity 2012', *Construction World*, 11 May 2012, https://www.constructionworld.in/gold/transport-infrastructure/highways-and-roads-infrastructure/infrastructure-today-india-opportunity-2012/4347.

8 'Unprecedented Development in the Road Transport Sector', *Press Information Bureau*, 11 October 2002, https://archive.pib.gov.in/archive/releases98/lyr2002/roct2002/11102002/r111020021.html.

9 Ejaz Ghani, Arti Grover Goswami and William R. Kerr, 'Highway to Success: The Impact of the Golden Quadrilateral Project for the Location and Performance of Indian Manufacturing', *National Bureau of Economic Research*, November 2012, https://www.nber.org/papers/w18524.

10 'LOK SABHA UNSTARRED QUESTION NO-1205: LOANS WRITTEN OFF BY BANKS', 11 December 2023, https://sansad.in/getFile/loksabhaquestions/annex/1714/AU1205.pdf?source=pqals.

11 Read more at: 'Rs 10.4 lakh crore NPAs, 9 years: Which banks wrote off, recovered how much?', *Newslaundry*, 1 March 2024, https://www.newslaundry.com/2024/03/01/rs-104-lakh-crore-npas-9-years-which-banks-wrote-off-recovered-how-much.

12 "Pranab Mukherjee, Chidambaram used to pressurise RBI to present rosier picture of growth,' claims ex-Governor Subbarao', *Business Today*, 16 April 2024, https://www.businesstoday.in/latest/economy/story/pranab-mukherjee-chidambaram-used-to-pressurise-rbi-to-present-rosier-picture-of-growth-claims-ex-governor-subbarao-425610-2024-04-15.

13 'RBI liquidity tweaks won't hit infra investment', *The New Indian Indian Express*, 16 May 2012, https://www.newindianexpress.com/business/2010/Jan/23/rbi-liquidity-tweaks-wont-hit-infra-investment-163692.html.

14 PTI, 'Haven't done anything wrong: Sheila on CWG', *The Hindu*, 3 August 2011, https://www.thehindu.com/news/cities/Delhi/havent-done-anything-wrong-sheila-on-cwg/article2319529.ece.

15 'Top 10 facts about Kalmadi's Commonwealth Games scandal', *NDTV*, 19 January 2012, https://www.ndtv.com/india-news/top-10-facts-about-kalmadis-commonwealth-games-scandal-568261.

16 'Verdict of Supreme Court on 2G Spectrum Allocations – Pre Consultation Comments (Preliminary) of CUTS to TRAI', https://trai.gov.in/sites/default/files/CUTS_plimanry.pdf.

17 'CAG report: RPower says had EGoM nod for use of surplus coal', *Business Today*, 17 August 2012, https://www.businesstoday.in/industry/energy/story/cag-report-rpower-says-had-egom-nod-for-use-of-surplus-coal-33165-2012-08-17.

18 'What is coal scam?', *The Indian Express*, 22 May 2017, https://indianexpress.com/article/what-is/manmohan-singh-cbi-coalgate-coal-block-allocation-cag-report-what-is-coal-scam-4668265/.

19 P.R. Sanjai, 'GVK terminates NHAI contract', *Mint*, 14 January 2013, https://www.livemint.com/Companies/riFD3qgxoYN4kBtpNuuU2L/GVK-terminates-NHAI-contract.html.

20 Rahul Chandran, 'GMR Infrastructure walks out of Rajasthan-Gujarat road project', *Mint*, 7 January 2013, https://www.livemint.com/Politics/3YzOpHQCqxAHxibKdi6uWK/GMR-Infrastructure-walks-out-of-RajasthanGujarat-road-proje.html.

21 Avinash Celestine and Shantanu Nandan Sharma, 'GMR, GVK exit from NHAI's mega-road projects: What went wrong?', *The Economic Times*, 20 January 2013, https://economictimes.indiatimes.com/news/economy/infrastructure/gmr-gvk-exit-from-nhais-mega-road-projects-what-went-wrong/articleshow/18091357.cms?from=mdr.

22 Ibid.

23 Anusha Subramanian, 'Cabinet reshuffle: Jairam Ramesh shifted but raises the green bar for Jayanthi', *Business Today*, 27 July 2011, https://www.businesstoday.in/opinion/perspective/story/cabinet-reshuffle-jairam-ramesh-22330-2011-07-12.

24 Sangeeth Sebastian, 'I have been under pressure to overlook environment violations: Jairam Ramesh', *India Today*, 7 May 2011,

https://www.indiatoday.in/india/north/story/jairam-ramesh-violated-environment-rules-under-pressure-133296-2011-05-06.

25 PTI, 'High Court dismisses Vodafone tax case', *The Hindu*, 8 September 2010, https://www.thehindu.com/business/companies/High-Court-dismisses-Vodafone-tax-case/article15907554.ece.

26 'Vodafone wins Rs 11,000 crore tax case, to get Rs 2,500 cr with interest', *The Economic Times*, 20 January 2012, https://economictimes.indiatimes.com/industry/telecom/vodafone-wins-rs-11000-crore-tax-case-to-get-rs-2500-cr-with-interest/articleshow/11565473.cms?from=mdr.

27 'Vodafone wins Rs 11,000 crore tax case, to get Rs 2,500 cr with interest', *The Economic Times*, 20 January 2012, https://economictimes.indiatimes.com/industry/telecom/vodafone-wins-rs-11000-crore-tax-case-to-get-rs-2500-cr-with-interest/articleshow/11565473.cms?from=mdr.

28 PTI, 'USIBC President Ron Somers slams slow pace in India's economic reforms', *The Economic Times*, 13 May 2012, https://economictimes.indiatimes.com/news/economy/policy/usibc-president-ron-somers-slams-slow-pace-in-indias-economic-reforms/articleshow/13119826.cms?utm_source=contentofinterest&utm_medium=text&utm_campaign=cppst.

29 'Clarification by Dr. Kaushik Basu, Chief Economic Advisor, Regarding his Lecture at the Carnegie Endowment in Washington', *Press Information Bureau*, 20 April 2012, https://pib.gov.in/newsite/PrintRelease.aspx?relid=82414.

30 Devjyot Ghoshal and Piyali Mandal, 'Natarajan: Success abroad, domestic challenges manifold', *Business Standard*, 12 September 2012, https://www.business-standard.com/article/economy-policy/natarajan-success-abroad-domestic-challenges-manifold-112091202005_1.html.

31 'Nearly 350 environment ministry files held back by ex-minister Jayanti Nataraja', *DNA India*, 13 January 2014, https://www.dnaindia.com/delhi/report-nearly-350-environment-ministry-files-held-back-by-ex-minister-jayanti-nataraja-1950255.

32 Vikas Dhoot, 'Did Jayanthi Natarajan delay big-ticket projects worth around Rs 10 lakh crore?', *The Economic Times*, 23 December 2013, https://economictimes.indiatimes.com/news/economy/policy/

did-jayanthi-natarajan-delay-big-ticket-projects-worth-around-rs-10-lakh-crore/articleshow/27760881.cms?from=mdr; PTI, 'India imports coal worth Rs 2.3 lakh crore in Apr-Sep FY23', *Financial Express*, 12 December 2022, https://www.financialexpress.com/business/industry-india-imports-coal-worth-rs-2-3-lakh-crore-in-apr-sep-fy23-2910151/.

33 PTI, 'New project announcements slumped in September 2012 quarter: CMIE', *The Economic Times*, 4 November 2012, https://economictimes.indiatimes.com/news/economy/indicators/new-project-announcements-slumped-in-september-2012-quarter-cmie/articleshow/17085302.cms?from=mdr.

34 Mansi Taneja, 'PM sets up project monitoring group to track large investment projects', *Business Standard*, 13 June 2013, https://www.business-standard.com/article/economy-policy/pm-sets-up-project-monitoring-group-to-track-large-investment-projects-113061300656_1.html.

35 PTI, 'Projects worth Rs 1.46 lakh crore pending, PM Manmohan calls meet on June 6', *India Today*, 4 June 2012, https://www.indiatoday.in/india/north/story/projects-pending-manmohan-singh-calls-meet-infrastructure-104490-2012-06-03.

36 PTI, 'High-powered panel under PM to clear mega projects', *Rediff.com*, 13 December 2012, https://www.rediff.com/money/report/high-powered-panel-under-pm-to-clear-mega-projects/20121213.htm.

37 'Top Priority Projects', *Construction World*, 1 February 2013, https://www.constructionworld.in/transport-infrastructure/highways-and-roads-infrastructure/Top-Priority-Projects/8613.

38 'Monitoring Group: The Breaker of Deadlocks', *Forbes India*, 10 June 2014, https://www.forbesindia.com/article/real-issue/project-monitoring-group-the-breaker-of-deadlocks/37924/1.

39 T.C.A. Sharad Raghavan, 'Backstage: The Story Behind India's High Growth Years' review: Strategist at work', *The Hindu*, 15 March 2020, https://www.thehindu.com/books/books-reviews/backstage-the-story-behind-indias-high-growth-years-review-strategist-at-work/article31050116.ece.

40 S.C. Garg, 'State of Infrastructure', *Infrastructure Statistics*, pp. 174–5.

41 Abhishek Banerjee and Karuna Gopal, 'India's lost decade: Falling behind BRIC economies between 2004 and 2014 and the subsequent recovery', *Firstpost*, 4 September 2023, https://www.firstpost.com/opinion/indias-lost-decade-falling-behind-bric-economies-between-2004-and-2014-and-the-subsequent-recovery-13073382.html.

Chapter 3: Annual Perspectives

1 Pratap Padode, 'Editorial', *Infrastructure Today*, January 2012.

2 Sarita C. Singh, 'Coal Ministry to bar captive miners from producing beyond approved level', *The Economic Times*, 15 December 2011, https://economictimes.indiatimes.com/industry/indl-goods/svs/metals-mining/coal-ministry-to-bar-captive-miners-from-producing-beyond-approved-level/articleshow/11113346.cms.

3 PTI, 'Jayanthi Natarajan raises green objections to National Investment Board', *India Today*, 9 October 2012, https://www.indiatoday.in/india/north/story/jayanthi-natarajan-manmohan-singh-national-investment-board-118229-2012-10-09.

4 PTI, 'Coal sector in thick of controversies in 2013 over allotment', *The Economic Times*, 30 December 2013, https://economictimes.indiatimes.com/industry/indl-goods/svs/metals-mining/coal-sector-in-thick-of-controversies-in-2013-over-allotment/articleshow/28133445.cms?from=mdr.

5 'Modi government's measures to boost business investment: Moody's', *The Economic Times*, 12 August 2014, https://economictimes.indiatimes.com/news/economy/indicators/modi-governments-measures-to-boost-business-investment-moodys/articleshow/40119946.cms?from=mdr.

6 M.G. Arun, 'Narendra Modi harps on governance, growth and GST in India Inc meet', *India Today*, 27 February 2014, https://www.indiatoday.in/india/north/story/narendra-modi-india-inc-indian-economy-gst-bjp-india-economic-conventi on-2014-183001-2014-02-27.

7 'MoEF for mining ban in 1kn buffer', *The Times of India*, 8 March 2014, http://timesofindia.indiatimes.com/articleshow/31627084.

cms?utm_source=contentofinterest&utm_medium=text&utm_campaign=cppst.

8 *Twelfth Five Year Plan (2012–2017) Faster, More Inclusive and Sustainable Growth (Vol. 1)*, Planning Commission, 2013, https://www.niti.gov.in/sites/default/files/2023-08/12fyp_vol1.pdf.

9 'Recent Developments and Prospects, Chapter 1 - World Economic Outlook (WEO)', April 2014, https://www.imf.org/external/pubs/ft/weo/2014/01/pdf/c1.pdf.

10 *World Investment Report 2014*, UNCTAD, https://unctad.org/system/files/official-document/wir2014_overview_en.pdf.

11 'India's urban awakening: Building inclusive cities, sustaining economic growth', McKinsey Global Institute, April 2010, https://www.mckinsey.com/~/media/McKinsey/Business%20Functions/Operations/Our%20Insights/Urban%20awakening%20in%20India/MGI_Indias_urban_awakening_executive_summary.pdf.

12 'Report of the Sub-Committee on Financing Urban Infrastructure in the 12th Plan', Ministry of Urban Development, March 2012, https://mohua.gov.in/upload/uploadfiles/files/Report%20of%20the%20Sub-Committee%20on%20Financing%20Urban%20Infrastructure%20in%20the%2012th%20Plan%20_0.pdf.

13 PTI, 'India's infra market to reach $6.6 trillion by 2025, says PwC report', *Business Today*, 16 September 2014, https://www.businesstoday.in/industry/infra/story/india-infra-market-pwc-housing-telecom-healthcare-education-135834-2014-09-16.

14 Lutz Killian, 'What caused the big fall in oil prices?', *World Economic Forum*, 25 February 2015, https://www.weforum.org/agenda/2015/02/what-caused-the-big-fall-in-oil-prices/.

15 'Government stares at Rs 1 lakh crore tax deficit, but may hike spend to boost growth', *The Times of India*, 20 December 2014, https://timesofindia.indiatimes.com/business/india-business/government-stares-at-rs-1-lakh-crore-tax-deficit-but-may-hike-spend-to-boost-growth/articleshow/45581795.cms.

16 PTI, 'Services sector growth picks up in January on new business orders, says HSBC', *Business Today*, 4 February 2015, https://www.businesstoday.in/latest/economy-politics/story/services-sector-grows-in-january-on-new-business-orders-hsbc-143479-2015-02-04.

17 'LED lights at Marine Drive: Piyush Goyal hits back at Sena', *Hindustan Times*, 24 March 2015, https://www.hindustantimes.com/mumbai/led-lights-at-marine-drive-piyush-goyal-hits-back-at-sena/story-ywFISKkRA5GHzIKG1jlQSI.html.

18 IANS, 'Earlier land law hugely anti-farmer: Arun Jaitley', *Business Standard*, 6 April 2015, https://www.business-standard.com/article/news-ians/earlier-land-law-hugely-anti-farmer-arun-jaitley-115040600278_1.html.

19 'Indian Railway Budget Speech 2015-16: Speech of Shri Suresh Prabhakar Prabhu introducing the Railway Budget for 2015-16 on 26th of February, 2015', https://indianrailways.gov.in/railwayboard/uploads/directorate/finance_budget/Budget_2015-16/Railway_Budget_Speech_2015-16%20(English).pdf.

20 'Indian Railways: Lifeline of a Nation', *Ministry of Railways*, February 2015, https://indianrailways.gov.in/railwayboard/uploads/directorate/finance_budget/Budget_2015-16/White_Paper-_English.pdf.

21 'Bure din gaye', Construction World, 1 June 2015, https://www.constructionworld.in/transport-infrastructure/ports-and-shipping/Bure-din-gaye/12800.

22 'Business Confidence Survey', *FICCI*, July 2015, https://www.slideshare.net/slideshow/business-confidence-survey-july-2015-ficci/51988660#4.

23 'Government looking to spur public spending to provide momentum to economy: Arun Jaitley', *The Economic Times*, 6 August 2015, https://economictimes.indiatimes.com/news/economy/policy/government-looking-to-spur-public-spending-to-provide-momentum-to-economy-arun-jaitley/articleshow/48367141.cms?utm_source=contentofinterest&utm_medium=text&utm_campaign=cppst.

24 Amiti Sen, 'Ahead of visit, US industry asks Modi to deliver on reforms', *The Hindu Businessline*, 20 January 2018, https://www.thehindubusinessline.com/economy/policy/ahead-of-visit-us-industry-asks-modi-to-deliver-on-reforms/article8557194.ece.

25 The report can be accessed from this link: http://finmin.nic.in/reports/ReportRevisitingRevitalising%20PPPModel.pdf

26 Mayank Aggarwal, 'Forest clearances for only 6% of road projects since Jan 2015', *Mint*, 27 April 2017, https://www.livemint.com/Politics/xznuWSDzz1snTEYCMPFdgO/Forest-clearances-for-only-6-of-road-projects-since-Jan-20.html.

27 Ravi Teja Sharma, Kailash Babar and Sobia Khan, 'Builders get realistic, increase delivery times up to 5 years from 3', *Realty.com*, 15 January 2016, https://realty.economictimes.indiatimes.com/news/industry/builders-get-realistic-increase-delivery-timelines-up-to-5-years-from-3-years/50585554.

28 'Up the ranks', *The Indian Express*, 25 December 2015, https://indianexpress.com/article/opinion/editorials/ease-of-doing-business-in-india-up-the-ranks/.

29 'Annual Survey of India's City-Systems 2016: Shaping India's Urban Agenda', *Jana Urban Space Foundation (India)*, https://www.janaagraha.org/reports/ASICS-2016.pdf.

30 Sahib Sharma, 'Projects worth Rs5.18 trillion completed in 2016-17, second highest in a decade', *Mint*, 12 April 2017, https://www.livemint.com/Companies/7qy5T8QBhlw6pUdXbXcdhJ/Projects-worth-Rs518-trillion-completed-in-201617-second.html.

31 PTI, 'Uttar Pradesh tops in PPP project investments: Study', *Business Standard*, 18 April 2016, https://www.business-standard.com/article/pti-stories/uttar-pradesh-topper-in-ppp-project-investments-study-116041800381_1.html.

32 'Make Internet More Accessible, Affordable and Open to Accelerate Development, says New World Bank Report', *World Bank Group*, 10 May 2016, https://www.worldbank.org/en/news/press-release/2016/05/10/make-internet-more-accessible-affordable-open-accelerate-development-says-new-world-bank-report.

33 'Global Average Connection Speed Up 23% According to Akamai's "Fourth Quarter, 2015 State of the Internet Report "', *Akamai*, 22 March 2016, https://www.akamai.com/newsroom/press-release/akamai-releases-fourth-quarter-2015-state-of-the-internet-report.

34 Sahib Sharma, 'Projects worth Rs5.18 trillion completed in 2016-17, second highest in a decade', *Mint*, 12 April 2017, https://www.livemint.com/Companies/7qy5T8QBhlw6pUdXbXcdhJ/Projects-worth-Rs518-trillion-completed-in-201617-second.html.

35 PTI, 'Infrastructure deficit biggest hurdle for Make in India: S&P', *India Today*, 2 August 2016, https://www.indiatoday.in/pti-feed/story/infrastructure-deficit-biggest-hurdle-for-make-in-india-sandampp-677475-2016-08-02.

36 PTI, 'India needs $1.5 trillion for infrastructure: Jaitley', *The Hindu*, 17 November 2021, https://www.thehindu.com/news/India-needs-1.5-trillion-for-infrastructure-Jaitley/article60571811.ece.

37 PTI, 'India needs Rs 31 lakh crore for infra sector in five years: Crisil', *The Economic Times*, 17 December 2015, https://economictimes.indiatimes.com/news/economy/infrastructure/india-needs-rs-31-lakh-crore-for-infra-sector-in-five-years-crisil/articleshow/50218997.cms?from=mdr.

38 'Access to Justice survey 2015-16', Daksh, https://dakshindia.org/wp-content/uploads/2016/05/Daksh-access-to-justice-survey.pdf.

39 'Arbitration law would unlock the capital flow in construction sector: Assocham', *Business Standard*, 21 December 2015, https://www.business-standard.com/article/companies/arbitration-law-would-unlock-the-capital-flow-in-construction-sector-assocham-115122100719_1.html.

40 'NITI Aayog proposes easier arbitration norms for infra firms', *Indian Brand Equity Foundation*, 26 August 2016, https://www.ibef.org/news/niti-aayog-proposes-easier-arbitration-norms-for-infra-firms.

41 Rajat Arora, 'NHAI to give Rs 6,000 crore to firms stuck in litigation', *ET Realty.com*, 15 September 2016, https://realty.economictimes.indiatimes.com/news/regulatory/nhai-to-give-rs-6000-crore-to-firms-stuck-in-litigation/54346427.

42 PTI, 'India records 10-year low in public-private investments: World Bank', *The Hindu*, 14 June 2016, https://www.thehindu.com/business/Economy/India-records-10-year-low-in-public-private-investments-World-Bank/article14422100.ece.

43 PTI, 'Government study pegs face value of fake currencies at Rs 400 crore', *The Economic Times*, 2 August 2016, https://economictimes.indiatimes.com/news/economy/finance/government-study-pegs-face-value-of-fake-currencies-at-rs-400-crore/articleshow/53504738.cms?from=mdr.

44 PTI, '"Housing prices to fall up to 30%, wiping Rs 8 lakh cr in value"', *Business Today*, 24 November 2016, https://www.businesstoday.in/latest/economy-politics/story/housing-prices-to-fall-up-to-30-percent-demonetisation-66402-2016-11-24.

45 'India: Three Year Action Agenda 2017-18 to 2019-20', *NITI Aayog*, 2017, https://www.niti.gov.in/sites/default/files/2023-03/Three-Year-Action-Agenda-2017-19.pdf.

46 Chris Clague, 'Safe Cities Index 2017: Security in a rapidly urbanising world', *Economist Impact*, 26 February 2018, https://impact.econ-asia.com/perspectives/infrastructure-cities/safe-cities-index-2017-security-rapidly-urbanising-world.

47 'Doing Business 2017', *Doing Business Archive*, 25 October 2016, https://archive.doingbusiness.org/en/reports/global-reports/doing-business-2017.

48 'Cabinet approves Rs 2.11-lakh crore state bank recapitalisation plan to revive investment', *Hindustan Times*, 24 October 2017, https://www.hindustantimes.com/business-news/cabinet-approves-rs-2-11-lakh-crore-state-bank-recapitalisation-plan-to-revive-investment/story-dT1OUa6zdwfanV1qNL7TDM.html.

49 'A quarterly solutions-based project update report: Snapshot of projects under Lighthouse Smart Cities', *Amcham India*, December 2017, https://amchamindia.com/wp-content/uploads/2024/05/Snapshot-of-Projects-Under-Lighthouse-Smart-Cities-A-Quarterly-Solutions-Based-Project-Update-Report.pdf.

50 T.C.A. Sharad Raghavan, 'Private sector investment may see rise', *The Hindu*, 2 August 2018, https://www.thehindu.com/business/private-sector-investment-may-see-rise/article24584643.ece.

51 Ashutosh R. Shyam and Rajesh Naidu, 'E&C firms report sizable growth in FY18 order book', 15 June 2018, https://economictimes.indiatimes.com/markets/stocks/news/ec-firms-report-sizable-growth-in-fy18-order-book/articleshow/64598601.cms?from=mdr.

52 PTI, '358 infra projects show cost overruns of over Rs 3.37 lakh crore', *The Economic Times*, 19 November 2018, https://energy.economictimes.indiatimes.com/news/power/358-infra-projects-show-cost-overruns-of-over-rs-3-37-lakh-crore/66687200.

53 Pallavi Nahata, 'New Projects Fall to Lowest Level of Modi Government's Tenure, shows CMIE Data', *NDTV Profit*, 3 January 2019, https://www.ndtvprofit.com/global-economics/new-project-announcements-fall-in-december-quarter-shows-cmie-data.

54 Kaushik Deka, 'SOS Survey 2019: The Champion States', *India Today*, 2 December 2019, https://www.indiatoday.in/magazine/cover-story/story/20191202-the-champion-states-1621269-2019-11-22.

55 Nasreen Sultana and Ashwin Ramarathinam, 'Profit growth in Q3 FY19 slowest in 5 quarters, shows analysis', *Mint*, 14 February 2019, https://www.livemint.com/companies/company-results/q3-results-2018-19-analysis-of-listed-companies-1550166459028.html.

56 Chris Sleight, 'Global equipment sales hit record high', *Off-Highway Research*, 25 March 2019, https://offhighwayresearch.com/News/Global-equipment-sales-hit-record-high/208.article.

57 PTI, 'PM Modi announces "April 2019-March 2020' as Construction-Technology year", *The Economic Times*, 2 March 2019, https://economictimes.indiatimes.com/news/politics-and-nation/pm-modi-announces-april-2019-march-2020-as-construction-technology-year/articleshow/68231886.cms?from=mdr.

58 'Budget 2019-2020 Speech of Nirmala Sitharaman Minister of Finance', 5 July 2019, https://www.indiabudget.gov.in/budget2019-20/doc/Budget_Speech.pdf.

59 'Independent Verification of Swachh Bharat Grameen confirms over 96% usage of toilets', *Press Information Bureau*, 5 March 2019, https://pib.gov.in/PressReleaseIframePage.aspx?PRID=1567486#:~:text=The%20key%20findings%20of%20NARSS,access%20to%20toilets%20used%20them.

60 'An Open Letter to Finance Minister', *Construction World*, 27 March 2020, https://www.constructionworld.in/latest-construction-news/real-estate-news/an-open-letter--to-finance-minister/23378.

61 'Asian Development Outlook (ADO) 2020: What Drives Innovation in Asia?', *Asian Development Bank*, April 2020, https://www.adb.org/publications/asian-development-outlook-2020-innovation-asia.

62 '100th Project Implementation: An Overview – August 2020', Ministry of Statistics and Programme Implementation, http://www.cspm.gov.in/english/pio_report/PIO_August_2020.pdf.

63 Gireesh Chandra Prasad, 'Infrastructure project delays need a fix: Nitin Gadkari', *Mint*, 28 October 2020, https://www.livemint.com/news/india/infrastructure-project-delays-need-a-fix-nitin-gadkari-11603898295152.html.

64 'Large companies made a killing in Q2 despite Covid concerns: CMIE', *Business Today*, 13 November 2020, https://www.businesstoday.in/latest/economy-politics/story/india-inc-q1-profit-hits-record-high-of-rs-145-lakh-crore-278779-2020-11-16; Pratap Padode, 'Why public spending is the cure for the pandemic', *Construction World*, 29 December 2020, https://www.constructionworld.in/policy-updates-and-economic-news/why-public-spending-is-the-cure-for-the-pandemic/25147.

65 'Mumbai records over 12,000 property registration in March, thanks to stamp duty cut: Report', *Mint*, 25 March 2021, https://www.livemint.com/industry/infrastructure/mumbai-records-12-696-property-registrations-in-march-thanks-to-stamp-duty-cut-11616672702338.html.

66 'Staging a Strong Comeback: India Residential Real Estate (Annual Report 2021)', *Anarock*, https://websitemedia.anarock.com/media/ANAROCK_ANNUAL_REPORT_2021_Staging_a_Strong_Comeback_19d10c61a8.pdf; PTI, 'Housing sales up 71% in 2021 in top 7 cities; sales down 10% from 2019 pre-Covid level', *The Economic Times*, 2 January 2022, https://economictimes.indiatimes.com/industry/services/property-/-cstruction/housing-sales-up-71-in-2021-in-top-7-cities-sales-down-10-from-2019-pre-covid-level/articleshow/88645743.cms.

67 'Building of National Highways touches 34 km per day, crosses milestone of 12,205 km in current financial year so far'. *Press Information Bureau*, 22 March 2021, https://pib.gov.in/Pressreleaseshare.aspx?PRID=1706719.

68 'Capital Goods update - 11MFY21', *CARE Ratings*, 14 April 2021, https://images.assettype.com/bloombergquint/2021-04/e3249408-21de-4514-979d-4372a22a58f5/CARE_Ratings_Capital_Goods_Update_.pdf.

69 Shivani Khanna, 'Advance tax collection surges 146% despite pandemic led economic disruption', *The Indian Wire*, 17 July 2021,

https://www.theindianwire.com/business/advance-tax-collection-surges-146-despite-pandemic-led-economic-disruption-315384/.

70 'Digital Transformation: The Future of Connected Construction in India', *IDC*, July 2020, https://damassets.autodesk.net/content/dam/autodesk/www/apac/en-IN/assets/autodesk-idc-infobrief-digital-transformation-in-construction-india.pdf.

71 Anwesha Madhukulya, 'India overtakes US to become second-most sought-after manufacturing destination', *Business Today*, 24 August 2021, https://www.businesstoday.in/latest/economy/story/india-overtakes-us-to-become-second-most-sought-after-manufacturing-destination-305048-2021-08-24.

72 'Incentives of Rs.120 crore to be given in next 3 years under PLI scheme for drones and drone components: Civil Aviation Minister Shri Jyotiraditya M. Scindia', *Press Information Bureau*, 16 September 2021, https://www.pib.gov.in/PressReleasePage.aspx?PRID=1755452.

73 'World Investment Report 2021: Investing in Sustainable Recovery', *UNCTAD*, https://unctad.org/system/files/official-document/wir2021_en.pdf.

74 'India's Turning Point', *McKinsey Global Institute*, August 2020, https://www.mckinsey.com/~/media/McKinsey/Featured%20Insights/India/Indias%20turning%20point%20An%20economic%20agenda%20to%20spur%20growth%20and%20jobs/MGI-Indias-turning-point-Report-August-2020-vFinal.pdf.

75 PTI, 'Demand for housing continues to remain robust: Deepak Parekh, Chairman, HDFC', *ET Realty.com*, 17 February 2022, https://realty.economictimes.indiatimes.com/news/allied-industries/demand-for-housing-continues-to-remain-robust-deepak-parekh-chairman-hdfc/89644397.

76 Dhruvaksh Saha, 'Highway construction gains pace, 8,045 km constructed till Feb-end', *Business Standard*, 16 March 2022, https://www.business-standard.com/article/economy-policy/highway-construction-gains-pace-8-045-km-constructed-till-feb-end-122031601501_1.html.

77 PTI, 'Auction of minerals blocks stabilised in country; 186 mines put on sale so far', *The Times of India*, 25 May 2022, https://timesofindia.

indiatimes.com/auction-of-mineral-blocks-stabilised-in-country-186-mines-put-on-sale-so-far/articleshow/91790126.cms.

78 'Companies spent ₹2.6 lakh crore on setting up 57.7 GW solar capacity', *The Hindu BusinessLine*, 28 July 2022, https://www.thehindubusinessline.com/companies/companies-spent-26-lakh-crore-on-setting-up-577-gw-solar-capacity/article65694213.ece.

79 Puneet Wadhwa, 'India to be the fastest-growing Asian economy in FY23: Morgan Stanley', *Business Standard*, 10 August 2022, https://www.business-standard.com/article/markets/india-to-be-the-fastest-growing-asian-economy-in-fy23-morgan-stanley-122081000249_1.html.

80 Pragya Srivastava, 'Capex plans continue to slide in September quarter, shows CMIE data', *Mint*, 3 October 2022, https://www.livemint.com/economy/capex-plans-continue-to-slide-in-september-quarter-shows-cmie-data-11664739634467.html.

81 Pratap Padode, 'Metro neglect will cost us dear', *FIRST Construction Council*, 8 February 2023, https://firstconstructioncouncil.com/article/902428.

82 Twesh Mishra, 'Ratings of road contractors in the offing to curb errant operators: Nitin Gadkari', *The Economic Times*, 20 December 2022, https://economictimes.indiatimes.com/industry/transportation/roadways/rating-of-road-contractors-in-the-offing-to-curb-errant-operators-nitin-gadkari/articleshow/96349487.cms?from=mdr.

83 Raghavendra Kamath, 'We plan to capture just 4% of mkt in 4 yrs: Prestige Estates' Irfan Razack', *Business Standard*, 28 February 2023, https://www.business-standard.com/article/companies/our-plan-is-to-capture-only-3-5-4-of-market-prestige-estates-irfan-razaq-123022800765_1.html.

84 Janaki Krishnan, 'Qualification criteria for road projects has to be tightened, says IRB Infrastructure Developers' MD', *The Hindu BusinessLine*, 27 March 2023, https://www.thehindubusinessline.com/companies/qualification-criteria-for-road-projects-has-to-be-tightened-says-irb-infrastructure-developers-md/article66667028.ece.

85 Sachin P. Mampatta, 'New private projects decline 79% in second quarter, shows CMIE data', *Business Standard*, 1 October 2023, https://www.business-standard.com/industry/news/new-projects-from-the-private-sector-decline-79-2-shows-cmie-data-123100100621_1.html.

86 Sohini Bagchi, 'Indian tech industry to grow 8.4% to $245 billion in FY23: Nasscom', *Mint*, 2 March 2023, https://www.livemint.com/industry/infotech/indian-tech-industry-to-grow-8-4-to-245-billion-in-fy23-nasscom-11677673202172.html.

87 'Shri Nitin Gadkari says under Parvatmala Pariyojana Government plans to develop more than 250 projects with Ropeway length of over 1,200 km in 5 years', *Press Information Bureau*, 19 April 2023, https://pib.gov.in/PressReleaseIframePage.aspx?PRID=1917864.

88 ANI, 'India will be the 3rd largest economy soon, says PM Modi', *The Economic Times*, 23 June 2023, https://economictimes.indiatimes.com/news/india/india-will-be-the-3rd-largest-economy-soon-says-pm-modi/videoshow/101201024.cms?from=mdr.

89 Sanjeev Sinha, 'Residential sales in top 8 cities at nine-year high in 2022: Knight Frank India', *Financial Express*, 10 January 2023, https://www.financialexpress.com/money/residential-sales-in-top-8-cities-at-nine-year-high-in-2022-knight-frank-india-2942300/.

90 'KPMG Global Construction Survey 2023', *KPMG*, https://kpmg.com/xx/en/home/insights/2023/05/2023-global-construction-survey.html.

91 Yaruqhullah Khan, 'Seven of 10 most-delayed infrastructure projects in India are rail lines', *Moneycontrol*, 29 August 2023, https://www.moneycontrol.com/news/business/seven-of-10-most-delayed-infrastructure-projects-in-india-are-rail-lines-11273691.html.

Chapter 4: Why Aren't We There Yet?

1 PTI, 'FM Nirmala Sitharaman compares India Inc to Hanuman, asks why not invest in manufacturing', *Mint*, 13 September 2022, https://www.livemint.com/economy/fm-nirmala-sitharaman-india-inc-hanuman-asks-why-not-invest-in-manufacturing-11663059534491.html.

2 Sandeep Soni, 'Over 35,000 MSMEs shut so far post Covid; Maharashtra, TN, Gujarat see highest closures', *Financial Express*, 12 February 2024, https://www.financialexpress.com/business/sme/over-35000-msmes-shut-so-far-post-covid-maharashtra-tn-gujarat-see-highest-closures/3391309/.

3 'India falls in global FDI ranking; inflows drop 43% to $28 billion', *Fortune India*, 21 June 2024, https://www.fortuneindia.com/macro/india-falls-in-global-fdi-ranking-inflows-drop-43-to-28-billion/117255.

4 Abhijeet Kumar, 'Pvt sector investment in FY23 fell to Covid-year levels, govt's share up', *Business Standard*, 7 May 2024, https://www.business-standard.com/economy/news/pvt-sector-investment-in-fy23-fell-to-covid-year-levels-govt-s-share-up-124050700688_1.html.

5 'MULTIDIMENSIONAL POVERTY IN INDIA SINCE 2005-06: A Discussion Paper', *NITI Aayog*, https://www.niti.gov.in/sites/default/files/2024-01/MPI-22_NITI-Aayog20254.pdf.

6 PTI, 'Over 24.8 cr people moved out of multidimensional poverty in India in 9 years: NITI report', *The Hindu BusinessLine*, 15 January 2024, https://www.thehindubusinessline.com/economy/over-248-cr-people-moved-out-of-multidimensional-poverty-in-india-in-9-years-niti-report/article67743141.ece.

7 Nidhi Singhal, 'India achieved in 9 years what would have taken 47 years by traditional means: Nandan Nilekani', *Business Today*, 28 August 2023, https://www.businesstoday.in/latest/corporate/story/india-achieved-in-9-years-what-would-have-taken-47-years-by-traditional-means-nandan-nilekani-395801-2023-08-27.

8 PTI, '55% of all new bank accounts in the world opened from India, says World Bank report', *Hindustan Times*, 21 April 2018, https://www.hindustantimes.com/business-news/55-of-all-new-bank-accounts-in-the-world-opened-from-india-says-world-bank-report/story-PWrkB2X8pbHHHtP1DaMMaK.html.

9 'Address by Governor, Reserve Bank of India at the Digital Payments Awareness Week celebrations, March 4, 2024, RBI, Mumbai', *Reserve Bank of India*, https://www.rbi.org.in/Scripts/BS_SpeechesView.aspx?Id=1422#:~:text=We%20have%20seen%20retail%20digital,as%20per%202022%20data)%201.

10 Anirban Sarma, 'Imagining 2024: Digital Public Infrastructure's global footprint', *Observer Research Foundation*, 19 December 2023, https://www.orfonline.org/expert-speak/imagining-2024-digital-public-infrastructure-s-global-footprint.

11 M.G. Arun, 'Why private investment in India remains tepid post pandemic', *India Today*, 7 March 2023, https://www.indiatoday.in/india-today-insight/story/why-private-investment-in-india-remains-tepid-post-pandemic-2343779-2023-03-07.

12 Ajay Chhibber and Akshata Kalloor, 'Reviving Private Investment in India: Determinants and Policy Levers', Institute for International Economic Policy Working Paper Series, Working Paper No. 181, March 2017, https://www2.gwu.edu/~iiep/assets/docs/papers/2017WP/ChhibberIIEPWP2017-5.pdf.

13 M.G. Arun, 'Why private investment in India remains tepid post pandemic', *India Today*, 7 March 2023, https://www.indiatoday.in/india-today-insight/story/why-private-investment-in-india-remains-tepid-post-pandemic-2343779-2023-03-07.

14 Ibid.

15 M.G. Arun, 'Why private investment in India remains tepid post pandemic', *India Today*, 7 March 2023, https://www.indiatoday.in/india-today-insight/story/why-private-investment-in-india-remains-tepid-post-pandemic-2343779-2023-03-07.

16 'Monthly Economic Review August 2023', *Department of Economic Affairs*, August 2023, https://dea.gov.in/sites/default/files/Monthly%20Economic%20Review%20August%202023_0.pdf

17 Ruchika Chitravanshi, 'India sees 43% decline in FDI inflows in 2023, drops to 15th spot', *Business Standard*, 20 June 2024, https://www.business-standard.com/economy/news/india-sees-43-fall-in-fdi-inflows-in-2023-drops-to-15th-spot-unctad-124062000868_1.html.

18 Prasanna Mohanty, 'Is private investment in the economy on revival path?', *Fortune India*, 17 October 2023, https://www.fortuneindia.com/opinion/is-private-investment-in-the-economy-on-revival-path/114485.

19 K.S. Badri Narayanan, 'Why India's manufacturing sector will be a rising star', *The Hindu Businessline*, 12 August 2023, https://www.pressreader.com/india/businessline-delhi-9WVW/20230812/281878712901825.

20 K.S. Badri Narayanan, 'Is India's manufacturing sector a rising star?', *The Hindu Businessline*, 11 August 2023, https://www.thehindubusinessline.com/economy/is-indias-manufacturing-sector-a-rising-star/article67184730.ece; Amiti Sen, '10 years

of NDA: PLI scheme, a promising start but yet to reach its potential', *The Hindu Businessline*, 19 April 2024, https://www.thehindubusinessline.com/news/elections/10-years-of-nda-pli-scheme-a-promising-start-but-yet-to-reach-its-potential/article68080625.ece.

21 Surabhi, 'India's disinvestment agenda: Why hasn't the policy taken off?', *Business Today*, 1 October 2023, https://www.businesstoday.in/magazine/deep-dive/story/indias-disinvestment-agenda-why-hasnt-the-policy-taken-off-398928-2023-09-19#:~:text=As%20many%20as%20159%20disinvestment,and%20joint%20ventures%-20since%202016.

22 Surabhi, 'India's disinvestment agenda: Why hasn't the policy taken off?', *Business Today*, 1 October 2023, https://www.businesstoday.in/magazine/deep-dive/story/indias-disinvestment-agenda-why-hasnt-the-policy-taken-off-398928-2023-09-19.

23 T.V. Mohandas Pai, X, 13 June 2023, https://x.com/TVMohandasPai/status/1668617861387124737.

24 Prime Minister's Office, 'India has Moved from Tax-Terrorism to Tax-Transparency: Prime Minister', *Press Information Bureau*, 11 November 2020, https://www.pib.gov.in/PressReleasePage.aspx?PRID=1671979.

25 PTI, 'I-T dept found unaccounted sales of Rs 1,000 cr during raid against Polycab', *Business Standard*, 10 January 2024, https://www.business-standard.com/companies/news/i-t-dept-found-unaccounted-sales-of-rs-1-000-cr-during-raid-against-polycab-124011000928_1.html.

26 Shoumojit Banerjee, 'Ex-CAG Vinod Rai apologises to Sanjay Nirupam over charges in 2G spectrum case', *The Hindu*, 28 October 2021, https://www.thehindu.com/news/national/other-states/ex-cag-vinod-rai-apologises-to-sanjay-nirupam-over-charges-in-2g-spectrum-case/article37211881.ece.

27 Ajit Ranade, 'Pending cases cross 5-crore: Justice delayed is justice denied', *Deccan Herald*, 27 July 2023, https://www.deccanherald.com/opinion/pending-cases-cross-5-crore-justice-delayed-is-justice-denied-1241077.html.

28 Marie Chêne, 'The Impact of Corruption on Growth and Inequality', *Transparency International*, 15 March 2014, https://knowledgehub.

transparency.org/helpdesk/the-impact-of-corruption-on-growth-and-inequality.

29 Shilpa Jamkhandikar and Ira Dugal, 'Mumbai gets a makeover as India binges on bridges, roads and rail', *Reuters*, 11 January 2024, https://www.reuters.com/world/india/mumbai-gets-makeover-india-binges-bridges-roads-rail-2024-01-11/.

30 Gautam Chikermane and Rishi Agarwal, *Jailed for Doing Business*, *ORF*, 2022, https://www.orfonline.org/public/uploads/posts/pdf/20221222133420.pdf.

31 'How India could rise to the world's second-biggest economy', *Goldman Sachs*, 6 July 2023, https://www.goldmansachs.com/insights/articles/how-india-could-rise-to-the-worlds-second-biggest-economy.

32 'One factor that can put India ahead of the US as the 2nd biggest economy', *The Economic Times*, 12 July 2023, https://economictimes.indiatimes.com/news/economy/policy/one-factor-that-can-put-india-ahead-of-the-us-as-the-2nd-biggest-economy/articleshow/101668658.cms.

33 Shruti Deora, 'What's going on with India's female labour force participation?', *Sattva*, 24 March 2023, https://www.sattva.co.in/news-media/whats-going-on-with-indias-female-labour-force-participation/; 'UNEMPLOYMENT RATES FALL FROM 5.8 PER CENT IN 2018-19 TO 4.2 PER CENT IN 2020-21', *Press Information Bureau*, 31 January 2023, https://pib.gov.in/PressReleasePage.aspx?PRID=1894913#:~:text=The%20Labour%20Force%20Participation%20Rate%20for%20males%20has%20gone%20up,18.6%25%20in%202018%2D19.

34 Shruti Deora, 'What's going on with India's female labour force participation?', *Sattva*, 24 March 2023, https://www.sattva.co.in/news-media/whats-going-on-with-indias-female-labour-force-participation/#:~:text=Unlike%20the%20downward%20trend%20India,32.8%20in%202020%E2%80%9321.

35 'The Global Talent Competitiveness Index 2023', *INSEAD*, https://www.insead.edu/system/files/2023-11/gtci-2023-report.pdf .

36 'Infrastructure projects in turmoil: Massive cost overruns and delays shake foundations of 411 key ventures', *Financial Express*, 19 November 2023, https://www.financialexpress.com/business/

infrastructure-infrastructure-projects-in-turmoil-massive-cost-overruns-and-delays-shake-foundations-of-411-key-ventures-3311070/.

37 PTI, 'Nitin Gadkari aims for road infrastructure to match US in next 5 years', *Business Standard*, 20 December 2023, https://www.business-standard.com/india-news/nitin-gadkari-aims-for-road-infrastructure-to-match-us-in-next-5-years-123122000436_1.html.

38 Rahul Kapoor and Chris Rogers, '"Make In India" Manufacturing Push Hinges on Logistics Investments', *S&P Global*, https://www.spglobal.com/en/research-insights/special-reports/look-forward/make-in-india-manufacturing-push-hinges-on-logistics-investments

39 Ibid.

40 Abhishek Law, 'Fast-forwarding freight. Dedicated freight corridor: 18-year mission on track', *The Hindu Businessline*, 14 April 2024, https://www.thehindubusinessline.com/economy/logistics/dedicated-freight-corridor-18-year-mission-on-track/article68061589.ece; Richa Sharma, 'Indian Railways to roll out tender for 10,000 km of "Kavach"', *Business Today*, 16 June 2024, https://www.businesstoday.in/india/story/indian-railways-to-roll-out-tender-for-10000-km-of-kavach-433487-2024-06-16.

41 'Cities as Engines of Growth: Executive Summary', NITI Aayog, May 2022, https://www.niti.gov.in/sites/default/files/2022-05/Mod_CEOG_Executive_Summary_18052022.pdf.

42 Mansi Jaswal, 'India's construction sector to employ 100 million, requires skilled workforce for economic growth: Report', *Mint*, 3 August 2023, https://www.livemint.com/industry/infrastructure/indias-construction-sector-real-estate-jobs-employment-gdp-economy-civil-engineers-11691047850783.html.

43 'National Infrastructure Pipeline project gets no mention in FM's Budget speech', *Moneycontrol*, 1 February 2024, https://www.moneycontrol.com/news/business/budget/national-infrastructure-pipeline-project-gets-no-mention-in-fms-budget-speech-12042931.html.

44 'First Advance Estimates of National Income, 2023-24', *Press Information Bureau*, 5 January 2024, https://pib.gov.in/PressReleaseIframePage.aspx?PRID=1993550.

45 'India's economy to be worth $30 trillion by 2047: FM Nirmala Sitharaman at Vibrant Gujarat Summit 2024', *Business Today*, 10 January 2024, https://www.businesstoday.in/latest/economy/story/indias-economy-to-be-worth-30-trillion-by-2047-fm-nirmala-sitharaman-at-vibrant-gujarat-summit-2024-412645-2024-01-10.

46 Akhileshwar Sahay, 'Opinion | India in 2024: Dreams, Aspirations, Agendas and Actions', *News18*, 4 January 2024, https://www.news18.com/opinion/opinion-india-in-2024-dreams-aspirations-agendas-and-actions-8728005.html; Melissa Cyrill, 'India's Economy in 2023: A Year-End Review', *India Briefing*, 15 December 2023, https://www.india-briefing.com/news/indias-economy-in-2023-a-year-end-review-30561.html/; 'India Vision 2036-37 – A Macro econometric Approach', NITI Aayog, https://www.niti.gov.in/sites/default/files/2023-03/India%20Vision%202036-37%20A%20Macro%20Econometric%20Approach.pdf.

Chapter 5: Fast Forward to Viksit Bharat

1 'India emerges as world's services factory: Goldman Sachs report', *The Times of India*, 30 April 2024, https://timesofindia.indiatimes.com/business/india-business/india-emerges-as-worlds-services-factory-report/articleshow/109707130.cms.

2 Swaminathan S Anklesaria Aiyar, 'This brainpower flex is India's best-kept secret', *The Times of India*, 25 May 2024, https://timesofindia.indiatimes.com/india/this-brainpower-flex-is-indias-best-kept-secret/articleshow/110424727.cms.

3 'Annual Status of Education Report 2023: Beyond Basics', *ASER*, 17 January 2024, https://asercentre.org/aser-2023-beyond-basics/.

4 Knight Frank India and RICS, 'Skilled Employment in Construction Sector in India', 2023, https://www.knightfrank.com/publications/skilled-employment-in-construction-sector-in-india-2023-10450.aspx.

5 A.M. Jigeesh, 'Employment scenario in India grim, says ILO report', *The Hindu Businessline*, 26 March 2024, https://www.thehindu.com/business/Economy/employment-scenario-in-india-grim-says-ilo-report/article67995387.ece.

6 'Why is India's female labour force participation ratio below that of Saudi Arabia?', *Moneycontrol*, 8 March 2021, https://www.moneycontrol.com/news/opinion/why-is-indias-female-labour-force-participation-ratio-below-that-of-saudi-arabia-6619621.html.

7 Sunaina Kumar, 'The female workforce in India: Emerging trends and insights', *Observer Research Foundation*, 7 March 2024, https://www.orfonline.org/expert-speak/the-female-workforce-in-india-emerging-trends-and-insights#:~:text=There%20has%2C%20however%2C%20been%20an,survey%20(2021%2D22).

8 Goutam Das, 'At 0.7% of GDP, India's R&D expenditure in science is less than BRIC nations', *Business Today*, 22 November 2019, https://www.businesstoday.in/latest/world/story/india-gdp-randd-expenditure-in-science-is-less-than-bric-nations-239968-2019-11-22.

9 Meghna Mittal, 'Budget 2024: India's scientific advisor to PM holds stakeholder discussions to boost R&D spend by private sector', *Moneycontrol*, 24 November 2023, https://www.moneycontrol.com/news/business/budget/budget-2024-indias-scientific-advisor-to-pm-holds-stakeholder-discussions-to-boost-rd-spend-by-private-sector-11806001.html.

10 'How BOCW boards were used to help unorganised workers in pandemic and what issues remain', *Outlook*, 1 May 2022, https://www.outlookindia.com/national/how-bocw-boards-were-used-to-help-unorganised-workers-in-pandemic-and-what-issues-remain-news-194348.

11 'Estimated data of Indian students studying abroad', https://www.mea.gov.in/Images/CPV/lu3820-1-mar-25-22.pdf.

12 'All-India Survey on Higher Education 2021-22', *Ministry of Education*, https://cdnbbsr.s3waas.gov.in/s392049debbe566ca5782a3045cf300a3c/uploads/2024/02/20240719952688509.pdf.

13 'NITI Aayog targeting half a million foreign students in India for higher education by 2047: CEO Subrahmanyam', *The Hindustan Times*, 1 December 2023, https://www.hindustantimes.com/education/news/niti-aayog-targeting-half-a-million-foreign-students-in-india-for-higher-education-by-2047-ceo-subrahmanyam-101701326482555.html.